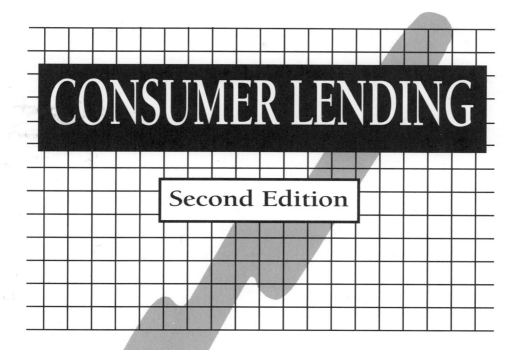

CONSUMER LENDING

Second Edition

Paul R. Beares
Vice President
First National Bank of Maryland

AMERICAN
BANKERS
ASSOCIATION

1120 Connecticut Avenue, N.W.
Washington, D.C. 20036

This publication is designed to provide accurate and authoritative information in regard to the subject matter covered. It is sold with the understanding that the publisher is not engaged in rendering legal, accounting, or other professional service. If legal advice or other expert assistance is required, the services of a competent professional person should be sought.

From a Declaration of Principles jointly adopted by a Committee of the American Bar Association and a Committee of Publishers and Associations.

Library of Congress Cataloging-in-Publication Data
Beares, Paul.
    Consumer lending/Paul R. Beares.—2nd ed, p.   cm.
    Includes bibliographical references and index,
    ISBN 0-89982-334-3
    1. Consumer Credit—United States,   2. Loans, Personal—United States.
    3. Bank loans—United States.   I. Title.
    HG3755,B39   1992
    332.1'753'0685—dc20

                                         92-5831
                                          CIP

Printed in the United States of America

Contents

Exhibits

Acknowledgments

I want to thank the following reviewers who have generously given both their time and guidance to help shape the updating and revision of this popular textbook.

John W. Carroll
Vice President (retired)
South Carolina National Bank
Columbia, South Carolina

Barry Chandler
Senior Vice President
Ponte Vedra National Bank
Ponte Vedra Beach, Florida

Landon L. Davis, III
Vice President
Small Business Group
Crestar
Vienna, Virginia

Richard A. Groeneman
Assistant Vice President
Lemay Bank and Trust
St. Louis, Missouri

Ronald M. Krause
Vice President and Manager
Loan Services
Bank One Milwaukee NA
Milwaukee, Wisconsin

Jim Matthews
Banking Consultant
Broomfield, Colorado

Robert A. Norris
Senior Vice President
New England Division Head
Fleet Bank
Bangor, Maine

Bill Young
Vice President
Citizens and Southern National Bank
Conyers, Georgia

I would also like to recognize the contributions of the ABA staff who have brought this new edition to life: Deborah Corsi, product manager; Tanja Lian, editor; and Andrea James-Parks, book designer.

About the Author

Paul Beares has been involved in the consumer credit business for over 20 years. He began his career with Commercial Credit Corporation and moved into banking in 1976. He has spent most of his career with The First National Bank of Maryland, where he acquired extensive experience in the management of credit, sales and marketing, collection, and customer service. Since 1988, Beares has served as vice president of the bank's Corporate Marketing Division.

Beares is also an active writer and teacher, having served on the faculty of the Stonier Graduate School of Banking and the American Bankers Association National Consumer Credit School for the past 10 years. He authored the 1987 *Consumer Lending* text, developed ABA's Professional Development Program for Consumer Credit, and has published a number of articles on consumer credit.

He holds a Master of Business Administration from the University of Baltimore and is a 1981 graduate of the Consumer Banking Association's Graduate School of Retail Bank Management.

In the midst of a sea of change, the banking industry has watched its consumer credit function swell in importance, evolving from a low-profile source of fixed-rate, closed-end loans to a dynamic operation delivering a panoply of products and services to a credit-reliant consumer market. In addition to other retail services, consumer credit has assumed strategic importance in the banking industry's efforts to stay profitable in a financial services marketplace that has become intensely competitive.

To function effectively in such an environment, as a consumer credit lender today, you'll need an impressive store of knowledge, skills, and intuition to succeed. These attributes are not magically bestowed. You can acquire this expertise by gaining an in-depth understanding of the consumer credit business: how it has evolved, the nature of the marketplace, and the legal environment that shapes lending practices. These broadly stated subjects are covered in Part I of *Consumer Lending*. Here, you'll be introduced to basic, historical, and regulatory material before exploring the details on products and services, the lending process, and proper administration.

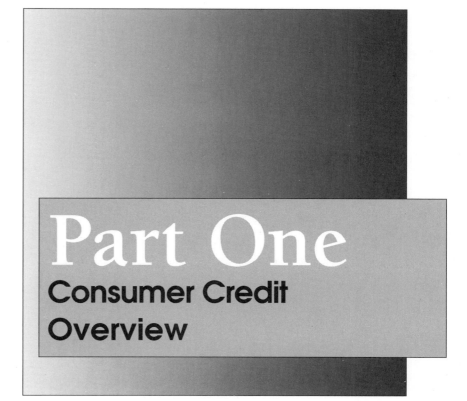

Part One
Consumer Credit Overview

1 Evolution of Consumer Credit

After reading this chapter, you will be able to

- ❏ define the term consumer credit and give examples of the types of loans that are and are not included in the definition
- ❏ discuss retail banking and give examples of how banks have sought to improve their efficiency and effectiveness in the market
- ❏ give examples of how deregulation in the 1980s affected bank consumer lending
- ❏ discuss how consumer attitudes have affected the use of credit in the United States
- ❏ identify two geographic/demographic trends that have significantly affected consumer lending from 1950 to today and describe their impact

Consumer Credit Defined

The legal definition of consumer and consumer credit varies from law to law and state to state, and there is no single, generally accepted definition. For example, the *Consumer Credit Protection Act,* a federal law designed to make credit terms clear and uniform, provides the following definitions:

- ❏ A **consumer** is a natural person who is primarily or secondarily liable on a credit contract.
- ❏ A **consumer credit** is borrowed funds that are used primarily for personal, family, household, or agricultural use, and not for business or commercial purposes.

A different definition of consumer is contained in the *Equal Credit Opportunity Act,* a federal law designed to provide equal access to credit, which describes an *applicant* as any person who is or may be contractually liable for an extension of credit, other than as a *guarantor, surety, endorser,* or similar secondarily liable party.

A practical definition of consumer credit, which will be used throughout this text, is as follows:

> Consumer credit includes all types of credit extended to individuals primarily for the purpose of buying goods and services for their personal consumption.

Consumer credit includes

- *installment loans,* which are repaid in two or more periodic payments
- *single-payment loans,* such as *demand loans* or those that have a specific payment date (a 90-day *note,* for example)
- *credit card transactions*
- *home equity lines of credit*
- loans to purchase cars, boats, planes, recreational vehicles
- loans for bill consolidations, vacations, home improvements
- loans for other services and durable goods used by the consumer

Not included in this definition of consumer credit are residential, purchase-money, and first mortgage loans, the proceeds of which are used to buy a home. Mortgage loans are separated from other forms of credit extended to consumers because the nature of the market for these loans is quite different in its legal requirements, competitive forces, and operation. Therefore, mortgage loans are normally handled by a specialized mortgage lending unit rather than the consumer credit department.

A Brief History of Consumer Credit

The use of credit has become so pervasive in the United States that it is hard to imagine our lives without it. We use credit cards to purchase everything from airline tickets to zoom lenses for cameras, and to help purchase goods that would otherwise be beyond our economic reach. Automobiles costing $20,000, boats costing $75,000, and that well-deserved European vacation costing $15,000 are all brought within the reach of many consumers because they have access to credit.

The credit services available to consumers have evolved over the course of history; however, the pace of change has accelerated in the 1980s and 1990s. This evolution has been driven by the desire of consumers to find better ways to manage their finances. Credit products available today offer consumers a wide range of options concerning when, how much, where, how, and for what purposes they borrow.

Financial institutions that serve the consumer credit market have played an important role in the growth of credit services. Regulatory change in recent years has stimulated greater variety and availability of credit and sparked the creative energies of lenders seeking to achieve a niche in the market.

New consumer credit products are continually being developed and added to traditional product lines, presenting new challenges and opportunities for both consumers and lenders. Home equity lines of credit, currently the fastest growing consumer credit product, were first offered during the 1980s. Leasing and credit cards have been widely available since the 1970s. The features and uses of these and other credit products are expanding and changing. For example, variable rates and lines of credit are now available on many consumer credit products, and credit cards are now accepted for doctor bills, food purchases—and even tickets to the movies. These rapid changes make it difficult for consumers to keep up-to-date on new financial services. Lenders, on the other hand, are challenged to anticipate and respond to consumers' needs, while learning to effectively manage an increasingly complex and competitive consumer credit product line.

The Beginnings of Consumer Credit

Consumer credit has had a long and varied history. Using credit to obtain goods and services is rooted deeply in our culture, and many current practices, philosophies, and attitudes toward credit have evolved out of thousands of years of borrowing and lending. Until guidelines and laws were developed in the early 1900s to regulate the credit industry, many unfair and illegal transactions occurred. Because of the unethical behavior of some lenders and borrowers, society has been more wary than accepting of the credit industry. Many societal attitudes towards credit are reflected in these quotations:

- *The wicked borrow, and payeth not again: but the righteous showeth mercy, and giveth.*
- *The rich ruleth over the poor, and the borrower is servant to the lender.*
- *Neither a borrower nor a lender be.*
- *For the love of money is the root of all evil.*
- *Creditors have better memories than debtors.*
- *He who does not have to borrow lives without care.*

Against this rather discouraging background, is it any wonder that some people have been reluctant to borrow or lend money? Could it be that these thoughts still influence people today? Anyone who has been around the lending business for even a short time can tell you that many people still think this way. But credit can and should be viewed in a more positive light. Using credit responsibly can provide consumers with economic and psychological benefits. For example, a line of credit can assure a customer that funds are available to meet emergencies, pay medical bills, or finance a college education. Benefits such as these, combined with the responsible provision of credit by financial institutions, have helped change consumer attitudes and values regarding credit.

Credit has been extended by merchants and other lenders throughout history. Educator Irving Michaelman noted in his study on consumer credit that "Lending money is one of the world's oldest professions."[1] He states:

> In the earliest days of primitive societies, lending was purely philanthropic, almost a duty, as tribes owning communal property could hardly conceive of charging anything for the use of such property. . . . In time the concept of private property evolved. . . . Here began the opportunity to offer something of value for loans, namely security, and the story of lending begins. At the same time, those who did not have land to borrow on had conceived the idea of offering themselves in servitude to secure loans. It did not take much ingenuity to substitute the concept of paying interest to replace servitude as recompense to the lender.
>
> The idea of interest, however, was resisted, if not forbidden, in laws calling for loans without interest to the poor and the cancellation of debts every seventh year.[2]

The Romans were among the first to add provisions to loan contracts to cover some of the risks of credit. Selling other services, such as *credit life insurance,* along with providing credit—a practice known as *tie-in selling*—was begun by the Romans. Roman lenders ". . . could add a handsome premium for the peril of shipwreck and additional lesser trivial risks. The practice of tie-in charges thus has a notable genealogy . . ."[3]

Early American Consumer Credit

Leaping forward to the 1700s in colonial America, we find that Benjamin Franklin philosophized, "A penny saved is a penny earned," but he also believed in credit. He extended credit liberally in his printing and bookselling business. His personal records show chattel mortgages (loans *secured* by a pledge of property) made to customers.[4] In Franklin's autobiography, he tells of calling off marriage plans because the bride's parents were unwilling to give him a *dowry* large enough to pay off his printing house debts.

The demand for credit increased significantly during the Industrial Revolution. Leaps in technology enabled consumer goods to be mass-produced for the first time in history. It was soon clear that mass production could not succeed without developing a solid base of consumers who were willing and able to purchase a wide variety of goods and services. Credit programs were soon needed to help consumers pay for higher priced goods. Many citizens were not ready, however, to accept the idea of credit; some had been the victims of *loan sharks* and *usurers.* Abraham Lincoln voiced concern about rising credit usage, reflecting rural America's lively antagonism for city people: ". . . one of the reasons being that they associated with bankers, loan sharks, and land sharks."[5]

Lenders of the late 1800s used some very strong-handed techniques to collect debts. Their practices were no doubt effective in recouping money, or at least persuading consumers to *refinance* their debts, usually with an upward adjustment in the interest rate. One particularly onerous practice involved the use of female employees, nicknamed "bawlerouts." A bawlerout would visit past-due debtors at their jobs and loudly bawl them out in front of fellow employees, an action that had a strong psychological impact on the debtor.[6]

An advertisement in the November 23, 1890, issue of the *Chicago Tribune* captures the flavor of the consumer credit market during the Gay 90s.

Any amount of money from $20 to $10,000 to loan on furniture, pianos, teams, etc. The property to remain in your undisturbed possession. At a lower rate of interest than you get elsewhere. Everybody who wants money, call and see us.

We are just as happy to make you a $25 loan as one for $2,500; we will give you plenty of time to pay the money back; in fact, we let you make the payments to suit yourself; as we do not ask for references or make inquiries of your neighbors, the transaction is sure to be private; no fear of losing your goods as we loan money for the interest and not to get the goods; we take up loans from other loan men; if you now have a loan on your goods, call and get our rates.[7]

Now isn't that a reassuring advertisement? You may notice that some of the themes are still present in consumer credit advertising today.

Emergence of Regulated Consumer Lending (1901-1945)

A formal, regulated consumer finance market began to emerge around 1900. Finance companies and *Morris Plan banks* were among the earliest financial institutions making credit plans more widely available to consumers. A major step came in 1916, when the Russell Sage Foundation—a charitable institution with the goal of improving social and living conditions in the United States—devised the *Uniform Small Loan Law.* This law provided the important early framework for the licensing of consumer lenders, and it established guidelines that provided some credibility for the emerging industry. That same year, an advertisement, shown in exhibit 1.1, appeared in the April 8 issue of the *Saturday Evening Post.* It announced the new concept of *retail installment loan* programs *(indirect lending)* for automobile dealers. Indeed, Henry Ford's mass production of the automobile was to provide the credit industry with its biggest opportunity for growth over the next few decades.

With new loan programs emerging, the movement to regulate consumer credit became intense. As the ad in exhibit 1.2 illustrates, the loan shark had become a target of the reform effort.

EXHIBIT 1.1   Indirect Automobile Dealer Ad

THE SATURDAY EVENING POST

Time Payments

Look for this emblem
on dealers' windows.

The First Organized National Service To Help Dealers Sell Automobiles

Guaranty Securities Corporation is the first organization of its kind in the world.

Its purpose and service is to directly assist automobile dealers to sell and the public to buy motor cars.

It has no cars of its own to sell.

It has nothing but service to offer automobile dealers.

This service is absolutely free.

And there is virtually no added expense to the car buyer beyond ordinary six per cent interest on the deferred payments.

For months we have been endeavoring to reach every dealer in the cars listed on the opposite page, with the details of the Guaranty Plan.

Hundreds of dealers all over the country are already selling thousands of cars on the Guaranty Plan.

It is sound, secure and safe.

Any dealer (in cars listed on opposite page) who has not received full particulars, may have them promptly for the asking.

The Guaranty Plan enables dealers to sell their cars on time payments—one down payment followed by monthly installments until the car is paid for.

Guaranty Securities Corporation will finance for any dealer (in cars listed on opposite page) any number of sales he makes on this basis.

It makes no difference how large or how small your business is—we will handle it.

Whether you sell one car a week or a hundred cars a month is beside the point.

All you can sell on this liberal installment plan, we will finance for you as fast as the mails will carry the papers to us and our check back to you.

Every dealer knows the tremendous automobile market just waiting to buy cars on the time payment plan.

Every dealer knows that this market is and always has been practically unlimited.

Many dealers have tried to work out their own plans but such a plan takes a lot of money or uses up a lot of bank credit and that in most cases has been the big stumbling block.

So we have worked out a plan for all dealers—large and small.

From now on, with the service of the Guaranty Securities Corporation you will be able to sell as many cars as your factory can supply you with—on this new and practical Guaranty (time payment) Plan.

The Guaranty Plan has been worked out and is backed by a group of capitalists some of whom are among the largest in the country.

Its soundness is vouched for by many of the leading banking and financial institutions in America.

As to the standing of the Guaranty Securities Corporation, we refer you by permission, to the following banks:

Metropolitan Trust Co., N. Y.
Liberty National Bank, N. Y.
First National Bank, Chicago
Corn Exchange National Bank, Chicago
Continental & Commercial National Bank, Chicago

The quicker you adopt this new Guaranty Time Payment Plan, the quicker you and your customers can enjoy its benefits.

Right now thousands of people in every state are waiting to buy cars on the Guaranty Plan.

If you are not fully informed about our service, fill out this coupon, mail it to us and we will send full particulars—or, better yet, telegraph.

Dealers—Send Us This Coupon

Buick —	Chevrolet—	Hudson —	Oldsmobile—	Overland —
Cadillac —	Dodge —	Hupmobile—	Maxwell —	Paige —
Chalmers—	Ford —	Jeffery —	Mitchell —	Reo —
Chandler—	Franklin —	Kissell —	Oakland —	Studebaker—
				Willys-Knight

GUARANTY SECURITIES CORPORATION,
    Equitable Building,
      New York, N. Y.

I am an authorized dealer in the cars which I have checked (√) in the above list.

Please send me complete information about the Guaranty Plan.

Name

Address

City   State

Guaranty Securities Corporation, Equitable Bldg., New York

EXHIBIT 1.2   **Pass the Loan Shark Bill!**

The Baby Boom and Movement to Suburbia (1946-1965)

The consumer credit market was still relatively new in 1945. Installment *loan outstandings*—the amount of money consumers owed on credit obligations—were estimated by the *Federal Reserve* to be $1.3 billion. Major growth, though, was just around the corner.

The end of World War II was followed by shifting geographic patterns and changing attitudes and values which fueled consumer demand for products and services. This demand, combined with industry's need to convert from wartime production, fueled a consumer products explosion unparalleled in history. By the end of 1949, *consumer credit outstandings* had jumped 939 percent to $12.2 billion.

The post-war baby boom between 1946 and 1963 resulted in the largest number of births in U.S. history. As this population bubble makes its way through life, it has stimulated a tremendous demand for credit and an unprecedented demand for material goods and services.

New attitudes, values, and social patterns also emerged in the 1950s. The decade was characterized by themes like: "Be the first person on your block to own . . ." and "Keep up with the Joneses." The messages expressed by these slogans helped to bring about a major shift in attitudes regarding credit usage. During the decade, total consumer credit rose 337 percent, reaching $41.1 billion. *Commercial banks,* which had captured the largest share of the consumer credit market in the 1940s, continued to increase their share, reaching nearly 43 percent of total consumer credit outstandings by the end of the decade.

Geographic population patterns also changed significantly during this time. A movement to the suburbs created demand for housing, automobiles, and all of the other products and services desired by new households. Banks, which rely heavily on providing convenience to attract customers, followed the population movement by establishing branch networks or forming new banks.

Economic and social stability encouraged continued market growth. Civilian employment reached high levels and became more steady. No longer did major segments of the population remain unemployed for substantial portions of the year. *Disposable personal income*—the amount of money that consumers have left after paying for basic food, clothing, and shelter needs—also rose. Consumers who could look forward to a gradually rising level of income and could count on steady employment were much more willing to undertake credit obligations. Lenders were also much more willing to lend in an environment where income and employment patterns were stable and more predictable.

Movement toward Change (1966-1979)

By the late 1960s, the Vietnam War was fueling inflationary pressures which made funds more expensive and harder for banks to attract. *Disintermediation*—the flow of funds out of depository institutions to sources paying higher rates—drained funds available for lending and drove up the cost of funds. Banks were not always able to raise lending rates to match the higher costs of deposits since loan rates were controlled by state law, and state legislators have rarely been anxious to raise rates. This resulted in severe earnings pressures on consumer loans which were virtually all on a fixed-rate basis and which generally were subject to low state usury limitations.

Social upheavals that characterized the 1960s had far-reaching effects. Much of our current consumer protection regulation stems from this time. Truth in Lending, which is a major part of the Consumer Credit Protection Act of 1968, rang the opening bell for many legislative bouts to follow. The consumer movement was highly successful in bringing about legislative changes. At the same time new laws allowed lenders to develop new consumer credit products and make larger loans with longer terms; they also permitted rates that were both fair and essential to the continued availability of credit.

Deregulation and Change (1980-Present)

The consumer credit market faced a major trauma in 1980. First, profit margins were severely squeezed as a result of a 1979 change in Federal Reserve policy that allowed interest rates to float freely at the same time as the rates banks were allowed to pay for deposits were being deregulated. As the cost of deposits soared, fixed-rate consumer loan portfolios became an albatross around the necks of bank managers. Exhibit 1.3 shows the effect on profit margins when loans made at a fixed rate are funded with variable rate deposits.

The 1980 *Consumer Credit Restraint Program* created other problems. This federal program was intended to stem the high level of consumer demand for credit, particularly unsecured loans such as credit cards, by imposing penalties on financial institutions that sought to increase their unsecured portfolios.

Bank reactions to these events included

- discontinuing credit accommodations to marginal indirect dealers (auto dealer outlets dropped by 3,783 locations during the period from 1979 to 1982, with the biggest drop in domestic auto dealerships)
- discontinuing issuance of new credit cards and terminating *lines of credit* for marginal customers
- ceasing all consumer loans to nonbank customers
- discontinuing some loan programs, particularly *unsecured lines of credit*
- relocating some consumer credit operations to other states

The impact on the consumer credit market was substantial. Financial institutions reacted by increasing pressure on state legislators to provide relief from unrealistic *usury rate caps.* Banks also sought the freedom to offer a wider variety of products and features to meet the changing credit needs of consumers. State legislation authorizing the widespread introduction of home equity line of credit products and variable rate consumer loans, as well as providing interest rate relief, was enacted in most states soon after 1980.

Conspicuous consumption reached a zenith in the 1980s. Consumers embraced debt enthusiastically as a tool to obtain immediate gratification for their desire for goods and services. The use of debt by consumers was matched by the federal government and the business community. During the 1980s, the United States went from being the world's biggest creditor nation, to its biggest debtor nation. Some business leaders dramatically embraced debt with practices such as leveraged buyouts, junk bonds, and numerous ill-conceived real estate ventures. Unwary financial institutions, did their part to facilitate the expansion of the debt balloon by

EXHIBIT 1.3   Fixed-Rate Loan Yield vs. Variable Cost of Funds

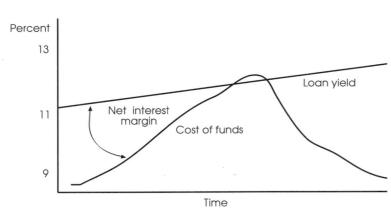

making credit widely available. This expansion of debt and free spending contributed to eight years of strong economic growth.

By the end of the 1980s, the debt balloon developed some slow leaks—higher loan losses, delinquencies, and bankruptcy problems. Credit excesses and problems in the banking industry were met with regulatory tightening and more conservative lending practices. By the early 1990s, it was apparent that the balloon had burst. The credit excesses on the part of both borrowers and lenders were over.

Retail Banking Is Defined

The concept of retail banking developed during the 1980s. Financial institutions that formerly had relationships primarily with businesses and only limited accounts with individual consumers began to recognize a whole new market in the range of consumer financial service needs:

- methods of exchange (checking accounts)
- store of wealth (savings and investments)
- purchasing power (credit services)

Banks discovered they could optimize sales and profits by seeking to fully serve consumer needs by taking a broader approach to the market. Rather than focusing on selling individual products, banks began packaging (grouping a number of services together to be sold as a single product) all appropriate services to sell to consumers. At the same time, deregulation and other external changes greatly increased competition. Banks adjusted to the realities of the marketplace by developing a sales culture with the goals of

- increasing the sales of products to the customer
- developing a close relationship with each customer
- retaining and better serving the customer's needs

Banks increasingly turned to technology to support the sales culture and improve the efficiency and effectiveness of retail banking units. Customer information systems (CIS) and marketing information systems (MIS) were developed to hold more extensive customer information, giving customer service representatives the tools they needed to cross-sell bank products and create targeted marketing programs. Personal computers and other automated terminals enabled banks to expedite credit decisions, improve customer service by enhancing the speed and accuracy of transaction processing, and increase employee productivity.

Summary

Lending and borrowing money are practices that have roots in ancient history and many of the values, attitudes, and practices associated with modern consumer credit stem from that time.

Substantial growth of the consumer credit market, though, was galvanized by the mass marketing of consumer products and services, a base of consumers willing and able to purchase those products, the willingness of consumers to use credit to help make purchases, a sound regulatory environment, and the existence of financial institutions willing to lend money. As these elements evolved over time, the consumer credit market has grown and thrived, providing an attractive market for financial institutions and a reliable source of credit for qualified individuals.

Review Questions

1. Define consumer installment loans. Which types of loans made to consumers are not included in this definition? Why?
2. What actions did banks take to implement a new definition of retail banking?
3. How have people's attitudes changed toward the granting and use of credit?
4. What effect did deregulation of the banking industry during the 1980s have on bank consumer credit programs?
5. What combination of events in the late 1900s contributed to a sudden upsurge in consumer credit demand?
6. What effect did the consumer movement in the 1960s-70s have on the consumer credit industry?

Optional Research

1. How do you feel about the use of credit? What are your attitudes and values in this regard?
2. Which types of credit have you used? What do you like, or not like, about each type?

2 Consumer Installment Credit Market

After reading this chapter, you will be able to

❏ list four benefits that consumer loans offer financial institutions

❏ define the terms loan outstandings and loan volume and describe the trends in the size and maturities of consumer loans

❏ identify the principal factors affecting consumer loan demand and describe how the family life cycle influences the use of credit

❏ identify the types of institutions that compete for consumer loans, their market share, and industry trends

❏ discuss the advantages and disadvantages that commercial banks have in the consumer credit market

Benefits of Consumer Credit

The existence of a well-developed consumer credit market increases the ability of consumers to purchase goods and services. Many people would not be able to buy a new car, add a room to their home, or pay for a private college education without the use of credit. If you had to wait to buy a new car until you had saved enough cash to buy it, chances are you wouldn't be able to buy a car very often and automobile manufacturers would sell a lot fewer cars. Thus, the widespread availability of credit makes it possible for more consumers to enjoy a higher standard of living by enabling them to obtain more goods and services than would be possible in a cash only economy. Credit also enables people to purchase items today and avoid paying a higher cost in the future. This benefit is particularly valuable in periods of high inflation, when the cost of goods is increasing rapidly.

Newer consumer credit products have greatly increased consumers' control over their personal finances. Credit cards enable people to take advantage of unexpected sales, make impulse or planned purchases, handle emergency needs, and have a convenient and safe means of purchasing a wide range of goods and services. Home equity lines of credit give consumers access to substantial amounts of credit to help them meet major borrowing needs such as college tuition payments.

Traditional loans, such as automobile, boat, and unsecured personal loans help consumers keep debt payments in balance with their income because they can spread the cost of products over their useful life. For example, a car loan can be spread over 5 years, while a loan for remodeling a kitchen might extend for up to 10 years.

Financial service providers have found the consumer credit market offers

- a source of sound loan assets
- a base of retail customers who are prospects for other products
- an attractive return on investment
- highly liquid portfolios

These characteristics have not only encouraged traditional lenders to expand the business but also have attracted new competitors such as AT&T and Merrill Lynch into the market.

Federal and state governments have often subsidized and encouraged the use of consumer credit through their tax policies. Federal tax laws used to allow consumers to deduct interest on all consumer loans. However, the Tax Reform Act of 1986 retained full deductibility for interest paid on loans secured by real estate only. This change undoubtedly contributed to the significant growth in home equity loans after 1985, though factors such as lower rates, convenience, and wider availability have also played a major role in the product's growth. However, the phaseout of the tax deduction for interest on other consumer loans (with total elimination in 1992) has **not** significantly altered consumers' use of credit cards and other loan products.

Consumer credit has been a positive factor in the economic development of the United States. The country enjoys one of the highest material standards of living in the world, and credit has been extended to a broad base of the population. It is critical to remember, though, that credit is a privilege not a right, and that the inappropriate or careless use of credit can lead to serious problems. Personal bankruptcies, family financial strains, and fraud are problems that present continuing challenges to the industry. These challenges must be met if responsible consumers and financial institutions are to continue to benefit from the consumer credit market.

Size of the Consumer Credit Market

The size of the consumer credit market is generally measured by

- ❏ the level of loan outstandings, the dollar amount of money owed on credit obligations
- ❏ *loan volume*, the amount of money borrowed by consumers during a given period of time

Since loan outstandings represent *interest-earning assets*, we will look first at the size and trends within that measure, then focus on trends and patterns in loan volume.

Loan Outstandings

Consumer loans may be divided into two major categories, closed-end loans and open-end or revolving loans. *Closed-end loans* extend a fixed amount of credit at the beginning of the transaction to be repaid in regular payments over a predetermined term. *Open-end,* or *revolving,* loans make a specified amount of credit available for use at the consumer's discretion. The consumer may use any or all of the credit line at anytime. Required payments vary depending upon the amount of credit being used at any given time, and the customer may repay all or any part of the balance, subject to a required minimum amount. Exhibit 2.1 shows the dollar amount of consumer installment credit outstandings for selected years.

EXHIBIT 2.1   **Consumer Installment Credit Outstandings, 1945-90**

In billions of dollars, not seasonally adjusted

	1945	1950	1960	1970	1980	1990
Total	2.6	15.5	45.1	105.5	302.1	750.9
Automobile	.4	6.0	18.1	36.3	112.0	284.9
Revolving	N/A	N/A	N/A	5.1	58.5	230.5
Mobile Home	N/A	N/A	N/A	2.5	18.7	21.7
Other	2.2	9.5	27.0	61.6	112.9	213.8
Securitized Assets	0	0	0	0	0	75.4

Source: Federal Reserve *Statistical Release G.19*

Closed-End Loans

Automobile loans have accounted for large and steadily growing outstandings; at the end of 1990, they accounted for nearly $285 billion in loans, 38 percent of the total market. Mobile home loans accounted for only 3 percent of 1990 outstandings, with $21.8 billion. The "Other" category includes all other types of closed-end loans: unsecured, second mortgage, boat, recreational vehicle, and similar loans. This category accounted for 28.5 percent of 1990 year-end outstandings—$214 billion. Generally speaking, the market share for closed-end loans has declined as consumer demand increasingly favors open-end credit products.

Open-End/Revolving Credit Lines

The revolving credit category was not tracked by the Federal Reserve until 1968, reflecting the more recent development of these products. This category is predominantly composed of credit card receivables, but also includes check overdraft and other unsecured revolving accounts. It has been the fastest growing product line until the recent surge in home equity lines of credit. By the end of 1990, nearly 31 percent—$208 billion— of consumer credit outstandings were in this category, up from 10 percent in 1980.

Home Equity Loans

Home equity loans (HELs) were first introduced in the 1980s and quickly became the fastest growing loan type. The value of HELs outstanding was estimated by the Fed to be $102 billion at year end 1990, with banks holding roughly 60 percent of the market. These loans grew 27 percent in 1989, and an additional 21 percent in 1990, the highest growth rate of any consumer credit product during those years.

Major Holders of Consumer Outstandings

The role and importance of different institutions in the consumer credit market has also changed over time. Exhibit 2.2 shows market share data for the major groups. Commercial banks continue to hold the dominant share of the market, though the mix of loans held has shifted over time. Competitor trends will be discussed more fully later in this chapter.

Loan Volume

Aggregate data for loan volume are not readily available.
However, some characteristics and trends in loan volume can be
identified by examining selected data. Exhibit 2.3 presents
selected volume data for several types of commercial bank
closed-end loans.

EXHIBIT 2.2   **Market Share of Major Holders of Consumer Credit, 1945-90**

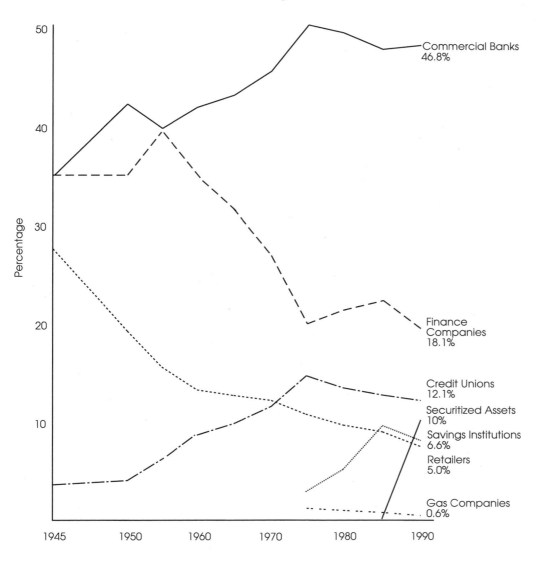

Source: Federal Reserve *Statistical Release G.19*

EXHIBIT 2.3 Portfolio Distribution of Closed-End Loan Volume for Commercial Banks

	1985 Percentage Distribution*		Average Loan	1990 Percentage Distribution*		Average Loan
	Number	Dollar		Number	Dollar	
Personal—unsecured	25.9%	14.6	$ 3,786	13.9	6.5	$ 3,978
Automobile—direct	18.3	18.6	6,849	12.0	10.9	7,890
indirect	29.5	39.9	9,093	44.0	47.2	8,560
Mobile home—direct	0.5	0.9	10,840	0.6	1.3	18,934
indirect	0.6	1.3	15,984	0.5	1.1	15,800
Recreational vehicle	2.0	2.8	11,528	1.4	1.7	11,418
Aircraft	0.2	0.3	29,375	0.1	0.1	41,900
Second mortgage	1.9	6.4	22,818	5.1	15.5	24,320

Source: *1991 Installment Credit Report,* American Bankers Association
*Percentages do not add to 100% because some loan types are excluded.

Unsecured loans were typically the smallest loans averaging ($3,978) in 1990, while automobile ($8,560), second mortgage ($24,320) and aircraft ($41,900) loan averages were significantly larger. The portfolio distribution also demonstrates the trend toward steadily increasing loan size. Note that the average direct auto loan rose from $6,849 in 1985 to $7,890 in 1990.

Exhibit 2.4 shows volume comparisons for VISA and MasterCard. These data reflect the high level of acceptance credit cards have achieved.

Seasonal Patterns

Demand for each type of consumer credit product has a seasonal pattern. These patterns are important to credit managers because they affect everything from staffing requirements to workflows to advertising campaigns. For example, banks typically increase credit card marketing activities in the early fall so they can capitalize on the Christmas season spending boom. They may also anticipate increased authorizations, customer service questions, and delinquencies, which also tend to rise late in the year.

Recent Growth Rates

The consumer credit growth rate during the 1980s is shown in exhibit 2.5. After a virtually stagnant growth rate of 0.4 percent

EXHIBIT 2.4   Card Volume Market Shares, 1991

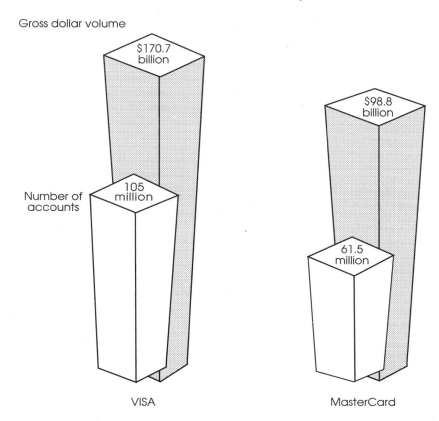

Gross dollar volume

$170.7 billion

$98.8 billion

Number of accounts

105 million

61.5 million

VISA

MasterCard

in 1980 and modest growth in 1981 and 1982, the market resumed double-digit growth rates in 1983 with a 15 percent increase. Growth was very strong in 1984 and 1985, when gains of 20.6 and 18 percent respectively were achieved. Revolving credit products continue to experience the highest rate of growth, with home equity lines of credit showing the strongest growth rates.

Factors Affecting Consumer Loan Demand

Demand for consumer credit has been very high in recent years; however, the level of demand is never constant. The need for credit is influenced by income, age, *family life-cycle* stage, attitude toward the use of credit, life-style, and financial condition. At the market level, total demand is influenced by prevailing sociological, economic, and competitive conditions.

EXHIBIT 2.5   Consumer Credit Growth Rate

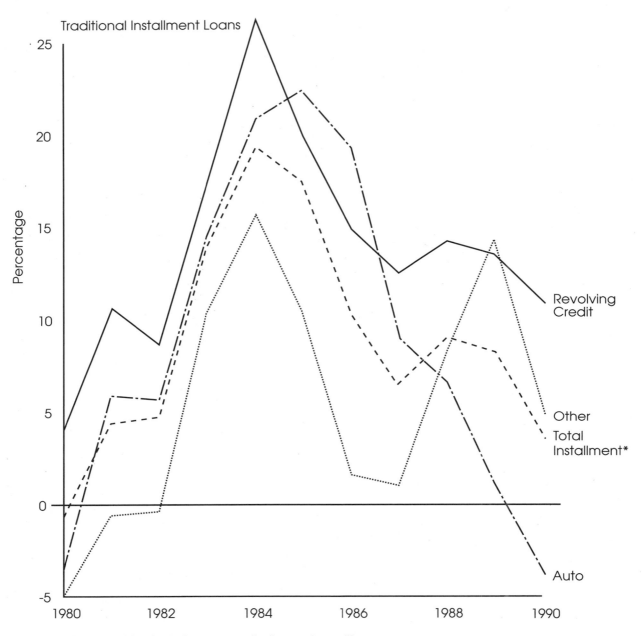

*Does not include home equity lines of credit.

Source: Federal Reserve *Statistical Release G.19*

Sociological Environment

We noted in chapter 1 that the attitude of consumers toward the use of credit has significantly shifted. This change in attitude was pointed out by the late Sylvia Porter in *Money Book:*

> It is no exaggeration to say that almost uninter-
> rupted buying on the installment plan has
> become a way of life in American homes to a
> point where a hefty percentage of families we
> consider as representing the "ideal" in our nation
> are never out of debt and another hefty propor-
> tion seldom are. In fact, I'll go beyond this and
> submit that the fundamental reason Americans
> have been borrowing so much today is precisely
> because they have had so much. This has intensi-
> fied your desire to satisfy your aspirations rather
> than simply finance your needs. And this in turn
> has led to unprecedented borrowing to achieve
> your aspirations at once.[8]

Indeed, borrowing has shifted from the basic needs to the luxuries of life. The lender today who is reluctant to lend money for vacations, upscale automobiles, and the latest electronic gadget may be considered out-of-date and certainly is not tuned in to the needs of contemporary consumers.

Marketers find they can segment the population into predictable patterns of credit behavior, based upon life-style characteristics. Factors such as residence location, types of cars owned, and past credit usage are frequently used by credit marketers to target credit prospects for their products. Gold cards, for example, were initially targeted to people living in high income residential areas and to professional groups, such as doctors and attorneys who would be attracted to the features and the ego-enhancing characteristics of the product.

The consumer's age and family life-cycle stage bear a direct relationship to the need for credit (see exhibit 2.6). Although the traditional family life cycle has undergone many variations in this country, a significant portion of the population still follows a predictable chronological pattern

- early household formation (ages 18-25)
- young family development (ages 25-35)
- the mid-life period (ages 35-55)

EXHIBIT 2.6   Life-Cycle Stage and Credit Usage

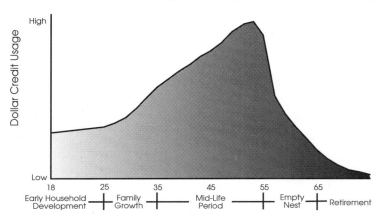

- the "empty nest" or "pre-retirement" period (ages 55-65)
- retirement (ages 65+)

Borrowing needs tend to be high relative to income at the beginning of a family's life cycle. New households desire durable goods such as cars, furniture, refrigerators, TVs, computers, VCRs, and all the other "essentials" of American life. From the mid-20s to mid-30s, incomes generally rise but this is matched by rising expectations and financial demands. Children create a significant demand on family finances. Some experts estimate that it costs in excess of $300,000 to raise a child from birth to college graduation.

College education and major household expenses face many people between the ages 35-55. They place a burden on the family budget and financial planning, but also generally occur when income levels are nearing a peak. This is a time when women frequently reenter the job market. Family credit outstandings tend to peak during this time.

Borrowing needs decline sharply after age 55. Typically, the consumer's income has peaked and most major borrowing needs and heavy cash flow requirements have been satisfied. Some find that this is the ideal time to buy a luxury car or a bigger boat. Generally, though, these are the years when consumers build their savings and investment accounts for retirement.

Economic Environment

The development of a large base of consumers living above a subsistence level is essential to the development of consumer credit. Peter Fousek, of the Federal Reserve Bank of New York, notes the following in his study of consumer credit:

> The shift in income distribution toward the lower income groups and the growth of a large middle class was also essential for the spread of installment credit. Among the other fundamental economic prerequisites for installment credit growth, the income security that comes with prosperous

times has been a major force in consumer credit expansion.[9]

Consumers are generally more willing to take on debt when they expect to have a continuing and steady or rising level of income over the *repayment period*. Consumers overwhelmingly tend to exercise self-discipline over their use of credit. Generally between 95 and 99 percent of all consumer loans are being paid as agreed. People borrow when they are confident about their income and comfortable with their monthly expenses, and reduce debt when they are less confident about their employment and income or are uncomfortable with their debt load. When consumers' income outlook is not favorable, not only will they be less likely to borrow, but lenders will also be less likely to make the loan requested. Thus, in recessionary periods, consumers are less likely to apply for loans, and lenders are more likely to tighten credit requirements and make fewer loans.

Regional economic difficulties in recent years have had material, and often completely unexpected, effects on consumers. Pessimists tend to point to rising delinquencies and bankruptcies as signs of serious problems in the consumer credit market, but while trends in these factors are important, they should be viewed objectively and against the total picture. Research reveals a tendency to self-control, although some consumers stretch their debt capacities:

> Other things being equal, households with large debts tend to reduce them, and households with small or no debts tend to increase their indebtedness. According to these results, there are certain equilibrium debt levels to which households tend to adjust their debt if their circumstances remain unchanged.[10]
>
> Although families tend to adjust their portfolios toward some desired level of installment credit, there are wide variations about this level over time. Our findings of large year-to-year changes in credit obligations . . . can be interpreted as evidence of potentially destabilizing effects on consumer credit.[11]

These observations help explain some of the variations in consumer credit demand over time. They also focus on a potential problem that can lead to delinquency and credit losses: some consumers can let their use of credit get out of control.

The level of consumer demand for credit is also influenced by economic trends, inflation, the level of interest rates, and the legal environment. Consumer credit can only develop when the economy of a country is stable. While credit exists in most cultures, the market remains stunted if there is instability within the government or the national economy. Lenders feel secure only when patterns of behavior are highly predictable. Lending in an unpredictable environment increases lenders' risk.

Inflation affects consumer credit in a number of ways. Consumers often react to high inflation by adopting the attitude "buy now before prices rise." Inflation also increases the average loan size, since goods and services will cost more. This results in a never-ending pressure on lenders to make larger loans and to increase the length of loan maturities to keep the monthly payments at desired levels.

Let's take a look at the automobile credit market. In 1976, the average new car cost $5,414. By 1990, the cost had risen to $14,500. Many banks increased the maximum *term* for a new car loan from an average of 36 months in 1976 (monthly payment $180) to 60 months in 1990 (monthly payment $322) to accommodate the increase in selling price. New car loans of up to 84 months, with 100 percent financing have been available in some upscale markets since the mid-80s. Previously, such terms were virtually unheard of.

The prevailing level of interest rates also influences credit demand. Consumers curtailed their borrowing significantly in 1980 and 1981, when interest rates hit peak levels. They dramatically stepped up borrowing in the 1984-1986 period in response to falling rates. In fact, much of the borrowing in 1986 was to refinance high-rate loans from prior years. This pattern of increasing and decreasing credit demand is directly affected by interest rate changes.

An example of the power of rates to stimulate borrowing was the use of *interest subvention programs* by captive automobile finance companies such as GMAC during the 1980s. In a subvention program, the manufacturer pays a portion of the cost of credit to the lender in order to offer below-market rates to consumers. Advertised rates of 3.9 and 4.9 percent strongly affected demand, particularly when regular rates were around 11 percent. These programs were powerful tools which the manufacturers used to stimulate product sales, sell slow-moving products, reduce inventory levels, and increase the captive companies' share of the market.

Legal Environment

The legal environment also affects the consumer credit market because it can either encourage or discourage borrowing and lending activities. In our review of the history of credit in chapter 1, it was obvious that consumer borrowing was limited when the lending business was unregulated and dominated by loan sharks and usurious lenders. Restrictive laws, though, have restrained credit use from time to time. One classic example is the *usury law* in the state of Arkansas. Until the 1980s, the state's constitution established a 10 percent usury limit on all consumer debt. The rate was acceptable for many years, but it became a major problem when deposit rates were deregulated. The rising cost of funds so narrowed the spread between the bank's cost and the maximum loan rate, that it was impossible to achieve an acceptable level of profitability. As a result, lenders either discontinued doing business in the state, or severely restricted the availability of credit.

Competitive Environment

The competitive environment continues to change as the consumer credit market is *deregulated*. Commercial banks, finance companies, credit unions, savings institutions, and retailers have traditionally been the primary suppliers of credit. In recent years, the distinctions between various lender groups has blurred and new competition has come from such unaccustomed sources as AT&T, which began offering credit cards in 1990. At the same time, most financial institutions enjoy greater freedom to develop and market a broader range of consumer credit products. In this section, we will review the major competitor groups within the market, focusing on their advantages, disadvantages, and relative market shares.

Commercial Banks

There is a wide divergence in the importance attributed to consumer credit by different banks. However, the mix of loan business held by banks has steadily shifted to the point where the industry now has more of its total assets in consumer loans than in any other category of loans.

EXHIBIT 2.7 **Commercial Bank Portfolio Distribution* of Consumer Installment Credit**

Percentage of Outstandings at Year End

	1970	1980	1985	1990
Automobile	45.8%	41.9%	39.5%	35.9%
Revolving	10.5	20.3	32.1	37.9
Mobile Home	8.0	7.0	3.8	2.8
Other	35.7	30.8	24.6	23.4

*Excludes home equity loans

Source: Federal Reserve *Statistical Release G.19*

Commercial banks have held the dominant share of the consumer credit market since 1946. Their market share peaked in 1979 at 51.5 percent, declining to 43.3 percent in 1986, before beginning to rise to 46.8 percent by the end of 1990, when banks held nearly $412 billion in consumer loans (including home equity loans). Banks have traditionally dominated the credit card and home equity market and hold the largest dollar outstandings in every loan category.

The mix of consumer loan business held by commercial banks has shifted significantly over the past 20 years (see exhibit 2.7). Revolving credit outstandings have climbed dramatically and now account for the largest share of the portfolio, while automobile, mobile home, and "other" loans have dropped as a percentage of the total portfolio. Remember, however, that the mix of business in individual banks may vary substantially from this overall industry data.

Banks recently have enjoyed several advantages in the consumer credit market. These include a positive image, a larger base of retail customers, and a growing network of convenient branches. Branch personnel now are often viewed as experts in personal finance and have begun to establish credibility as reliable resources for loans. The industry's positive image has come under some pressure, however, as a result of banking problems in recent years, making these advantages more tenuous.

The industry's base of checking and savings account customers provides another important competitive advantage. Research consistently finds that satisfied customers are more responsive to marketing efforts than noncustomers. Thus, banks have emphasized building a sales culture and cross-selling to capitalize on these customers.

The branch distribution system is an important element in developing direct loan business and marketing other credit products. Much of the growth of bank consumer loans can be traced to the expansion of the branch network. Many consumers prefer borrowing from convenient loan sources, and may even be willing to pay a premium, such as higher interest rates, in order to gain convenience.

Yet commercial banks also face some challenges in developing their consumer credit business. The wide variety of services offered by banks creates a problem of priorities. Branch personnel are expected to wear many hats and must balance an ever-changing list of priorities. Consumer lending, sometimes a low priority for the bank, may not receive the amount of time and attention necessary to optimize lending opportunities.

Managing the risks related to consumer lending is a challenge that must be addressed. Some banks are extremely conservative in their lending practices, accepting only low-risk loans and offering new products only after thorough testing by others in the market. The result of this conservative stance may be a loss of market share, a failure to maximize profits, and the need to play catch-up with more aggressive competitors. On the other hand, overly aggressive lending practices can result in high delinquencies and losses, inefficient operations, and funding problems.

Another potential problem is the lack of consistent management support. Some banks cut off or substantially reduce certain types of loans only to aggressively pursue these loans at other times. This practice, characterized as "stepping on the gas, then hitting the brakes," generally reflects a short-term rather than a long-term market perspective, and it can adversely affect future lending efforts.

The nature of consumer loans themselves pose some problems for banks. The *fixed rates* and relatively long *maturity structures* of some consumer loans, such as boat, airplane, and recreational vehicles, can pose challenges from the viewpoint of matching assets with funding sources and affect profitability. Variable rate lending programs have helped overcome concerns about protecting interest rate margins, though their acceptance by consumers has been limited. *Secondary markets* have also been developed to give increased *liquidity* to the loan portfolio. In recent years, banks have sold off or securitized credit card, automobile, boat, mobile home, and other portfolios to a variety of investors. Selling loans in the secondary market allows the bank to serve its customer's credit needs without creating additional funding requirements.

Finance Companies

Finance companies can be divided into a number of different groups, depending upon who owns them. *Captive finance companies*—such as General Motors Acceptance Corporation (GMAC), Chrysler Credit, and Ford Motor Credit—were originally formed to help manufacturers sell the goods they produce. In recent years they have expanded their consumer credit product lines. GMAC, for example, offers a full range of loan services to customers throughout the country, while a Ford Motor subsidiary is one of the nation's largest credit card providers.

Another group of finance companies is owned by commercial banks. These holding company subsidiaries extend the bank's distribution network into desired geographic areas, usually beyond the home state. Finance company subsidiaries allow banks to reach segments of the consumer market they might not otherwise serve.

A third group of finance companies are independent finance or *personal loan companies,* such as Beneficial Finance and Household Finance. Many of these companies have either merged with other financial institutions or acquired bank franchises. Beneficial, for example, has aggressively acquired credit card portfolios through its Beneficial National Bank subsidiary, while Household has established a banking network in a number of states. The differences between banks and finance companies are likely to continue to blur as many financial institutions acquire licenses to operate under each type of charter.

Finance company market shares have been on a long downhill slide. This negative trend was reversed briefly during the 1980s, when captive automobile finance companies greatly expanded their portfolios. The effectiveness of their efforts to control domestic automobile financing through rate subsidy programs was dramatically demonstrated in 1986, when their automobile outstandings grew 39.7 percent (compared with a 5.7 percent gain by banks). Overall, finance companies had the highest growth rate of any lender group that year—a 26 percent increase. However, finance company market shares began to decline once the subvention programs ended. By the end of 1990, they held an estimated $136 billion in consumer loans, or 18.2 percent of the market, making them a distant second to banks.

The ability to specialize gives finance companies a competitive advantage. Finance companies have developed highly efficient operational systems, skilled lending and collection personnel, and aggressive marketing practices. Some banks have also developed specialized lending units for indirect automobile, boat, and home equity loans to offer better service and products and improve sales.

Finance companies have also benefited by opening branches throughout the country. State laws limit branching, but they are less restrictive than the regulations governing banks. The freedom to branch has allowed finance companies to expand into desirable market areas and to develop national or regional distribution networks.

The biggest competitive disadvantage faced by the finance and personal loan industry has been a poor image. This problem stems from the fact that finance companies were perceived as charging higher rates and dealing with higher risk consumers. These companies often provide credit services to a segment of the population that otherwise might not have access to credit.

Another problem for the finance company industry is its need to fund loan portfolios with higher cost funds than those available to other lender groups. While banks, savings institutions, and credit unions obtain a significant portion of their loanable funds from savings deposits, finance companies must rely on commercial paper and other forms of funding. This results in a higher *cost of funds* which must be passed on to customers in the form of higher rates. These funding sources are also subject to problems of availability and greater volatility under some economic conditions.

Savings Institutions

Before 1980, savings and loan associations and mutual savings banks were only permitted to invest a small percentage of their assets in consumer loans. This constraint prevented most savings institutions from taking an active role in the market. When deregulation began, thrifts quickly became the fastest growing industry group in the consumer credit market. Their market share rose from 3.7 percent at the end of 1979 to a peak of 9.8 percent in 1987; however, by December 1990, the savings institution market share had fallen to 6.6 percent, with an estimated $50 billion in loan outstandings.

Savings institutions benefited from having a large base of retail customers who were interested in a range of products; this helped savings institutions build and diversify their loan portfolios. These firms also have a base of branch offices through which they can develop their direct loan business and *cross-sell* other loan products and related retail services. The relatively short maturities and high rates offered by consumer loans are also attractive to savings institutions accustomed to large portfolios of long-term, fixed-rate mortgage loans.

The troubled financial condition of many savings institutions has prevented some from embarking on the development of new product lines or even promoting basic loan services to their customers. In many cases, they lack the financial resources required to support a consumer credit operation or to attract the necessary expertise required to build a loan portfolio. Further, the image of some savings institutions has been severely damaged in recent years due to the great number of insolvencies in that industry. This will have a negative impact on their marketing efforts in the future.

Credit Unions

Credit unions are financial institutions specifically developed to serve individuals with something in common—a profession, a religion, or a company, for example. Some of the largest credit unions are organized by employees of United Airlines, AT&T, IBM, and Westinghouse; the military service; and state and local governments. In recent years, however, the definition of common bond has been extended to much more loosely defined groups—people who live in a certain area, for example. This broadening of the definition of eligible members, while an advantage to credit unions, is of concern to competitors, as it allows credit unions access to more consumers.

Credit unions enjoy an economic advantage over profit-driven competitors in that they operate on a not-for-profit basis. Excess earnings may be distributed to the members in a variety of ways, including higher rates on savings accounts or lower interest rates on loans. The not-for-profit status exempts the credit union from taxes, an expense that all of their competitors must cover in their pricing.

Credit unions also have access to relatively low-cost funds since they obtain loanable funds primarily from the savings accounts of their members. They are also able to offer their members a level of convenience generally not available to other lender groups. For example, both savings deposits and loan payments can often be handled on a *payroll deduction* basis by many credit unions. This feature is the ultimate in payment convenience and a positive feature from the standpoint of personal financial management. It also helps to reduce delinquencies and losses as well as some operating expenses.

Credit union market shares peaked in the late 1970s at nearly 17 percent, then fell to 12.1 percent at the end of 1990 when they held an estimated $91.2 billion in consumer loans. Their overall market share has been slowly declining over the past five years, but that does not reflect the impact these institutions have on specific areas. Indeed, when strong credit unions are present in a local market, they may control a significant share of the market.

The association between the credit union and its members is generally very strong. This relationship is a definite advantage in developing and maintaining a healthy consumer loan program as well as providing other financial services, such as savings and checking accounts.

The major disadvantage facing credit unions is their restricted customer base. Credit unions are limited to serving their memberships, and thus are not able to tap other desirable consumer groups.

Although some credit unions offer full financial services to their members, others do not have the resources to offer a full range of consumer credit products, particularly the popular open-end products. Small credit unions are often staffed by part-time or volunteer employees and, as a result, may not offer the privacy, convenience, and level of service that many customers want.

Retailers

Retail merchants were among the first groups to extend credit terms to consumers. They entered the credit business primarily to increase the sale of goods and services to their customers.

Among the major issuers of retail credit accounts are large department stores such as Sears, J.C. Penney, and Montgomery Ward. Many major department store chains still offer a private brand credit plan, one bearing the store's name, though most also accept *VISA, MasterCard,* and other credit cards, such as American Express and Discover. Much of the activity in retailer accounts has shifted to the major national bank card programs—VISA and MasterCard. In fact, many of the retailers who offer their own private brand credit plans use a bank or outside processor to handle their transactions.

The market share held by retailers has steadily declined over the last several decades, though actual dollar outstandings have continued to rise. At the end of 1990, retailers held $42.2 billion in consumer loans—less than 6 percent of total consumer credit outstandings.

One decisive advantage that retailers enjoy is their ability to package the sale of goods or services conveniently with the sale of credit. This not only makes the sale of credit easier, it also means that the retailer benefits both from the credit-related income and the profit made on the sale of goods or services. Because of this additional income potential, retailers tend to offer more flexibility in credit arrangements than other lenders. Plans such as "90 days with no payments" or "no payments until next year" are designed to maximize the sale of goods.

One disadvantage retailers face in extending consumer credit is that funds are tied up in customers' accounts receivable. The retailer may have neither the financial strength to carry the accounts nor the wherewithal to *service* them. Retailers that offer their own credit plans must be able to process loan applications, make credit approvals, and handle the processing of payments and collection activities relating to the accounts, or pay an outside vendor, such as a bank to provide these services. These functions represent an additional cost that must be covered by the interest income generated from the accounts or subsidized by the price of the goods sold.

Other Credit Sources

Credit has long been provided by families and friends. For the borrower, this may be the best possible source since the terms are likely to be informal, "Pay me when you have the money," or may be in the form of a gift rather than a credit transaction "Pay me back whenever you are able to, but if you can't, don't worry about it." However, there may be psychological costs associated with borrowing from one's family or friends. In the long run, it may be more comfortable to borrow from a financial institution than to opt for the more flexible terms, albeit with strings attached, available from one's family.

Loans may also be obtained from insurance companies. Individuals who own an insurance policy that builds cash value can borrow against the policy, usually at very favorable rates and with extremely flexible terms. A sample cash value table is shown in exhibit 2.8.

The policyholder may borrow against the cash value at an annual percentage rate set forth in the insurance policy, as long as the policy is in force. As the cash value builds, the consumer has a source of loan funds available at a rate of interest that is usually below market rates. The consumer must repay the interest on the borrowed funds; the principal may be repaid at the owner's discretion, or it may be paid out of the policy proceeds if it is still outstanding at the time of the policyholder's death. Insurance policy loans do not usually appear on credit reports, and thus do not affect other credit requests the consumer may apply for.

**EXHIBIT 2.8   Cash Value—Universal Life
Policy**

End of Policy Year	Cash or Loan Value
1	$ 81.90
5	3,007.02
10	6,854.21
15	10,411.09
20	12,470.03

Other sources of loans include employers, some of whom are willing to lend money to employees. Loans of this nature are more common in small companies where the owner has a close working relationship with employees. In some circumstances, employees may also borrow against vested funds in a pension plan. Such loans, while usually restricted to emergencies, college education expenses, and similar purposes, often provide a very low cost, flexible way to borrow. Loans may also be obtained from *real estate brokers,* who may provide *short-term equity advances* to facilitate the purchase of a new home; *securities brokers,* who provide *margin accounts* (loans to purchase stock) and other loan services to their customers; and trade people, many of whom provide short-term credit to facilitate specific purchases for home improvements or other needs. The use of these sources depends upon consumers' personal needs and are generally related to specific transactions.

Summary

Demand for consumer credit is influenced by many factors. The consumer's income, age, life cycle stage, life-style, attitudes about borrowing, and personal financial condition all affect the use of credit. Likewise, credit use is affected by circumstances in the economy at large. Economic factors, such as inflation, the level of interest rates, employment trends, and local economic conditions influence the level and timing of credit usage.

Consumer credit is a growing, multibillion dollar market. Loan outstandings—the amount of money owed by consumers on credit obligations—has maintained a relatively strong, though not steady, rate of growth since World War II. Automobile loans are the largest group of consumer loan outstandings, while revolving credit products, such as credit cards and home equity lines of credit, have achieved the highest rate of growth over the last decade.

The major lenders serving the consumer credit market are commercial banks, finance companies, credit unions, savings institutions, retailers, and gasoline companies. Commercial banks hold the largest share of the market, with nearly 47 percent of the total outstandings at the end of 1990. Banks have a dominant share of the credit card and home equity loan outstandings.

Review Questions

1. Name one of the family life-cycle stages and characterize it in terms of credit usage.
2. What advantages and disadvantages do commercial banks have in the consumer credit market?
3. What general trend is observable in the size and maturities of consumer loans? Can you pinpoint a reason for the trend?
4. Despite the fact that commercial banks have traditionally emphasized their business loan portfolios, what do the statistics say about the mix of their loan portfolios?
5. List four benefits which consumer loans offer financial institutions.
6. Why do retailers offer credit to their customers, and how has the market share of retailer credit plans fared over time?

Optional Research

1. How intense is the competition in your bank's market area? What types of credit providers compete directly with your bank? Make an appointment to talk to your consumer credit manager to find out the answers.
2. Try to locate some statistics from your consumer credit department that show installment credit outstandings for your bank. How have they changed over time? Can you identify a trend? What is the mix of consumer loans within your bank?

3 Regulation of Consumer Credit

After reading this chapter, you will be able to

❏ discuss the primary focus of federal and state laws relating to consumer credit

❏ list at least five key laws or regulations affecting consumer lending activities

❏ list nine bases on which a provider of credit may not discriminate under the Equal Credit Opportunity Act

❏ describe the primary purpose of the Truth in Lending law

❏ discuss the general requirements of the Community Reinvestment Act and cite the consequences of noncompliance

The Regulatory Environment

A sound legal environment is essential to the growth and stability of consumer credit. Laws that result in fair trade practices and provide for an equitable distribution of credit help build a relationship of trust between consumers and financial institutions, foster market acceptance of consumer credit products, and encourage responsible credit use.

Consumer credit laws and regulations are developed at the state and federal level. Each state develops its own set of lending laws that govern permissible types of loans, rates, and contractual terms. Legislative and regulatory action at the federal level was relatively limited until the 1960s when social concerns over equality, discrimination, and fair treatment led to a series of federal consumer credit laws. The two primary areas of focus for federal laws have been to

■ require uniform disclosures of important credit features

- provide credit on an equal basis to all qualified borrowers

The regulatory environment can be described as a circular process. Laws are proposed and passed that govern the marketplace. They are generally intended to address the specific legal framework for carrying out an activity. Based on the laws, regulations are issued to clarify and interpret the intent of the law. Regulators are also responsible for monitoring financial institutions for compliance. Violations and problems may be resolved administratively, or they may require intervention by the courts, which resolve issues in dispute. Changes in the market or in the regulatory and legislative environment itself may ultimately lead to further legislative activity.

Federal Regulation and Enforcement

The federal legislative process begins with the U.S. Congress. Congress is charged with the responsibility of enacting laws, some of which govern consumer credit. Federal law generally is concerned with the industry's trade practices, including consumer protection from unfair credit practices, elimination of unfair discrimination, and the types and manner in which disclosures regarding specific credit terms are made to consumers.

As exhibit 3.1 indicates, federal laws are monitored and enforced by a number of regulatory agencies. These agencies

EXHIBIT 3.1   Federal Banking Regulators and the Institutions They Supervise

Institutions* Supervised	Primary Federal Regulator
National banks	Comptroller of the Currency
State-chartered banks, (members FRB)	Federal Reserve Board (FRB)
State-chartered banks, (not members of FRB)	Federal Deposit Insurance Corporation
Savings associations	Office of Thrift Supervision (OTS)**, Department of the Treasury
Federal credit unions	National Credit Union Administration
Consumer finance companies, mortgage bankers, and certain other creditors	Federal Trade Commission

*All institutions listed, except finance companies, are assumed to be insured.

**Formerly the Federal Home Loan Bank Board. The Federal Home Loan Bank System still exists and has members ranging from insurance providers to commercial banks. Each of these members is supervised by one of the federal agencies listed above.

develop rules and regulations that specify how laws are to be implemented and then monitor the institutions under their purview for compliance. Some institutions are subject to review by more than one federal agency. For example, national banks are regulated by the *Comptroller of the Currency,* the Federal Reserve Board, and the *Federal Deposit Insurance Corporation.* Federal agencies do, from time to time, focus on particular regulations, and the intensity of exams vary based on the state of the economy and the political environment. For example, in recent years there has been a strong emphasis on compliance with the Community Reinvestment Act (CRA). This has been reflected in more stringent CRA examinations and in requirements for public disclosures of each bank's CRA rating.

State Regulation and Enforcement

Each state has its own laws regulating consumer credit. The state laws have primary control over

- rates lenders charge
- contract provisions that may be used in credit transactions
- maximum loan maturities
- fees that can be imposed on loans

The wide variety of legislation at the state level often makes it difficult for lenders from different states to communicate. Some states do not allow lenders to offer variable rates or to secure loans with second mortgages on a consumer's home. Others dictate restrictive interest rates.

Each state has regulatory agencies that monitor financial institutions chartered under state law. For example, the state banking commissioner regulates state-chartered banks. These banks may also be regulated by the Federal Reserve Board if they are members of the Federal Reserve System. State regulators routinely accept the examinations made by national regulatory agencies.

Federal Consumer Credit Laws

Federal laws primarily provide uniform disclosures of important credit features and ensure that credit is provided on an equal basis to all qualified consumers. We will focus on the major laws concerning credit laws passed since 1968.

The Equal Credit Opportunity Act

The Equal Credit Opportunity Act (ECOA) was passed by Congress in 1974 as Title VII of the Consumer Credit Protection Act. It was substantially amended and took its current form in 1976. The act, implemented by the Federal Reserve Board's *Regulation B,* covers all types of credit, including consumer and business credit.

The primary objective of ECOA is to prohibit discrimination regarding any aspect of a credit transaction on the basis of the applicant's race, color, religion, national origin, sex, marital status, or age. A lender may not treat one borrower or prospective borrower more or less favorably than another on the basis of these characteristics. ECOA also prohibits discrimination because all or part of the applicant's income is from a public assistance program, or because the applicant has in good faith exercised any rights under the Consumer Credit Protection Act.

ECOA provisions affect all aspects of consumer credit and some business transactions, including a bank's procedures for taking loan applications, credit evaluation criteria, adverse action notifications, and recordkeeping requirements. Thus, ECOA is probably the most pervasive of all consumer credit laws. The rationale for an antidiscrimination law is obvious: people were denied credit for all of the reasons specified in ECOA. Unfounded biases and undesirable practices did exist, and it was necessary to take strong action to change them.

Application Requirements

ECOA and Regulation B provide specific rules to define when an application is made, who an applicant is, and what other parties are covered. Specifically, ECOA protects

- ❏ any person who makes an oral or written request for credit made according to procedures established by a creditor for the type of credit requested
- ❏ persons who have already had credit extended to them, as well as individuals currently applying for credit
- ❏ any person who is or may be contractually liable for an extension of credit, other than as a guarantor, surety, endorser, or similar secondarily liable party

Furthermore, the ECOA says that an application is considered to have been made when

- a request for an extension of credit has been made in accordance with the procedures established by a creditor for the type of credit requested
- a conversation between an individual and a creditor turns to a discussion of the individual's creditworthiness and the creditor offers any opinion on the subject

These provisions have an impact on banks' policies and procedures. For example, if a bank has a policy of not accepting applications for credit over the phone, a consumer could not claim to have made an application in that manner. Indeed, to avoid potential ECOA problems, many banks have adopted such a policy without having evaluated the broader marketing implications of the decision. By requiring all applicants to complete and sign a written application form, the bank may be losing loan business to competitors who allow consumers to apply in more convenient ways.

The second part, which defines when an application has been taken, poses some additional concerns. If a woman, for example, tells a loan officer that she is divorced and asks whether that would affect her ability to obtain a specific loan, and the officer offers an opinion, an application has been made under the terms of the act, whether or not an application form has been completed. This provision was included to help prevent discouraging a potential applicant from applying for a loan.

Lenders could be deemed to have discouraged an applicant in several situations: by offering unfavorable opinions regarding the applicant's creditworthiness; by creating barriers that deter a potential applicant from completing a loan application; and by selectively advertising to avoid major groups within the bank's primary market area. A bank creates barriers when it does not provide application forms in the language predominantly spoken in its market area—Spanish language documents in parts of Florida, Texas, and California, for example—or when the bank does not employ loan personnel who speak the language of the area.

ECOA also deals with the types of questions asked of consumers on loan application forms and the order in which questions may be asked. To make it easier for banks to comply, the Federal Reserve provides model forms.

Credit Evaluation Requirements

The ECOA requires lenders to eliminate some of the criteria they may have previously used to evaluate the creditworthiness of applicants. Before the ratification of ECOA, some lenders denied credit because the applicant was

- not white
- divorced, separated, or unmarried
- over the age of 65 or would be during the course of the loan
- female
- on welfare or public assistance
- a member of a particular religious denomination

Basing a credit decision on these criteria is considered unfair discrimination under ECOA. The specific prohibited evaluative criteria are as follows:

- **Race and color** Questions regarding race may not be asked, except for government monitoring purposes, on a credit request for loans secured by residential property. This exception allows regulators to monitor lenders' compliance with credit availability requirements contained in equal housing regulations. Under no circumstances is race or color to be considered in the decision-making process.
- **Religion** Questions regarding religion are not permitted under any circumstances, nor is this factor to be considered in the credit decision.
- **National origin** The same rules apply to this category as for race and color. However, the creditor "may consider whether an applicant is a permanent resident of the United States, the applicant's immigration status, and such additional information as may be necessary to ascertain its rights and remedies regarding repayment." Thus, noncitizenship and/or immigration status may be considered in the decision-making process. Aliens who are not permanent residents or who are likely to return to their native country and could avoid being held accountable for the debt may be refused credit based upon their citizenship status.

❑ **Age**   Lenders may request the applicant's age or birthdate and consider it in the decision-making process "when such age is to be used to favor the elderly applicant in extending credit." Other rules state that age may be used as a variable in credit-scoring systems, provided that elderly applicants are not assigned a negative value. For example, age may be used if applicants over the age of 55 receive the highest score possible for this characteristic.

Creditors are subject to several rules regarding income that may be related to age. For instance, lenders may take into account the level and probable continuity of income over the term of the loan. Thus, if an applicant is eligible for retirement during the term of the loan, the creditor may evaluate the applicant's ability to pay based upon the likely postretirement level of income. If the applicant would be unable to meet the bank's *debt-to-income ratio* after retirement, the loan could be denied based upon insufficient ability to pay, but not due to age.

❑ **Marital status**   Whether a creditor may ask an applicant's marital status depends on the applicant's state of residency and the type of credit being sought. In a *community property* state, creditors may always inquire about the marital status of an applicant, no matter what type of credit is sought. In a noncommunity property state, creditors may not inquire about an applicant's marital status if the applicant is applying for an individual, unsecured credit account. Marital status may be asked if the applicant requests secured credit, and on all requests for joint, unsecured credit.

In situations when inquiries about marital status are permitted, only the terms "married," "unmarried," and "separated" are permitted. Additionally, questions about a spouse may be asked if

- the applicant resides in a community property state
- the spouse will use the account
- the applicant is relying on income from a spouse or former spouse to qualify for the credit

❑ **Income**   ECOA prohibits lenders from disregarding income from alimony, child support, or separate maintenance payments and from welfare or similar public support programs. The regulation also prevents lenders from disregarding income from part-time employment or income of a woman of child-bearing age. These provisions eliminated practices that had been used by lenders to judge an applicant's creditworthiness. Before ECOA, lenders often asked what a woman's child-bearing intentions were, and they did not count the wife's income in loan calculations because of the possibility that she might become pregnant and leave her job.

ECOA does allow lenders to consider the probability that these protected sources of income will continue over the term of the loan and to judge the reliability of the income source. This provision allows lenders to examine documents, such as divorce decrees and separation agreements, that verify income and show how long it is expected to continue. Of course, lenders are also allowed to investigate the borrower's employment, income, and credit history.

❑ **Sex**　The sex of the applicant may not be considered in making a credit decision. Given the trend toward more single-person households, more working women, and modern life-styles, few lenders have difficulty with this provision.

Credit Scoring

ECOA recognizes the development of *credit-scoring* programs as a legitimate means of evaluating credit risk. Accordingly, it has guidelines for how the programs are to be developed, the criteria that may be included in the system, and how the system is to be maintained. Scoring systems must be demonstrably and statistically sound and empirically derived. This means that each scoring system must be developed using actual data developed from the financial institution's loan accounts, and that the items included on the score card and the values assigned must be consistent with recognized statistical procedures. All credit scoring systems must be periodically monitored to validate their predictive ability. We will discuss credit-scoring systems in more detail in chapter 9.

Adverse Action

An *adverse action* is the refusal of a lender to grant credit to an applicant on the basis requested (by declining the same term and amount desired by the borrower). An applicant might request an unsecured loan, for example, but the lender denies the loan request or decides that the loan can be made, but only on a secured basis. In the latter case, the lender might make a *counteroffer,* meaning that it would offer credit on a basis other than that requested by the consumer. Both decisions—to reject a loan request or to make a counteroffer—are covered under Regulation B's adverse action provisions. (If the consumer accepts the counteroffer, no special disclosures need be made. On the other hand, if the terms of the counteroffer are not accepted by the consumer, the bank must send an adverse action notice.)

Regulation B states that lenders must notify applicants of an adverse action within 30 days of receiving a completed application or after taking adverse action regarding an existing account (for example, terminating a line of credit). A sample adverse action notice is shown in exhibit 3.2. If a counteroffer is not accepted, lenders have up to 90 days to send a formal adverse action notice.

From a practical standpoint, ECOA and Regulation B are concerned with the need to tell consumers why they failed to qualify for a loan. Knowing the reasons for a loan denial allows applicants to correct problems or at least to better understand why they do not qualify. Indeed, lenders have traditionally provided financial counseling to consumers who have been denied credit. Rejected applicants are not always the friendliest people, but sometimes the lender can provide them with information that will help them qualify for credit in the future, thereby preserving their goodwill.

Violations

ECOA violations can be extremely costly to the bank since the act provides for civil penalties and class action suits. A successful class action suit can cost the bank $500,000 or 1 percent of its net worth, whichever is less.

Truth in Lending Act

Enacted in 1968, the Truth in Lending Act was the first in a series of consumer credit protection laws. It was revised significantly in 1982 when Congress passed the *Truth in Lending Simplification and Reform Act.* The revisions were in response to the deregulation movement of the early 1980s and were passed in order to correct some of the complexities of the earlier law.

EXHIBIT 3.2   Adverse Action Notice

2. Date: _____

1. Applicant's Name: _____

    Applicant's Address: _____

3. Description of Account, Transaction, or Requested Credit:

    _____

4. Description of Action Taken:

    _____

    _____

5. **Part I — PRINCIPAL REASON(S) FOR CREDIT DENIAL, TERMINATION, OR OTHER ACTION TAKEN CONCERNING CREDIT.** This section must be completed in all instances.

    a. ____ Credit application incomplete
    b. ____ Insufficient number of credit references provided
    c. ____ Unable to verify credit references
    d. ____ Temporary or irregular employment
    e. ____ Unable to verify employment
    f. ____ Length of employment
    g. ____ Income insufficient for amount of credit requested
    h. ____ Excessive obligations in relation to income
    i. ____ Unable to verify income
    j. ____ Length of residence
    k. ____ Temporary residence

    l. ____ Unable to verify residence
    m. ____ No credit file
    n. ____ Limited credit experience
    o. ____ Poor credit performance with us
    p. ____ Delinquent past or present credit obligations with others
    q. ____ Garnishment, attachment, foreclosure, repossession, collection action, or judgment
    r. ____ Bankruptcy
    s. ____ Value or type of collateral not sufficient
    t. ____ Other, specify: _____

6. **Part II — DISCLOSURE OF USE OF INFORMATION OBTAINED FROM AN OUTSIDE SOURCE.** This section should be completed if the credit decision was based in whole or in part on information that has been obtained from an outside source.

    ____ Our credit decision was based in whole or in part on information obtained in a report from the consumer reporting agency listed below. You have a right under the Fair Credit Reporting Act to know the information contained in your credit file at the consumer reporting agency. The reporting agency played no part in our decision and is unable to supply specific reasons why we have denied credit to you.

    Name: _____
    Address: _____
    _____
    Telephone Number: _____

    ____ Our credit decision was based in whole or in part on information obtained from an outside source other than a consumer reporting agency. Under the Fair Credit Reporting Act, you have the right to make a written request, no later than 60 days after you receive this notice, for disclosure of the nature of this information.

    If you have any questions regarding this notice, you should contact:

    Creditor's name: _____
    Creditor's address: _____
    Creditor's telephone: _____

NOTICE: The federal Equal Credit Opportunity Act prohibits creditors from discriminating against credit applicants on the basis of race, color, religion, national origin, sex, marital status, age (provided the applicant has the capacity to enter into a binding contract); because all or part of the applicant's income derives from any public assistance program; or because the applicant has in good faith exercised any right under the Consumer Credit Protection Act. The federal agency that administers compliance with this law concerning this creditor is (name and address as specified by the appropriate agency).

The Truth in Lending Act, implemented by Regulation Z, is intended to protect borrowers involved in a credit transaction of less than $25,000 that is primarily for personal, family, or household use by requiring uniform and detailed disclosures. Primary emphasis is placed on disclosures that allow consumers to determine the exact cost of the credit transaction and to compare rates and other credit costs to make informed decisions.

Annual Percentage Rate

The Truth in Lending Act requires that all lenders disclose the cost of borrowing in one standard manner. Rates must be quoted as an *annual percentage rate* (APR) using formulas contained in Regulation Z. The APR represents the cost of a loan, including the finance charge and any other mandatory charges such as the cost of any mandatory insurance coverage. The APR, therefore, is not just the interest rate, but the total cost of borrowing expressed as an annual percentage.

Finance Charge

The *finance charge* is defined as the dollar amount that the credit will cost the consumer. This item, along with the annual percentage rate, is regarded as essential for the consumer who wishes to compare the costs of different financing arrangements. One of the main things the finance charge reflects is how much will be paid in interest over the full term of the loan. For example, a $3,000 loan for 36 months at an annual percentage rate of 15 percent will incur interest charges of $743.64. Reducing the term to 24 months reduces the interest to $491.04, a reduction of $252.60.

Lenders must disclose the APR and finance charges, along with the amount financed and total of payments, in a section known as the *"federal box"* (see exhibit 3.3). These disclosures must be more conspicuous than other disclosures since they are the primary factors that the borrower can use to compare credit costs.

Closed-End Loan Disclosures

Truth in Lending disclosures must be made before a closed-end loan is consummated. *Consummation* is defined as the time when the consumer becomes contractually liable on a credit transaction. In addition to the disclosures shown in the federal

EXHIBIT 3.3   Federal Box Disclosures

ANNUAL PERCENTAGE RATE The cost of your credit as a yearly rate.	FINANCE CHARGE The dollar amount the credit will cost you.	Amount Financed The amount of credit provided to you or on your behalf.	Total of Payments The amount you will have paid after you have made all payments as scheduled.
15½%	$2,046.24	$5,256.24	$7,503.00

You have the right to receive at this time an itemization of the Amount Financed.
☐ I want an itemization.   ☐ I do not want an itemization.

Your payment schedule will be:

Number of Payments	Amount of Payments	When Payments Are Due
60	$120.05	January 16, 1992

Insurance
Credit life insurance and credit disability insurance are not required to obtain credit, and will not be provided unless you sign and agree to pay the additional cost.

Type	Premium	Signature
Credit Life Jt.	256.24	I want credit life insurance. Signature
Credit Disability		I want credit disability insurance. Signature
Credit Life and Disability		I want credit life and disability insurance. Signature

You may obtain property insurance from anyone you want that is acceptable to   (creditor). If you get the insurance from   (creditor),   you will pay $ _____ .

Security: You are giving a security interest in:
    ☐ the goods or property being purchased.
    ☐ (brief description of other property). *Your residence*

Filing fees $ _29.50_____   Non-filing insurance $ _____

Late Charge: If a payment is late, you will be charged $ _5.00_____ / _____ % of the payment.

box, Regulation Z requires that the consumer have the option of receiving a detailed explanation of the items that make up the amount financed, which is the amount of money loaned to the consumer and subject to a finance charge. Consumers may waive the requirement for an itemization. As a practical matter, the itemization is helpful when the loan includes the

EXHIBIT 3.4 Sample Itemization of Amount Financed

Itemization of the amount financed of $ _____

$_____ Amount given to you directly
$_____ Amount paid on your account with the bank

Amount paid to others on your behalf

$_____ To (public officials, credit bureau, appraiser, and/or
insurance company)
$_____ To (name of other creditor)
$_____ To (other)
$_____ Prepaid finance charge

distribution of funds to a number of parties; this will be the case on a bill consolidation loan, when the bank is issuing checks to other institutions. However, on a straightforward loan in which the borrower will be receiving all of the funds, it seems less necessary. Exhibit 3.4 shows a sample itemization of the amount financed.

Disclosures for variable rate loans must also conform to provisions in Regulation Z. Sample disclosures are shown in exhibit 3.5. They specify the various changes that could occur on loans with variable rates. The intent of the variable rate disclosures is to give consumers a clear understanding of the effect a change in rate will have on the loan. Because of the wide variety of variable rate programs, it is very difficult to develop one disclosure to cover all programs. For example, some programs fix the monthly payment at the time the loan is made, passing rate changes along to the consumer in the form of more or fewer monthly payments. Other variable rate programs pass on rate changes in the form of higher or lower monthly payments.

Truth in Lending also establishes specific requirements for advertising credit products. It requires sets of disclosures if certain triggering terms are used in the advertisement. These *triggering terms* include the following:

EXHIBIT 3.5 Sample Variable Rate Disclosures

The annual percentage rate may increase during the term of this transaction if:
(the prime interest rate of (creditor) increases)
(the balance in your deposit account falls below $ _____)
(you terminate your employment with (employer).)

The interest rate will not increase above _____%
The maximum interest rate increase at one time will be _____%
The rate will not increase more than once every (time period)

Any increase will take the form of:
(higher payment amounts)
(more payments of the same amount)
(a larger amount due at maturity)
If the interest rate increases by _____% in _____ (time period) your regular payments will increase to
$ _____

- the amount or percentage of any down payment required
- the amount of any installment payment
- the dollar amount of any finance charge
- any reference to the rate
- the number of monthly payments required
- the period of repayment

No advertisement can give any triggering term without providing all other required credit terms. Triggering terms also apply to conversations with potential borrowers. Thus, if a lender or dealer uses these terms, then all required disclosures must be made. This is a very challenging requirement for lenders to monitor and one which must be addressed in training programs. These disclosures must meet the requirements for clarity and conspicuousness specified by Regulation Z.

Open-End Credit Disclosures

Since open-end accounts remain open for an indefinite period of time and borrowers are permitted to use the credit at any time in the future, different disclosure requirements apply. The Truth in Lending Act requires that disclosures must be made to the borrower when the account is opened and periodically during the life of the account.

The initial disclosures must be made before the first transaction. This is a flexible provision that allows banks to use a wide variety of marketing approaches without being overburdened with the need to make lengthy disclosures. The consumer must also be provided with all necessary disclosures before ever using the account. If the customer does not like the information in the disclosures, the account may be canceled before incurring any expense. The required open-end disclosures include

❑ a statement of when finance charges begin to *accrue,* including an explanation of whether or not any period exists during which credit may be used and repaid without incurring a finance charge

❑ a disclosure of each *periodic rate* that may be used to compute the finance charge, the range of balances to which it is applicable, and the corresponding annual percentage rate; when different periodic rates apply to different types of transactions (some banks charge more for cash advances than for merchandise purchases on credit cards)

❏ an explanation of the method used to determine the balance on which the finance charge may be computed

❏ an explanation of how the amount of any finance charge will be determined, including a description of how any finance charge other than the periodic rate will be determined

❏ a statement of the consumer's rights and a notice of procedures to be used to resolve a billing error

The disclosures must state any security interest—claims against the property purchased under the account or otherwise pledged as collateral—that the bank will have. For example, in the case of a home equity line account, the fact that the creditor is taking a security interest in the customer's residence must be disclosed.

Periodic disclosures are required for each billing cycle in which there is activity on the account or a remaining balance. These disclosures, generally contained on the customer's billing statement, are illustrated in exhibit 3.6.

The *periodic statement* must contain

■ *account balance* at the beginning of the *billing cycle*

■ an identification of each credit transaction and any credit to the account during the billing cycle

■ each periodic rate and corresponding annual percentage rate and the balances to which each applied during the billing cycle

■ the finance charge

■ the minimum payment due and the date it is due

■ the closing date of the billing cycle

■ the outstanding balance as of the closing date

Consumers entitled to a periodic statement must be notified at least 15 days prior to the effective date of any change in credit terms. This provision is frequently triggered by changes in state law or the bank's marketing program. For example, if the bank decided to raise its rates, customers would need to be notified 15 days in advance of the change. State laws often provide for much more advance notice before a bank can implement a change. Some states may also limit changes in

EXHIBIT 3.6   Sample Monthly Billing Statement

AMOUNT
ENCLOSED

MAKE CHECK
PAYABLE TO BANK

REVOLVING CREDIT ACCOUNT STATEMENT

ACCOUNT NUMBER

H

CLOSING DATE	PAYMENT DUE DATE
02/15/	03/10/
MINIMUM PAYMENT DUE	NEW BALANCE
$54.87	$1,848.00

PLEASE RETURN THIS PORTION OF THE STATEMENT WITH PAYMENT.

PERSONAL LINE:

FINANCE CHARGE CALCULATION

FINANCE CHARGE	AVERAGE DAILY LOAN BALANCE	DAILY PERIODIC RATE	NO. OF DAYS	**ANNUAL PERCENTAGE RATE**
$23.95 =	$1,819.33 X	.042465% X	31	15.500%
NEXT BILLING PERIODS RATE		.040410%		14.750%

POSTING DATE	REVOLVING CREDIT ACTIVITY 01/15/ TO 02/15/	DEBITS/ADVANCES CREDITS/PAYMENTS
01/21	ADVANCE	93.24
01/23	ADVANCE	49.09
02/06	PAYMENT THANK YOU	51.70-

SUMMARY

ACTIVITY	PREVIOUS BALANCE	PAYMENTS CREDITS	ADVANCES DEBITS	FINANCE CHARGE	NEW BALANCE
LOAN ADVANCES	1,713.33	31.61	142.33	.00	1,824.05
FINANCE CHARGE	20.09	20.09	.00	23.95	23.95
OTHER CHARGES	.00	.00	.00	.00	.00
TOTALS	1,733.42	51.70	142.33	23.95	1,848.00

PRINCIPAL PAYMENT	CURRENT CHARGES			OTHER/PREVIOUS UNPAID PAYMENTS	MINIMUM PAYMENT DUE
	INTEREST	INSURANCE	LATE CHARGES		
30.92	23.95	.00	.00	.00	54.87

ACCOUNT NUMBER	CREDIT LIMIT	AVAILABLE CREDIT	CLOSING DATE	PAGE
	2,000	175	02/15/	1 OF 1

NOTICE: SEE REVERSE SIDE FOR IMPORTANT INFORMATION

terms only to future loans. The customer must be given the option to pay off the balance on the account under the old terms or to accept the new terms. The customer may accept the new terms and continue to use the account, either by signing a new agreement or by using the account after the effective date of the change. Customers who use the account after the new terms go into effect are generally subject to all of the new terms.

Special Credit Card Provisions

The Truth in Lending Act prevents banks from mailing *unsolicited credit cards* to consumers, a practice that flourished in the late 1960s. The act also states that a customer must sign a specific request form before an account can be opened.

Credit cardholders may be held liable for up to $50 of any *unauthorized transaction* if the bank tells consumers of this liability and provides them with a telephone number they should call in the event a card is lost, stolen, or used without a cardholder's authorization.

Rescission Rights

The provisions of the Truth in Lending Act apply to all loans in which the lender takes a security interest in the borrower's primary residence. A primary residence can be a mobile home, boat, trailer, or traditional housing, but the term does not include vacation and second homes.

Each borrower who owns and lives in the residence securing the loan must be given the required disclosures. The right to rescind the loan lasts until midnight of the third full business day following consummation. For example, if the customer signs the loan documents on a Monday, the loan could be canceled on Tuesday, Wednesday, or Thursday. Any one of the borrowers eligible to rescind may void the transaction by notifying the lender that he or she is exercising that option. If the loan is not rescinded, it could be finalized in this example on Friday. This provision is designed to give consumers the opportunity to examine all of the disclosures in greater detail before becoming legally obligated to repay the loan.

The right to rescind delays the disbursement of funds until the three-day period has elapsed. If any party to the loan executes the right to rescind, the entire contract is void. The bank must cancel the transaction and is not entitled to receive any finance charges on the loan.

The consumer may waive the right to rescind only under both of the following conditions:

❏ The consumer determines that the extension of credit is needed to meet a bona fide financial emergency.

❏ The consumer provides a signed and dated *statement of waiver* or modification explaining the nature of the emergency.

While provision has been made for waiving the right of rescission, lenders usually avoid any exceptions to the three-day waiting period. An incorrectly performed rescission cannot be subsequently corrected and allows the consumer to extend the rescission period for up to three years.

Fair Credit Reporting Act

The Fair Credit Reporting Act (FCRA) is Title VI of the Consumer Credit Protection Act. Effective since 1971, the FCRA is directed primarily at *credit reporting agencies*—firms that supply credit information to third parties like banks and other lending institutions. Some of the better known credit reporting agencies are Credit Bureau International, TRW Credit Data, and Trans Union.

The FCRA has four primary objectives:

❏ to establish acceptable purposes for which a consumer credit report may be obtained

❏ to define consumers' rights regarding credit reports, with particular emphasis on giving consumers access to their reports and a procedure for correcting inaccurate information

❏ to establish requirements for handling any adverse credit decision that resulted in whole or in part from information contained in a credit report

❏ to define the responsibilities of a credit reporting agency

A consumer credit report is defined as information on an individual's handling of their personal credit accounts. The information is gathered by a credit reporting agency and passed to third parties with a legitimate business need for the information. When a bank reports factual information to another bank or to a credit reporting agency regarding its experience with its own customers, it is not covered under the definition. If the bank passes along information regarding the customer's accounts with another bank, it would then be in the business of supplying consumer reports, according to the FCRA's definition.

Lenders may obtain a credit report from a credit reporting agency when they have received a bona fide application for credit. They may also obtain updated reports on consumers who have an open loan account with them. For example, the bank may obtain a report on credit card customers at the time of their card expiration date to determine whether the account should remain open. Lenders may also run customer names against credit bureau files when they are legitimately considering offering credit, such as on a preapproved credit offer. A report may be obtained on all the individuals who are applying for a loan. Randomly obtaining credit reports to check on friends, adversaries, neighbors, relatives, and fellow employees is prohibited. Such uses of credit reports violate the right to privacy guaranteed all consumers.

The FCRA does not prohibit banks from using prescreening programs to market credit products. *Prescreening* is a process in which the bank matches a list of names against a credit bureau file to identify consumers who meet certain predetermined credit characteristics. As a result of the prescreening process, the requesting bank receives a list from the credit reporting agency of the names of potential customers who meet the bank's qualification criteria. The bank does not see the individual credit reports for these consumers, though, so the practice does not fall within the scope of the FCRA.

The rules for prescreening changed in 1990. The new provisions state that if a bank uses a prescreening program to identify potential customers, it must offer to extend credit to all who meet the defined requirements, and that additional "back-end" requirements could not be used to further eliminate prospects. This has had a strong impact on marketing programs, which had come to rely on the ability to verify income and employment before extending a final offer.

If the bank obtains an actual credit report and the report contributes to an adverse action, it must disclose the source and nature of the adverse information to the consumer within 30 days of the date of the application.

Consumers have the right to see their credit bureau file and to have corrected any erroneous information. Credit reporting agencies may charge for this service.

Community Reinvestment Act

The Community Reinvestment Act (CRA) was passed in 1977 as Title VIII of the *Housing and Community Development Act*. While it has no direct effect on individual loan decisions, it does affect the bank's overall loan strategy, marketing efforts, and lending policies. CRA has been increasingly emphasized in recent years. Regulators and community action groups have intensified their examinations of bank performance in meeting the needs of local communities. Bank ratings on CRA examinations are now a matter of public record, and poor performance can adversely affect the bank's image and even prevent it from acquiring or merging with another bank or expanding its branch network.

CRA is designed to encourage regulated lending institutions to make available enough funds to meet the full and legitimate credit needs of all communities, and all segments of those communities, within their market areas. A particular emphasis in CRA is placed upon serving low- and moderate-income areas.

CRA requires a bank's board of directors to develop a written plan outlining objectives and strategies for meeting the credit needs of its communities. The bank is also required to take steps to inform the public of its general plans and performance in areas covered by CRA and to invite the public to review relevant bank documents for comment.

CRA empowers supervisory agencies to deny banks permission to establish new branches or to block banks' acquisitions and mergers if they have not complied with the act. In practice, CRA reminds banks that they have a special relationship with their communities and that it is not acceptable to serve the credit desires of foreign countries or remote businesses while neglecting the borrowing needs of local businesses and individual customers.

Real Estate Transaction

The consumer movement of the 1960s and 1970s led to the passage of a number of laws directed at real estate lending. Most of the laws focused on *purchase-money, first mortgage loans,* although second-mortgage lending, nonpurchase-money first mortgages, and home improvement loans were also affected to some degree. The advent of home equity line of credit products has served to increase legislative focus on these transactions. While securing loans with the equity in a home has given consumers access to the largest amount of credit possible, it also raises concerns that people may not repay these loans if real estate values decline as they have recently in many parts of the country.

Real Estate Settlement Procedures Act

The Real Estate Settlement Procedures Act, known as RESPA, was enacted in 1974 and is implemented through *Regulation X*. The act was substantially amended in 1975 in response to concerns expressed by the mortgage lending industry.

RESPA requires that mortgage lenders give disclosures to applicants similar to those required by the Truth in Lending Act. The required disclosures include a good faith estimate of *closing costs* and a special information booklet covering the various aspects of mortgage loans. These disclosures provide the consumer with a much better understanding of all of the costs associated with the impending mortgage loan transaction. In addition, RESPA gives borrowers some control over those costs by allowing them to select the title company that will be used.

RESPA applies to any loan secured by a residence intended for one to four families and that involves the purchase of a home. Its coverage does not extend to nonpurchase-money first mortgages or to second mortgage and equity line accounts.

The act places some restrictions on the amount of money mortgage lenders can require in an *escrow account*. It also prohibits *kickbacks* and *fee-splitting*—the practice of paying people for referring potential loan customers—on covered transactions. According to the provision, no person can give or accept any fee or kickback for referring business to or from a specific person incidental to the transaction. For example, an attorney may not offer to pay a lender for business referred to him for services such as title checks.

Fair Housing Act

The *Fair Housing Act* was passed as Title VIII of the *Civil Rights Act of 1968*. It prohibits discrimination in the sale or rental of housing, the financing of housing, and the provision of brokerage services.

In framing the Fair Housing Act, Congress was concerned about two practices that were prevalent at the time: *blockbusting* or *steering*, which involves directing groups of consumers into specific neighborhoods and away from others; and discrimination in providing real estate loans to protected groups. Discrimination took the form of

■ refusing to sell or rent a dwelling to members of certain groups

- discrimination in the terms or conditions of sale or rent
- falsely informing a person a dwelling was not available
- denying a loan for purchase, construction, or repair of a dwelling

The Fair Housing Act affects consumer credit lenders if they extend loans for home improvements and home maintenance. Lenders covered by the Fair Housing Act are required to display the *Equal Housing Lender poster* and to submit reports to regulators regarding their real estate loans. They must maintain a log of all applications covered by the Fair Housing Act and provide required data to regulatory agencies as requested. Those agencies monitor the portfolios of banks under their jurisdiction to ensure they are not discriminating or engaging in the practice of redlining.

Home Mortgage Disclosure Act

The *Home Mortgage Disclosure Act* (HMDA) was adopted in 1975 and is implemented by *Regulation C.* HMDA was revised in 1980, with further changes in 1986 and 1989 in response to the dramatic increase in home equity programs.

HMDA is strictly a disclosure law. It requires banks to report the geographic area where real estate and home improvement loans have been made. This information is then used by regulators to evaluate a bank's compliance with the Community Reinvestment Act and to evaluate whether or not the bank is engaging in discriminatory lending practices. Information is furnished to regulators showing the number of real estate related loans (mortgages, second mortgages, equity lines, and home improvement loans) made by census tract. If, from the data, it is evident that the bank is not serving certain areas, it may be an indication that the bank is *redlining* or engaged in other unacceptable practices. HMDA helps detect and, therefore, control illegal mortgage lending practices.

Home Equity Loan Consumer Protection Act (Amendments to Regulation Z, Truth in Lending)

Truth in Lending was amended in 1989 to address specific concerns about home equity line of credit programs. The amendments expand the disclosures made to consumers considering a home equity loan product.

Specifically, lenders are required to

- give specified disclosures and a home equity line booklet at the time of application
- adhere to advertising requirements established for these loans
- restrict the conditions under which a line of credit could be terminated or the amount of the line reduced

The primary focus of this regulation is to ensure that consumers fully understand that they are pledging their home as collateral for the credit service, and that all of the terms are clearly disclosed in advance.

The major effects of the regulation have been to

- increase the cost of offering these programs due to the necessity of making more detailed disclosures
- eliminate the *"evergreen"* provisions on lenders' line of credit programs, substituting a limited draw period for the line, forcing consumers to renew the line periodically—every ten years, for example

Flood Disaster Protection Act

The Flood Disaster Protection Act, passed in 1973, established the National Flood Insurance Program. The purpose of the program is to provide reasonably priced flood insurance to persons residing in flood-prone areas. This act was passed following a particularly difficult year in which hurricanes and other natural disasters destroyed millions of dollars' worth of homes.

The act requires banks to determine whether a property is located in a flood hazard zone before making a loan secured by real estate or a mobile home. If the home is in a flood zone, the bank must disclose this fact to the consumer and, if the property is in a community participating in the National Flood Insurance Program, it must require that the consumer obtain federal flood insurance. When flood insurance is required, it can not be waived under any circumstances. Further, the burden for ensuring coverage is on the lender, not the borrower.

Consumer Credit Compliance Program

The rash of consumer credit regulation that occurred from the late 1960s through the early 1980s made it necessary for banks to establish *compliance programs*. The complexity of many of the regulations, combined with the requirements for reporting and record retention, have imposed significant additional costs and administrative burdens on all financial institutions. Further, in recent years, regulators have increased the emphasis on compliance as part of their regular bank examinations. Banks have responded by developing and maintaining self-auditing compliance programs to address the full range of compliance issues, including employee training, documentation, and internal controls.

Compliance programs are designed to achieve a variety of objectives. These include

- improving customer service by having procedures in place to resolve inquiries and problems in an efficient manner
- increasing bank efficiency by standardizing some tasks and providing clear direction regarding actions to be taken
- ensuring compliance with all applicable regulations
- avoiding costly penalties and litigation resulting from regulatory violations

Responsibility for compliance begins with the bank's board of directors and extends to tellers and customer service representatives. Without a commitment from all employees, the bank may be exposed to compliance problems.

Some of the key steps involved in developing and maintaining a compliance program are

- documenting the bank's policies
- developing formal procedural manuals
- training lenders and support personnel in the requirements of the law
- conducting internal audits

The importance of well-documented policies and procedures and an effective compliance program is spelled out clearly in the following excerpt from Regulation B:

Failure of compliance. A failure to comply with this section shall not constitute a violation when caused by an inadvertent error; provided that, on discovering the error, the creditor corrects it as soon as possible and commences compliance with the requirements of this section.

The compliance program helps to ensure that the bank remains in compliance by subjecting it to periodic formal review. If an inadvertent error or violation is detected, it can be corrected before major problems develop.

Summary

Consumer lending is a highly regulated business. Lenders are subject to a variety of federal and state laws governing trade practices, the provisions in credit contracts, and the distribution of credit to all qualified consumers. Compliance with these laws is monitored and enforced by a variety of regulatory agencies as well as by financial institutions themselves, and the judicial branch of government is instrumental in interpreting the law.

A series of federal laws has been directed at protecting the consumer credit market since 1968. These laws have focused primarily upon the need to provide consumers with uniform disclosure of key credit features and to ensure that credit is provided on an equal basis to all qualified consumers. These laws have resulted in significant changes in the policies, procedures, and practices within the industry.

Review Questions

1. Give some examples of practices that led to the development of consumer credit laws and regulations.
2. What types of consumer loan provisions do state laws generally regulate?
3. How are federal laws implemented and enforced? Give some examples.
4. Name the nine bases on which a provider of credit may not discriminate under the Equal Credit Opportunity Act.
5. What is the basic intent of the Truth in Lending Act?

6. Why are the requirements for disclosures on closed-end credit different from those on open-end credit? What are some of the major differences?
7. What are banks specifically required to do in order to comply with the Community Reinvestment Act? What are the consequences of non-compliance?

Optional Research

1. Does your bank have a formal consumer credit compliance program? Take a look at your bank's compliance policy statement or make an appointment to talk to the compliance officer and find out the organization and scope of the program.
2. Read the loan documents your bank uses, or the documents for the loans which you have made. Is there anything in them which is not clear? Have you ever read them before?
3. Who is your bank's CRA officer? What is your bank's CRA rating? What is your bank doing to meet the community's borrowing needs?

The universe of consumer credit products and services offered by commercial banks is always expanding. But it was not until recently that the word "universe" could have been applied at all. Once, banks looked to areas like commercial lending to bring in profits. Now consumer credit operations have taken a prominent place in the family of financial services offered by contemporary banks, proving to be not only a producer of interest income from loans, but also a major provider of fee income and liquidity.

This part of *Consumer Lending* introduces you to the many types of consumer credit products and services marketed today. Consumer installment loans comprise two broad product groups: closed-end and open-end loans. Closed-end loans have a term that ends at a stated time, when the principal and interest payments have been made in full. Open-end loans, sometimes known as revolving credit, remains available to the borrower up to a certain limit, for as long as the consumer handles the account in a satisfactory manner.

By looking at the features of these credit products, you will get an appreciation of the vastness and diversity of the universe of consumer credit products.

Part Two
Consumer Credit Products and Services

4   Closed-End Loans

After reading this chapter, you will be able to

❏ list three characteristics of closed-end loans and discuss how each affects borrowers and lenders

❏ describe the most important consideration in making an unsecured loan and how lenders can limit risk on these loans

❏ name the four types of secured loans based on the behavior of their collateral value over time and give examples of each type

❏ discuss the benefits direct lending offers lenders and consumers

❏ discuss the disadvantages of direct lending and describe ways in which institutions seek to minimize them

Characteristics of Closed-End Loans

Closed-end loans accounted for nearly 70 percent of the dollars outstanding on consumer installment credit accounts at the end of 1990. At that time, Federal Reserve estimates show that the total dollar outstandings in closed-end loans reached $520.5 billion. Banks held the largest share of these loans, but other financial institutions, such as finance companies, credit unions, and savings institutions held large closed-end loan portfolios.

Closed-end loans are most easily recognized by the fact that they have a predetermined term and number of payments. Closed-end loans can run for 90 days, 12 months, or any specified number of months or years, with a variety of payment schedules possible (monthly, quarterly, annual). The length of the loan term is generally associated with a particular type of loan. For example, car loans typically run up to 48 or 60 months, while boat and home improvement loans may run as long as 10 years. Competitive conditions and the ever-increasing price of items consumers purchase on credit have led to a seemingly endless lengthening of maturities. One of the primary reasons for extending maturities is to keep monthly payments at a level affordable and attractive since the amount of monthly payments is a key consideration for consumers shopping for a loan.

The fixed nature of a closed-end loan contract allows the consumer to plan the family budget, knowing exactly what amount must be set aside for loan payments, when the payments are due, and how long the loan will be open. Most consumer loans provide for equal monthly payment amounts, though some variable rate programs may call for periodic payment adjustments.

Another characteristic of closed-end loans is that they are usually related to a specific borrowing need such as purchasing a car, consolidating bills, or making home improvements. The close association between the loan request and the specific need makes the purpose of the loan a variable often evaluated in the decision-making process. Lenders are in a position to evaluate whether or not the loan purpose is appropriate. Many lenders want to have some say in what the loan will be used for, while others are content to let consumers decide.

Since many closed-end loans are made for the purpose of purchasing a particular item, it is customary to use the item as collateral for the loan. These goods provide some measure of protection for the lender. Goods such as automobiles, boats, airplanes, recreational vehicles, and savings accounts are common forms of collateral. Collateralized loans have had a significant impact on the credit program which we will discuss in greater detail later in this chapter.

Types of Closed-End Loans

One approach to grouping loans is to combine the purpose of the loan and the collateral securing it. Exhibit 4.1 shows the different types of loans which may be included in a bank's closed-end loan portfolio. This approach is helpful in monitoring the mix of loans (the number and dollar amount of loans within the portfolio) and the characteristics (average loan size) of specific loan types. While the mix of closed-end loans may vary widely from bank to bank, the characteristics and trends for each individual loan type will be similar.

Personal, unsecured loans and state- or federally-insured student loans, often account for a high percentage of the number

EXHIBIT 4.1 Portfolio Distribution of Closed-End Loan Outstandings at Commercial Banks

Selected Loan Types	1985			1990		
	Number	Dollar	Average Amount	Number	Dollar	Average Amount
Personal—unsecured	18.8%	11.2%	$ 3,283	9.7%	4.1%	$ 3,120
Automobile—direct	18.6	16.9	5,003	11.7	8.9	5,362
indirect	32.3	36.5	6,246	47.5	46.0	6,815
Home improvement	4.7	4.8	5,719	2.2	1.8	7,220
Recreational vehicles	2.0	2.9	9,047	1.5	1.8	9,274
Student loans	14.9	8.4	3,097	12.4	8.4	3,097
Second mortgage	3.2	9.4	16,271	3.2	16.2	21,600
Aircraft	0.1	0.3	31,936	0.1	0.1	35,846

Source: *Installment Credit Report* (1985 and 1990 editions), American Bankers Association

of loans in the portfolio but a lower percentage of dollar outstandings. This is because the loans are typically for smaller amounts. On the other hand, second mortgage, aircraft, and mobile home loans are larger, accounting for a relatively high percentage of the dollar outstandings and a lower percentage of the number of loans.

Grouping loans by the type of collateral will help illustrate the issues consumer credit managers face as they develop their programs.

Unsecured Loans

This category is composed of the many loans made to consumers in which the lender does not require collateral to extend credit. Some banks follow very conservative practices regarding unsecured loans, often referred to as personal loans, restricting them to only the highest quality customers. Other banks take a much more aggressive posture and are comfortable extending personal loans to a broader range of consumers. The key to success is learning how to effectively manage the unsecured loan portfolio to meet the bank's marketing and asset quality objectives.

Unsecured lending is based on trust in the honesty and integrity of the consumer and upon the lender's ability to properly evaluate the credit risk associated with a given loan request. The borrower pledges to repay the loan under the terms set forth in the loan agreement. In the event the borrower can no longer pay off the loan, he or she is in *default,* the bank must work with the customer to resolve the problem, rather than rely on some form of collateral for repayment of the debt. Lenders normally charge higher rates and require shorter terms on unsecured loans because of the higher risk factor.

Comaker Loans

Another category of loans, which may be unsecured or secured, involve someone who signs the loan documents with the applicant to strengthen the loan request and induce the bank to make the loan. This person is the *comaker* and is fully liable for repayment if the primary borrower is unable or unwilling to repay the loan. Comakers receive no direct benefit from the loan; that is, they do not receive any of the funds from the loan proceeds, nor do they acquire any ownership interest in collateral that may be purchased with the loan proceeds. The comaker's status may be contrasted to the status of the co-applicant who is an equal party to the loan, sharing in the proceeds from the loan and typically receiving a share of ownership in goods purchased with the loan funds.

The fact that a comaker receives no benefit from the loan has significant implications for the decision-making process. Since the comaker is simply guaranteeing the obligation, they have a strong tendency to refuse responsibility for the loan if the bank develops problems in collecting payments from the *primary borrower.* For this reason, banks tend to limit comaker loans to situations in which they want to add strength for an applicant who has very limited credit experience or limited background due primarily to age, usually a young person who has just started to work. Lenders prefer to have comakers who are closely associated with the applicant, such as parents, rather than casual acquaintances, since the former tend to take the obligation more seriously if problems develop.

Home Improvement Loans

Unsecured loans are often made for the purpose of making improvements to the borrower's residence. It is normal for lenders to try to secure large home improvement requests with a *second mortgage* or home equity line of credit and recording a lien on the property. Smaller requests and requests from customers with very strong credit characteristics may be unsecured.

Home improvement loans are generally perceived as sound loans since the funds are used to improve the borrower's residence. This, in turn, should increase the value of the borrower's home. Banks often have policies that recognize a favored status of home improvement loans over other types of unsecured loans—maximum maturities are often longer, loan amounts higher, and rates lower than comparably sized personal and comaker loans.

Secured Loans

Collateral is customarily taken on consumer loans to reduce the level of risk. If the consumer encounters problems and is unable to repay a secured loan under its contractual terms, the lender may take possession of the collateral, subject to provisions in the *loan contract* and *security agreement,* and sell it to satisfy the debt.

The various types of secured loans are grouped below according to the behavior of the collateral's value over time: *depreciating value, fluctuating value, stable value,* and *appreciating value.* Each group has unique considerations that should be addressed when setting the bank's lending policies and procedures.

Depreciating Value Collateral

Depreciating value collateral covers all goods that decline in value from the moment they are sold. Goods in this group include automobiles, boats, trucks, airplanes, recreational vehicles, mobile homes, motorcycles, and equipment.

Exhibit 4.2 illustrates the relationship between the collateral value of goods that depreciate and the balance on a loan they secure. The gap between the collateral value and the loan balance represents the area of credit risk on the loan. If it were necessary to *repossess* the goods during the early stages of the loan, the bank could not recover the full amount of the loan by selling the goods. The difference represents an unsecured portion of the debt.

Individual products within each type of goods decline at different rates. For example, a Chevrolet Cavalier may decline in value faster than a Ford LTD. This difference in the rate of depreciation is another factor affecting risk in the loan. The more rapidly the units depreciate, the greater the credit risk. The rate of depreciation is affected by

EXHIBIT 4.2   **Depreciating Value Collateral: Credit Risk**

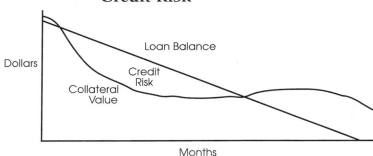

factors such as market demand, unit condition, color, image, and location.

When securing a loan with depreciating value collateral, it is important to determine the item's value at the time the loan is made. The value of some goods may be determined by referring to *valuation guidebooks*. Used automobile values may be obtained from National Automobile Dealers Association (NADA) or Blue Book publications, while new car values may be determined directly from dealer invoices or from services such as Automotive Invoice Service. Boat values can be obtained from BUC Book or, in some cases, from a marine survey. Values for mobile homes, recreational vehicles, motorcycles, and airplanes may also be obtained from similar publications. Some items require a special inspection or formal survey to establish their value. This is particularly true of airplanes, boats, and classic automobiles. Such surveys should only be conducted by qualified people. The valuation of goods is not a precise science, and the credit analyst should be aware of the limitations of each valuation source used.

Fluctuating Value Collateral

The value of some forms of collateral rises and falls over time (see exhibit 4.3). These fluctuations may increase collateral risk and make risk management difficult. Collateral in this category includes *stocks, bonds,* and other types of *securities.* The value of securities changes constantly, making careful analysis and control essential. Further, some securities are riskier than others. The stock of a well-established company with solid earnings is more predictable than that of a company experiencing significant problems or a new company without an established earnings record. Therefore, it is important that each bank establish very clear guidelines regarding what it will and will not accept as collateral.

Many banks only accept securities as collateral for demand loans, which allow the bank to call the balance due in full at any time. To avoid collateral risk if the value of the stocks or bonds deteriorate during the term of the loan, the bank should include in its loan documents a provision that allows

EXHIBIT 4.3   **Fluctuating Value Collateral: Credit Risk**

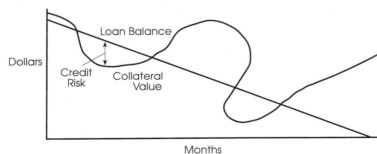

EXHIBIT 4.4   Sample Stock Listing

52 Weeks			Today's			
Hi	Lo	Volume	Hi	Lo	Close	Net Chg.
139¾	96¼	15704	109⅜	108⅛	108½	−1

the lender to ask for additional collateral if the value of the original collateral decreases beyond a certain point.

The value of actively traded stocks and bonds can be determined from data published in newspapers and from sources such as stock brokers. The value of privately held securities, those not traded in public markets such as the New York or American Stock Exchanges, is more difficult to determine and using them as collateral may be riskier, since there is a less predictable value and less demand for them. Exhibit 4.4 shows a stock market quotation for IBM. The value of each share is equal to the closing amount. If the consumer had 500 shares, they would have a total value of $54,062.50 (500 x 108.125).

All bank loans secured by margin stock and made for the purchase of margin stock are subject to the limitations of Regulation U. Margin stock is listed on exchanges, and on the Federal Reserve Board's list of marginable over the counter stocks. Regulation U requires the bank to take a purpose statement for all loans in excess of $100,000 secured by margin stock. Further, no bank may extend more than the maximum loan value of the collateral securing the credit (presently 50 percent of the current market value of margin stock).

Stable Value Collateral

Stable value collateral significantly reduces the level of risk on a loan. Collateral in this category includes savings accounts, certificates of deposit, and *cash value life insurance*. The collateral's value may be determined directly from the account record, passbook account, or insurance policy. Loans secured by this form of collateral are generally regarded as loss-free, although lenders will tell you that losses sometimes do occur due to operational errors. For example, if the *hold* placed on a savings account serving as collateral is accidentally released, a customer may take advantage of the opportunity to remove all of the funds from the account, leaving the bank in an unsecured position.

Barring operational errors, this category of loans has a very low risk, a fact that helps explain why loans secured by stable value collateral generally carry the lowest interest rates of all types of consumer loans. Exhibit 4.5 portrays the credit risk

EXHIBIT 4.5   Stable Value Collateral: Credit Risk

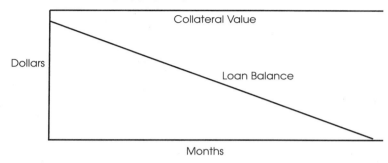

Appreciating Value Collateral

Appreciating Value Collateral

Some collateral actually appreciates—increases—in value over time. This category of secured loans is usually confined to real estate collateral, primarily the borrower's residence. While homes normally increase in value, it is absolutely clear that this is not always the case. Therefore, prudence and sound practices are required to manage portfolios secured by residential loans.

The build-up of *equity*, due to rising home values, is the source of most of the *net worth* reflected on the average consumer's *balance sheet*. This equity is increasingly being used to give consumers access to large amounts of credit, and to provide security for consumer loans.

The value of appreciating value collateral is usually obtained from an appraisal performed by a qualified appraiser. In theory, loans made using appreciating value collateral would exhibit the relationship to the loan balance illustrated in exhibit 4.6. However, there are no guarantees that all real estate will appreciate in value. Properties can go down in value due to neglect, a decline in the surrounding community, natural or man-made disasters, or the general state of the local economy. Further, loan collectors can tell you that homes and other collateral sold under quick-sale situations (auctions and foreclosures) rarely bring their full value. These facts demonstrate that even loans secured by appreciating value collateral are not completely risk free.

EXHIBIT 4.6   Appreciating Value Collateral: Credit Risk

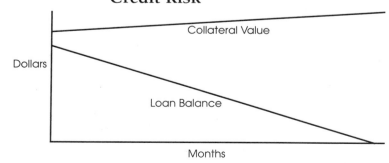

Guaranteed Loan Programs

Numerous governmental and quasigovernmental organizations offer specialized loan programs to meet the borrowing needs of certain groups. The level of risk varies among the programs, as do the specific program requirements.

Guaranteed student loans, designed to help students finance a college education, are the most common type of guaranteed loans handled by consumer credit departments. One of the best known programs is the Department of Education's Guaranteed Student Loan (GSL) Program. Loans are guaranteed up to established dollar limits as long as the bank fully complies with the requirements. GSLs also enjoy a very active secondary market made up of banks and other institutions that are willing to buy loans from the originating lender. This allows banks to make student loans to their customers without needing to keep them in their loan portfolio.

Other *guaranteed loans* often handled by a bank's consumer credit department include programs offered by state and local governments, the Farmers Home Administration, the Department of Housing and Urban Development, and the Small Business Administration (SBA). Some of these programs provide for full protection against loan losses, while others, such as SBA loan programs, provide partial guarantees.

In most cases, lenders do not compromise their credit requirements for guaranteed loans since the potential for collection problems and losses still may exist. While these programs do not generally offer high yields for the bank, making guaranteed loans plays an important part in fulfilling the bank's obligation to serve the legitimate borrowing needs of its community. In particular, participation in programs that benefit the community and serve the needs of the less fortunate help a bank meet its obligations under the Community Reinvestment Act.

Direct Loans

Direct loans are loans that are normally made in the offices of the financial institution. The consumer deals directly, in person, by phone, or by mail, with bank personnel at each stage of the lending process. The resulting personal contact presents many opportunities and challenges to the bank.

Since direct loans are almost always *closed* in the bank's offices, a convenient location is a very important factor in developing a successful direct loan program. It is difficult to get consumers to drive past competitors to obtain a direct loan from the bank unless the bank has something special to sell, such as lower rates, better service, or better loan products, and is able to differentiate itself from competitors based on these factors. The close relationship between branch location and the ability to attract loan and deposit customers at least partially explains the proliferation of bank branches between 1950 and 1980.

The Bank's Perspective

Direct lending offers financial institutions a number of advantages. These include

- a high level of control over the loan process
- personal contact with the customer
- loan structuring and selling opportunities

Direct lending brings the customer in personal contact with bank employees. The bank's employees answer inquiries regarding credit products, take applications, communicate the credit decision, and handle the loan closing. This means that the bank must train and develop its personnel to handle each loan function in a customer-oriented, efficient manner. The higher level of control results in better quality loan decisions, enhanced profit opportunities, and reduced credit risk.

The opportunity to establish a personal relationship with the customer is an important benefit of direct lending. Many individual lenders have a following of customers who are loyal, not necessarily to the bank, but to them. This relationship develops from providing high-quality service to people over a period of time and can be a very powerful tool in building a solid customer base. Consumers tend to be more receptive to marketing efforts by individuals and organizations with whom they have already had a satisfactory experience and in whom they trust. If the bank can offer high-quality personal service in its direct lending program, it may be able to enhance its total retail banking effort. Traditional direct lending is a natural fit with *personal bankers* and *relationship banking* offered by many retail-oriented banks.

Direct loan applications make it possible for the lender to recommend a variety of borrowing structures to the consumer. It is not at all possible to offer structuring options with indirect loans, and it is significantly restricted in most forms of open-end credit. Once the application is taken, the lender usually *qualifies* the borrower for the specific loan requested. If the applicant qualifies for a loan, the lender may then proceed with a full analysis of the applicant's financial needs in order to "recommend the best loan for the customer and the bank." This may involve recommending a different type of loan and a substantially different loan size and structure than that initially requested. For example, suppose an applicant requests a $1,000 loan to pay for college expenses. The lender might determine in the interview that this will be an ongoing need since the applicant's daughter is entering her freshman year. An analysis of the facts may lead the lender to recommend a home equity line of credit account, rather than the $1,000 loan. The home equity line account, where permitted by state law, would allow the applicant not only to meet the immediate borrowing need, but also to provide a flexible source of funds and repayment terms to meet future borrowing needs while providing the possibility of tax deductions on the interest. This type of structuring provides numerous benefits to both the bank and the customer. Moreover, it is an example of how lenders can provide valuable financial advice.

Another advantage of direct lending is that it gives the bank the opportunity to initiate a total banking relationship with the retail customer. When an applicant's credit request is approved, he or she will be more receptive to learning about and purchasing the bank's other services. The banker also has the benefit of having more information available concerning the customer's financial condition and needs than is typically provided in any other type of account relationship with the bank. When opening a checking account, the bank knows the customer's name, address, and employer, but little else. In contrast, when a customer applies for a loan, the bank knows those facts plus the customer's income, credit history, debts, age, number of dependents, and other personal information. The extra information gained from the loan application can be used to target more specific and more effective cross-selling efforts.

There are a number of disadvantages for financial institutions offering direct loans. The labor-intensive nature of the process, as well as its reliance upon skilled lenders and attractive branch locations, poses significant management challenges. Personnel costs are the largest expense for banks, and it is essential that consumer credit managers carefully identify products and procedures that will increase staff productivity. Several options for reducing employee costs and/or enhancing productivity are to

- automate as much of the process as possible
- centralize as much of the process as possible
- emphasize indirect loans to shift some of the loan functions to dealers

- emphasize open-end credit products, which reduce the costs of handling future borrowing needs

The emphasis placed upon creating a sales culture within banking makes it critical for bank personnel to develop higher levels of selling skills and focus more intently on effectively delivering products and services designed to meet the financial service needs of consumers.

The Consumer's Perspective

Retail customers benefit in several ways from borrowing on a direct loan basis. First, financial counseling provided in connection with the lending process can help consumers better manage their personal finances. The direct lending process also gives the borrower the opportunity to learn about the broad range of financing options available, as well as other credit-related services, such as credit insurance. This cross-selling opportunity is particularly important in the current market, because new products are constantly being developed and bank marketers are working to achieve greater product differentiation. A lender might offer counseling in the form of suggestions regarding a particular loan or advice regarding debt structuring, other bank products, or how to build savings.

Positive, well-informed counseling is a vital element in developing positive customer relationships. It is a far more effective tool for building goodwill than simply taking the customer's order. Effective counseling requires a high level of product knowledge and communication skills, and it means not making the mistake of assuming that the consumer is aware of all of the financial alternatives available in today's rapidly changing banking environment. It is hard enough for us to keep up with new products, and that is our job.

In addition to the financial counseling opportunities that arise, the flexibility to structure loans in the direct loan process can significantly benefit the customer by

- lowering monthly payment requirements on outstanding loans
- reducing the number of debts
- lowering interest rates on loan accounts
- increasing borrowing flexibility in the future through the use of more versatile open-end credit programs

In some cases, the lender's ability to structure the loan allows a loan to be made rather than rejected. In many cases, the lender's flexibility also means enhanced profits for the bank.

One of the primary disadvantages of direct loans, from the consumer's perspective, is the possible inconvenience of having to make one or more trips to the bank during office hours. This time is in addition to the time it took to shop for the goods or services being financed. Direct loans are not as convenient for the consumer as indirect loans, where the dealer handles both the sale of goods and arranges for financing. Nor are they as convenient as open-end credit lines which, once the account is opened, allow the customer access to credit when, where, and for whatever purpose is deemed appropriate.

Another more subtle disadvantage of direct loans is potential exposure to lender bias. Many lenders subscribe to the "lending is an art" philosophy, which holds that the lender weighs *all* of the tangible and intangible variables and comes up with a decision regarding the loan request. While there is obvious merit in this philosophy, it must also be recognized that such an approach allows individual biases to creep in; even prohibited criteria, such as age, race, and marital status, can enter into the decision-making process. Lender biases can work to the benefit of some consumers, such as those the lender knows well, but to the disadvantage of others. Individual lender biases against bill consolidation loans, people who borrow from finance companies, applicants who don't bank with your bank, divorced people, women, truck drivers, and so on, occasionally are asserted outside of the bank's written lending policy. Often, if not most of the time, these variables have little correlation with whether or not consumers repay their loans. To some extent, lender bias is an unavoidable element in the direct lending process. It is gradually being rooted out, however, by means of better education of loan personnel and by the use of credit-scoring programs.

CONSUMER CREDIT AT WORK
The Annapolis Boat Show

Each year, the boating industry holds one of its largest in-water boat shows in the charming city of Annapolis, Maryland, home of the United States Naval Academy. On alternating weekends, dealers display sailboats, then powerboats, ranging from $500 inflatable craft to $1 million-plus luxury yachts. The shows attract thousands of visitors, many of whom are ready to buy the boat of their dreams.

The Annapolis boat shows are also popular with financial institutions seeking to develop retail boat loans. Banks and other lenders obtain display space on the grounds of the show, where they can vie for direct loan business. The shows are the culmination of loan development plans that were drawn up nearly a year before and are fine-tuned in the weeks just prior to the event.

One regional bank developed an aggressive marketing plan for the boat show that plan included direct mail and telemarketing efforts to potential retail customers and marine dealers, a cocktail party for all dealers participating in the show, and a booth at the show that offered one-hour credit approval. The direct mail and telemarketing for retail customers were directed to the bank's current boat loan customers and to boat owners whose names were obtained from a variety of mailing lists. The mailing offered consumers the opportunity to be preapproved for a specific dollar amount before they went to the show. This would allow customers to shop, knowing they had a loan and how much they could afford. The direct mailing effort and the cocktail party for dealers emphasized the bank's commitment to the marine industry and encouraged dealers to refer both direct and indirect boat loans to the bank's booth.

The week before the show, the bank's consumer credit marine specialists, supported by marketing department personnel, conducted training for the employees who would be working at the bank's booth. The training covered everything from how to dress—nautical but professional—to product knowledge and how to manage the booth. The final plan, including rates, maximum loan maturities, and down payment requirements, was set at the last possible moment to ensure that no competitors would find out and thereby gain an unfair advantage. The final rate was not set until the morning the show began, and then only after carefully checking the rates offered by competitors.

To accommodate one-hour loan approvals, a telephone and terminal for obtaining credit reports were located in the booth. Behind the scenes were lenders and support personnel who could be called into service as needed. Those handling the booth were skilled and highly motivated salespeople.

Once the show gates opened, a crush of consumers began the constant flow of opportunities that would last for three days. Many consumers came ready to buy and prepared to apply for credit, some carrying copies of their tax returns and personal financial statements. Once an application was taken at the booth, a support person would begin the process of investigating the application. A lender would then review the application and make a credit decision. If higher lending authority was needed, senior lenders were on call to handle that need. Customers could return to the booth within an hour, assured that they would have a decision.

At the end of the first show, the bank counted the results: millions of dollars in new direct and indirect boat loans, an enhanced image with marine dealers and consumers, and a sense of pride among the employees who contributed to the success of the show. The bank subsequently used this same kind of marketing program in other marine trade shows, as well as in other trade shows sponsored by home improvement dealers, recreational vehicle dealers, and automobile dealers.

Summary

Closed-end loans are classified in a number of different ways. The broadest categories are direct loans—loans in which the consumer deals directly with the bank—and indirect loans—loans in which the consumer deals with a third party who arranges credit through a lender. Loans may be further divided into groups based upon the type of collateral securing the loan, or the type of unsecured loan being made. Understanding the characteristics of each type of loan is helpful in monitoring the bank's loan portfolio and establishing lending policies.

Collateral behavior patterns are an important consideration when analyzing risk on loans. The lender should know how to determine the value of the collateral at the outset of the loan and understand how its value is likely to change over the loan term. While there is some collateral risk on all secured loans, risk is greatest on collateral that depreciates or fluctuates in value over the loan term.

Direct loan programs provide financial institutions with the greatest amount of control over the lending process. This control can be helpful in maintaining credit quality, developing other retail account relationships with the consumer, and structuring the best loan for the customer and the bank.

Review Questions

1. Name as many characteristics as you can that are peculiar to closed-end loans. What advantage do these characteristics hold for the borrower?
2. What intangible factor does unsecured lending depend on?
3. Does the requirement for a comaker on a loan really make a risky loan less risky? What type of applicant usually prompts a bank to ask for a comaker?
4. Why are home improvement loans, though often not secured, considered a relatively safe investment for the bank?
5. Identify the four categories of secured loans and discuss their effect on risk.
6. Name an advantage of direct lending for a bank and then name an offsetting disadvantage. Do the advantages and disadvantages overall balance out?

Optional Research

1. Does your bank offer guaranteed loans, for example, guaranteed student loans? What percentage of your bank's consumer credit portfolio is guaranteed by a government or quasi-government agency?
2. What is your bank's policy about the types of collateral it will accept on a secured loan? Are there any types of collateral your bank will specifically **not** accept?

5

Indirect Loans and Related Credit Products

After reading this chapter, you will be able to

- ❏ name the three parties involved in an indirect lending program
- ❏ list the options available to a lender when structuring an indirect loan
- ❏ describe the benefits indirect lending offers financial institution and dealers
- ❏ discuss the advantages and disadvantages of indirect lending from the consumer's perspective
- ❏ define floorplanning and describe how it works in an indirect lending environment

Overview

Indirect loans have been a significant part of the consumer credit business since the first national dealer plan was announced by the Guaranty Securities Corporation in 1916. This form of lending developed to help retailers—often referred to as dealers—increase their sales by providing a convenient source of credit for their customers and to help financial institutions make credit more readily available to customers who could not be as effectively served on a direct loan basis.

Merchants such as automobile, boat, recreational vehicle, and mobile home dealers have been the primary providers of indirect loans. Stores selling large appliances and furniture stores also offer indirect loan programs, though most purchases from these merchants are now handled more conveniently with credit cards. Home improvement companies are another group of service providers who often seek to provide indirect financing for their customers.

Floorplan lines of credit, commercial loan programs in which the bank finances the dealer's inventory, such as the cars on an automobile dealer's display lot, are often provided as part of an indirect lending program. Financial institutions that extend floorplan lines of credit generally have closer relationships with the dealer. This, in turn, enhances the possibility of obtaining other business from the dealer, such as deposit and cash management business, and usually gives the provider first shot at the retail loans generated.

Characteristics of an Indirect Loan Program

An indirect loan involves three parties: a financial institution, a dealer, a consumer. The dealer is also the financial institution's customer on an indirect loan program; thus, the lender must compete for both the dealer's business and then for the individual retail customer's business. Their relationship is depicted in exhibit 5.1. The relationship begins when the lender and dealer execute an agreement defining the terms and conditions to be used in offering credit to the dealer's retail customers. Once an agreement is signed, the dealer will begin to offer the lender's credit services to customers.

Essentially, indirect lending allows consumers to purchase goods and arrange for credit at the same time. When a consumer wishes to purchase a product and desires to finance a portion of the purchase price, the dealer will take a loan application and submit it to the lender. The credit analyst reviewing an indirect loan request has fewer loan structuring options, since the dealer can only offer financing related to the sale of a particular item. The analyst reviews the terms of the sale—signers, amount, rate, maturity, down payment, etc.—and makes a decision within those constraints. The lender might approve the loan subject to receiving a larger down payment, shorter loan term, or a loan with a cosigner. Unlike a direct loan transaction, however, the lender cannot offer any other loan products or loan structures, such as a bill consolidation loan. Once the

EXHIBIT 5.1   **Indirect Lending Relationships**

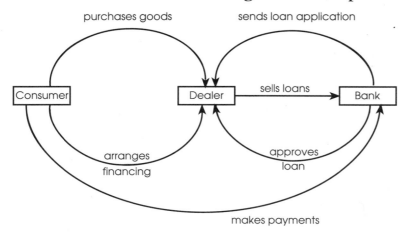

loan is approved, the dealer asks the customer to sign a loan contract and the customer receives the goods. The contract is subsequently assigned (sold) to the lender.

The lender does not have any contact with the loan customer until after the loan has been made. Consumers often do not know, nor care, which financial institution is providing the loan. The first contact the lender has with the customer usually occurs when a billing statement or coupon book is mailed. Some banks never try to develop any further business from their indirect loan customers, emphasizing only the profits from the indirect loan, while others seek to build relationships with these customers by marketing other products to them.

The Indirect Lending Process

Establishing a Dealer Network

An indirect lending relationship is developed as a result of sales efforts by bank personnel. The bank first determines which type of dealers it wishes to work with. A bank normally limits its indirect loan sources based upon the types of goods sold, the quality of dealers available, and the bank's specific objectives for this product line. Once these objectives are established, the bank develops strategies to attract and maintain the desired base of dealers. For example, in the face of strong domestic car competition from captive finance companies, many banks focused on developing a base of foreign car dealers. These dealers were attractive because many of them had high sales volumes, dealt with desirable consumers, and were not being served by finance companies.

The next step is to identify the particular dealers within each product group that the bank will target for an indirect relationship. Care is taken at this stage to solicit only dealers who will produce the kinds of loans desired by the bank and those who maintain the image, selling practices, and creditworthiness that are acceptable to the bank.

The bank may seek to diversify its loan portfolio by targeting dealers who handle different types of products—automobiles or boats, for example—and by seeking dealers who handle different brands of those products, such as Toyota and Chrysler automobile dealers, or powerboat and sailboat dealers. The type and number of dealers desired vary depending upon the bank's size, its objectives and capabilities, the type of dealers available in the bank's market area, and the competitive environment.

A successful sales effort results in establishing a formal business agreement. A contract defines the terms of the relationship and covers the specific services the bank will provide for the dealer. The agreement covering indirect retail loans is often referred to as the *dealer plan of operation,* or simply, dealer agreement. This agreement covers a wide range of topics relating to the business relationship including the bank's rates, maturities, down payment requirements, and other terms applicable to individual retail contracts. It will also specify how any income the dealer will receive from interest on retail loans will be paid. The agreement also details the dealer's rights and responsibilities regarding the loan program.

Exhibit 5.2 shows some of the kinds of information normally covered in a dealer plan of operation. Note that the plan establishes

- the rate the bank will charge on loans purchased from the dealer, called the *retention* or *buy rate*
- the maximum rate the dealer can charge retail customers
- the maximum loan term
- the down payment requirement
- the *dealer recourse* and *dealer reserve* option selected

It is common for dealers to have indirect lending agreements with more than one financial institution. The lender that is able to establish the closest relationship with the dealer,

EXHIBIT 5.2 Sample Retail Automobile Dealer Plan of Operation

Year Model	Bank Retention (Buy) Rate	Maximum Customer Rate	Term
New cars	10.00%	13.00%	48 months
	11.00	14.00	60 months
Current used	12.00	15.00	48 months
One-year old	13.00	16.00	48 months
Two-year old	13.00	16.00	42 months
Three-year old	13.50	16.50	36 months
Four-year old	14.00	17.00	30 months
Older models	16.00	18.00	24 months

Down payment: The minimum down payment on all vehicles is 20%.

Recourse option: All loans are on a nonrecourse basis.

Dealer reserves: Reserves are paid monthly on an earn-as-we-earn basis.

provides the quickest answers on credit applications, or offers the lowest rates or most liberal credit availability at any given time, is likely to obtain most of the dealer's business.

Processing Indirect Loan Applications

Once the dealer agreement is signed, the dealer may begin directing business to the bank. The dealer takes applications in the normal course of business and sends them to potential lenders. These applications are usually transmitted via fax machines, allowing the dealer to send the application to a number of lenders in a matter of minutes. Indeed, fax machines were in use for indirect loan programs long before they became widely used as a communication tool. Small dealers may still call the application into the bank.

Once transmitted, applications are generally processed by a centralized credit department that specializes in this type of lending. The applications are investigated and a credit decision is made by lending personnel. The decision is then communicated by telephone or terminal to the dealer. Given the highly competitive nature of indirect lending, it is usually necessary for loan decisions to be communicated as quickly as possible, generally within hours, if not minutes, of receiving the application. If more than one lender approves the application, the dealer will determine which financial institution will get the loan. Normally, it will go to the provider with the lowest buy rate.

The dealer prepares the legal documents for all approved loans. Large dealers usually prepare the documents on sophisticated equipment, and have loans closed by finance and insurance specialists. Smaller dealers, on the other hand, often have salespeople or office managers manually prepare the forms for closing. Whoever closes the loan will usually attempt to sell credit insurance and *warranty* services as part of the loan. The sale of these services usually provides an additional source of income for the dealer and the salesperson, who may be paid a commission on the sale.

Next, the dealer sends the completed loan documents, original application, and contract to the bank. Any documents required to obtain the title and record the lender's lien are processed by the dealer at this time. The contract is reviewed by bank personnel to ensure that it is properly executed and that the loan complies with the conditions of approval noted on the bank's records.

The final step in the process is for the bank to book the loan and *disburse* the loan proceeds to the dealer. Soon after, the bank sends a coupon book or billing statement to the customer. The bank may now begin direct contact with the customer.

The Bank's Perspective

Banks pursue very different strategies with regard to indirect loans. Some large banks have developed a broad base of dealers and actively compete for this business, while many others have chosen to leave the business. As with any product in the mature stage of its life cycle, indirect lending is subject to strong competition and is highly price sensitive. Thus, some providers simply are unable to obtain the desired return on their investment or find that this type of lending is not compatible with their overall goals. Those who remain active in the market are likely to control higher market share, but must deal with the challenge of achieving acceptable loan quality and profitability.

Advantages

The most important benefit to the bank is the role the dealer plays in selling the bank's credit services. Indirect loan programs not only help the dealer sell products, but also help the bank generate loan volume.

The bank's dealer base can be a powerful extension of its own sales force. Dealers enable the bank to reach consumers located in geographic markets that may be out of reach of the bank's offices, and to reach desired consumer life-style groups. For example, a Mercedes dealer is likely to produce a high net worth clientele that might be very attractive to the bank, while another dealer may generate a lot of business from young people, who are just beginning to build a household. In either case, the dealer can generate a significant number of customers and dollar loan volume for the bank.

Banks also benefit because the dealer handles some of the functions involved in the credit process and may also accept some liability for the performance of individual loans. The dealer takes the application, prepares loan documents, and closes the loan. This allows the bank to handle more applications with a smaller staff and increase productivity levels.

The bank may also be able to reduce the level of risk on indirect loans if the dealer is willing to accept some responsibility for the performance of loans generated by the dealership. This responsibility is usually referred to as dealer recourse, meaning the bank has recourse to the dealer to recover all or a portion of any loss it may suffer on a retail loan.

There are four basic recourse options:

- ❏ *Nonrecourse* or no liability   The dealer has no responsibility beyond normal warranties and recording the lien.
- ❏ Recourse or *full recourse*   The dealer is responsible for reimbursing the bank the full amount of any losses on its accounts.
- ❏ *Repurchase recourse*   The dealer is responsible for the full amount of any losses if the bank returns the collateral to them. There may be certain time constraints, such as within 90 days of delinquency on the loan.
- ❏ *Limited recourse*   This option may be used selectively. Dealers may agree to reimburse the bank for a flat dollar amount, $1000 for example, or for a specific period of time, such as for the first 12 months; any loss suffered above the dollar amount or beyond the agreed time is absorbed by the bank.

Note that the sample dealer plan of operation, shown in exhibit 5.2, provides for a nonrecourse arrangement. There has been a steady trend away from the other recourse options due to competitive pressures, though such plans are still found in some regional markets. The disappearance of this protection increases the bank's exposure to losses on indirect loans.

The value of a given recourse plan depends upon a number of factors, the most important being the strength and reliability of the dealer. If the dealer goes out of business or has no regard for its obligations, the bank can incur losses even if the dealer has signed a full repurchase agreement. At best, recourse can help the bank minimize credit losses and allow it to make loans to some slightly higher risk customers; at worst, it can lure the lender into a false sense of security, resulting in unexpected credit losses or unacceptably high delinquencies.

Another important feature of indirect lending is that it enables the bank to adjust its loan volume quickly. New dealers, particularly high-volume auto dealers, can generate hundreds of loans and millions of dollars in loan volume in a very short period of time. This volume can help the bank invest available funds quickly, thereby generating earning assets. On the other hand, volume from dealers can be slowed by a number of tactics which range from raising credit requirements to withdrawing the financing plan from selected dealerships. For example, in 1980, many banks elected to dramatically curtail their consumer loan business due to a severe profit squeeze. One response was to cut off indirect dealers, thus slowing new loan volume. On the down side, such tactics make it very difficult for the bank to get the dealer's business back if it decides to go back into the market at a later date.

Disadvantages

One disadvantage for banks is the profitability of indirect lending has come under severe pressure in recent years. As the product line has matured, competition has driven down lender profits by

- limiting the spread between the bank's cost of funds and the dealer buy rates
- forcing lenders to give up recourse protection
- stretching credit requirements in order to compete for retail business

Because of these changes, many financial institutions have withdrawn from the market and sold their indirect loan portfolios to those still actively in the business. The majority of indirect lending is now concentrated in a much smaller base of lenders.

The indirect market is often characterized by rapidly shifting loyalties. Dealers will shift business from one loan source to another at the slightest reduction in the dealer rate. Further, tactics such as the use of interest subvention programs by captive finance companies have caused severe disruption in the market. This marketing tactic, while rarely used in recent years, has severely cut domestic new car loan volume for many financial institutions during program periods and forced banks to reassess their positions in the indirect auto loan markets.

Some problems are unique to indirect lending. One problem is pressure exerted by dealers to induce the bank to make marginal loans. If the dealer sends a lot of business to the bank, it sometimes expects the bank to take a few marginal risk customers along with the good ones—especially when the dealer accepts some recourse on the loans. However, it is never a good practice for a bank to compromise its credit standards. Banks have adopted a number of strategies for tempering dealer pressure including

- requiring a higher authority for approval of nonstandard credit risks
- requiring dealer recourse endorsements on all high-risk applicants
- discontinuing relationships with dealers who apply undue pressure

Problems may develop for the bank because of the high pressure, deceptive, or otherwise unacceptable selling practices of some dealers. In some cases, banks might even suffer credit losses due to such practices. Banks need to determine that each dealer's practices are acceptable before establishing a relationship, and then continually monitor the relationship. When problems arise, such as customer complaints, failure to correct documentation problems, high delinquency on the dealer's retail loans, and discrepancies between the terms disclosed on the loan papers and information provided by the dealer, the bank should carefully review and correct each situation.

Sometimes banks experience serious problems handling indirect loans because of dealer fraud. Fictitious loans, double financing, misrepresentation of terms, and straw purchases might occur if a dealer is under financial strain. Since the salesperson's commission may be dependent on a loan approval, there is pressure to "doctor" or "beef up" the application. This can lead the bank to make credit decisions based on inaccurate information. Fraud generally does not go on very long but can result in considerable losses for the bank.

Dealers may submit *fictitious loans* from applications and contracts for nonexistent individuals or for real people who did not, in fact, enter into a contract with the dealer. This type of fraud can be detected by sound investigation practices, which verify the existence of the consumer, and audit confirmation programs, which detect any discrepancies on loan contracts.

Applications and contracts may also be submitted to and approved by more than one lender, resulting in the dealer being paid twice for one sale. This practice, known as *double financing*, usually surfaces quickly since the customer will receive two coupon books. The bank must respond quickly when such complaints arise.

Dealer personnel may also misrepresent some of the terms on a loan request to make a loan application appear more favorable. Selling prices, down payments, and other terms may be misrepresented, making it appear the customer has invested more in the sale than the dealer actually received. This problem may be minimized by relying on sound collateral valuation guides to determine the amount the bank will lend on various collateral. Random audits to verify loan terms also help curb misrepresentation.

Another fraudulent practice is the use of straw purchasers. A *straw purchaser* is an individual who allows his or her name and credit information to be used to obtain a loan for someone who does not qualify. While the straw purchaser actually signs the loan documents, they receive no direct benefit from the loan. This practice is extremely dangerous since it normally arises when the actual purchaser of the goods does not qualify for credit due to a bad credit history or some other significant problem. Straw purchasers, like comakers, often do not pay for loans if the primary user fails to make payments.

The Dealer's Perspective

The availability of an indirect financing program helps dealers close sales on the spot, enables them to sell monthly payments, and increases dealer profits.

Dealers are anxious to complete a sale as quickly as possible because it eliminates the possibility of losing a customer who may either find a better deal elsewhere or decide to postpone making a purchase. This is one reason why fast credit approvals are so important to the indirect lending process. Credit programs allow the dealer to offer monthly payments, which can bring the purchase of large-ticket items within the reach of more consumers. Thus, instead of trying to sell a car for $20,000, the salesperson can sell it for only $350 per month— sounds much more affordable, doesn't it? If a long-term repayment plan is available, dealers may be able to "sell customers up" to higher priced models, or, if necessary, down to less expensive models.

The extra profit dealers earn from credit sales (income from loans and insurance), is very important to them. Banks pay the dealer a portion of the interest charges on loans developed by the dealer. These funds compensate the dealer for its sales role and the tasks it performs in connection with taking the application and closing the loan. The dealer's portion of the interest income is the difference between the rate charged to the retail customer and the bank's buy rate. For example, if the dealer charges the customer 13.5 percent and the bank's buy rate is 12 percent, the dealer earns the difference—1.5 percent—over the term of the loan. Exhibit 5.3 shows the income a dealer might receive from a typical retail transaction.

The dealer's share of the finance income ($337.79 in the sample transaction) goes into a reserve account with the bank. The dealer reserve account is a checking account established for the dealer but controlled by the bank. Funds are added to the account during the month as new loans are booked and may be disbursed to the dealer at the end of the month on two basic schedules:

❏ **Earn as bank earns**   Under this schedule, the dealer receives income in the same manner as the bank receives its income. As payments are made, the interest income is split between the bank and the dealer based on their predetermined percentage.

❏ **Reserves paid up-front**   Under this schedule, the dealer receives the full amount of its share of the finance charge income for all loans booked the prior month. This amount is reduced by any income on prior loans that must be rebated when an account pays out ahead of time. For example, if a customer with a 48-month loan pays the loan off at the end of 24 months, the bank and dealer will not earn all of the interest anticipated on the loan. The dealer must, therefore, be charged for the unearned portion that has already been paid to it.

EXHIBIT 5.3   Dealer Income from a Retail Contract

Customer is purchasing a new Ford Escort, 48-month term.

	Contract Terms	Dealer Income
Amount financed	$9,000.00	
Bank retention rate	12.00%	
Customer rate	13.50%	
Total finance charge	$2,822.66	
Bank's retention	$2,484.87	
Dealer share of finance charge		$337.79
Life insurance premium	144.00	
Dealer commission: 32%		46.08
Accident & health premium	276.70	
Dealer commission: 32%		88.54
Warranty policy	585.00	
Cost to dealer	300.00	
Dealer profit on warranty		285.00
Total dealer earnings on this retail contract		$757.41

The Consumer's Perspective

Advantages

Retail consumers may derive several benefits from an indirect loan. Many consumers place a high value on convenience, and some are willing to pay extra for it. The ability to both buy a product and arrange financing at the same time is a definite benefit. Indirect lending programs have traditionally emphasized convenience. In fact, high-volume dealerships frequently sell vehicles, close loans, and send happy customers on their way before getting the final approval on the loan.

Another benefit that indirect loan programs may offer the consumer is flexible terms. Dealers frequently offer credit for longer terms with lower down payments than the bank offers on direct loans in response to competitive pressures in the market and the existence of dealer recourse plans.

Finally, consumers who lack a good credit record or characteristics that show stability—length of residence or employment—normally required for loan approval are occasionally able to obtain financing through a dealer. This benefit results primarily from either the dealer's willingness to accept some degree of recourse on the loan, thereby reducing the bank's risk, or from the pressure exerted on the bank by dealers to take some marginal customers.

Disadvantages

On the negative side, an indirect loan may not be the best loan alternative for a particular consumer if viewed from a total financial management perspective. Since each indirect loan request must stand on its own and there is no provision for restructuring the borrower's existing debts, it may be difficult to structure the best loan for the customer. The lender is not able to provide any financial counseling to the borrower, though this role is sometimes assumed by the dealer's finance and insurance representative. Information provided by these individuals, however, is primarily concerned with making a sale and not necessarily with what is the best loan for the customer.

Another drawback of an indirect loan program is that the customer may not have compared products and credit options. The result is often an impulse purchase that the consumer may regret later. A familiar story is of a car shopper falling in love with a car and wanting to take it home immediately. Salespeople are trained to recognize these strong urges and to help consumers realize their dreams without further ado. These decisions often come under closer scrutiny after it is too late. People usually do a good job of rationalizing their decisions, but sometimes they direct their anger at the nearest scapegoat. In the case of an indirect loan, the bank may be a convenient scapegoat for the disgruntled customer who realizes lower priced loans were readily available directly through the bank.

Finally, consumers may be harmed by unfair or deceptive selling practices by dealers. High-pressure sales approaches, deals packed with unwanted or unnecessary credit insurance or warranty policies, and unclear loan terms are all examples of sales practices that frequently come to light only after the contract is signed and the customer has gone home. Consumers are sometimes told that the bank requires them to take insurance or that the bank sets the rate on the loan. Worse yet, consumers occasionally sign blank or incomplete contracts, only to be surprised later.

Floorplan Financing

Floorplanning is a form of commercial lending that banks may offer independently or in connection with an indirect loan program. Floorplan financing is also known as inventory financing or wholesale line of credit programs, and it involves establishing a line of credit which the dealer uses to finance an inventory of products for sale and display purposes. For example, automobile dealers maintain relatively large inventories of vehicles on their lots. These vehicles may be sold immediately or may be used to show prospective buyers the options available to them.

The Floorplan Process

The operation of a floorplan line is illustrated in exhibit 5.4. The following steps will guide you through the floorplan process.

Line of Credit Is Established

The bank will follow its normal process for approving this type of commercial loan. Once the floorplan line is approved, the bank informs the manufacturers that supply goods to the dealer that it will now be providing floorplan financing. The amount of the line usually depends upon the dealer's sales volume, the variety of units available, the time it takes for the manufacturer

EXHIBIT 5.4 Operation of an Automobile Dealer Floorplan Account

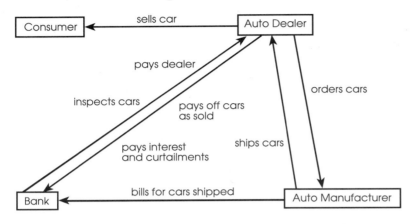

to deliver ordered units to the dealer, seasonal demand patterns, and the dealer's financial strength. A general rule of thumb is that dealers should maintain an inventory equivalent to 60 days of sales volume, this should be adjusted in accordance with seasonal demand patterns. For example, boat dealers in the northeastern part of the country experience their heaviest sales volume from March through June, while sales tend to be weak from November through January. Thus, dealers stock heavy inventories during peak periods to maximize sales and, generally, keep inventories low during slow periods to minimize floorplan interest costs.

Dealer Orders Inventory from Manufacturer

The dealer places orders with the manufacturer to fill specific customer orders or to replace units that have been sold out of inventory. Occasionally, the manufacturer will initiate the process by attempting to induce dealers to take delivery of units it wants to ship out of its inventory. In this case, the manufacturer may offer some incentive to the dealer for taking delivery of units, such as paying part of the interest cost or providing free financing for a period of time.

Manufacturer Requests Approval from the Bank

The manufacturer normally contacts the floorplanning bank before filling a dealer's order. The purpose of this contact is to verify that the floorplan line can cover the dollar value of the units to be shipped. If the order is within the maximum credit line, the bank gives the approval to ship the units. If, on the other hand, the new units would put the dealer over the maximum amount of the line, the bank may, at its discretion, refuse to pay for the units ordered. The dealer must then delay ordering the units or must seek approval from the bank to temporarily exceed the limits of the line.

Manufacturer Sends Approved Units to the Dealer and Bills the Bank

Once the bank approves shipment, the manufacturer sends the units to the dealer and sends the bill of sale to the bank. In most cases, the actual ownership documents (Certificate of Origin) for individual units are sent directly to the dealer, although some banks hold these documents, depending on state law and bank policy. The bank pays the manufacturer for units as invoices are received.

Bank Sets Up Unit under the Floorplan Line

The bank charges the dealer's floorplan line for each unit at the time it receives the bill or draft from the manufacturer. Unit numbers are recorded on the bank's floorplan list along with the amount of the invoice for that particular unit.

Dealer Pays Off Units as Sold

Units remain on the inventory list and floorplan account until they are paid in full by the dealer. Dealers are required to pay off units immediately after they are sold. When dealers have been paid but do not pay the bank in full for units sold, the bank is put at risk. The floorplan line is no longer secured by those particular units and essentially becomes an unsecured loan. In fact, banks have taken losses in the millions of dollars as the result of dealers selling inventory and failing to pay the bank.

Bank Conducts Monthly Inspection of All Units on Floorplan

Banks typically inspect the dealer's inventory every month. This task may be done by bank employees or by outside firms that provide such services. Inspectors go to the dealer's store with a list of all units that are open on the bank's records. They examine each unit in inventory, checking off the units they actually see. They also note anything unusual about the unit, such as damage or excessive mileage that could reduce the unit's value and expose the bank to loss. All units must be accounted for. If units are missing, the inspector determines whether they are sold, out on demonstration, or being traded to another dealer. Depending upon the bank's policies, the inspector may immediately require a check from the dealer to pay off all units that have been sold or cannot be accounted for.

The Bank's Perspective

The bank's ability to extend wholesale lines can help its efforts to attract business from a given dealer. The more financial services the bank can provide to the dealer, the more value the relationship has to both parties. When a dealer has a floorplan line with a particular bank, the dealer generally will arrange its indirect retail loans with the same bank. Dealers typically maintain their checking accounts and other cash management accounts with the same bank that handles their floorplan.

Floorplan lines of credit are typically priced in relation to the bank's prime commercial lending rate. The rate floats with changes in the bank's prime rate, sheltering the bank from the interest rate risk inherent in fixed-rate lending. Loan yields on floorplan lines are generally not as attractive as other types of loans; however, they contribute to total dealer profitability and play a key role in helping the bank become the dealer's primary source for other financial services.

Dealer floorplan lines can present some significant challenges to banks. One problem is their labor-intensive nature. A floorplan line can involve many transactions each day, the overall volume depending on the size of the dealership and the type of product financed. A car dealer with a $2 million floorplan line produces many more transactions daily than a dealer with a $500,000 line. Likewise, a sailboat dealer with the same $2 million line generates far fewer transactions, but each transaction involves larger amounts of money. Automation of the wholesale accounting system can help reduce processing costs, improve efficiency, and enable the bank to handle larger lines and more dealers than a comparably staffed manual system.

Profitability is a primary area of concern with floorplan lending. A major area of competition among banks are wholesale rates, which generally vary close to the prime lending rate offered by the bank. Thus, bank managers need to examine the total profitability of the dealer account to determine whether it meets competitive pricing initiatives.

Inventory financing also presents some significant credit risks. Risk is best controlled by carefully selecting the dealers to whom the bank extends floorplan lines. Line requests should be subjected to a thorough credit analysis and the dealer's selling practices, reputation, and experience should be carefully weighed before a floorplan line is extended. Once a dealer is approved, the bank must continue to monitor the dealer's financial health. It is in the face of strained business conditions, such as declining sales or operating losses, when dealers are most likely to resort to unacceptable and risky practices.

As noted earlier, collateral risk on a floorplan line is controlled by conducting regular inspections of the dealer's inventory. This essential control point will quickly identify any practices that are unacceptable to the bank or that could expose the bank to credit losses.

The Dealer's Perspective

Consumers shopping for goods, such as cars, boats, and appliances, often want to take immediate delivery of the item they select for purchase. If a dealer has the exact item the consumer wants in inventory, a sale may be closed without delay. Financing enables dealers to keep a well-stocked inventory and therefore make more sales. In contrast, a floorplan line also allows the dealership to use its funds elsewhere in the business, rather than tying them up in inventory, if appropriate.

A floorplan line is a debt obligation for the dealer. Interest must be paid on the outstanding balance used each month. Assuming a dealer has an average daily balance of $2 million on its floorplan account, and the floorplan rate is 9 percent, the monthly interest charges would be $14,795. Naturally, the dealer must cover this cost in the selling price of its products.

Dealers must also be prepared to reduce or curtail the amount owed to the bank for units that have been in inventory for extended periods of time. For example, the bank may allow the dealer to keep an automobile in inventory for up to 12 months without reducing the amount owed on the unit. However, after that time, it is prudent for the bank to require the dealer to reduce the amount owed on the unit since it is depreciating in value, thereby increasing the bank's exposure. The bank may require a *curtailment* of 10 percent of the unit's original costs each month until the unit is sold or paid in full.

Banks may find it necessary to cancel a dealer's floorplan line or restrict the line based on a number of factors. Declining economic conditions or shifts in bank objectives or strategies occasionally lead banks to reduce wholesale lending. Cancellations most frequently affect smaller or financially weaker dealerships, which, by virtue of their size or financial condition, have fewer options available to them when lines are canceled. Adding to the small dealers' burden is the probability that their floorplan line is more likely to be canceled during economic downturns when banks are less likely to be seeking new business.

The mix of automobile dealers in the United States has changed significantly over the past 30 years. The number of domestic automobile outlets has declined, while import outlets have grown. These changes reflect, among other things, changing buyer preferences over time. Many small dealers have disappeared in recent years and been replaced by large dealer operations that have multiple locations. These large dealers, sometimes referred to as "mega-dealers," are often very strong financially, and they offer new opportunities and challenges for lenders serving the indirect automobile market.

Leasing

Leasing is a financial arrangement in which one party, in this case the bank (*lessor*), owns the collateral and rents it to the consumer (*lessee*) for a specific period of time. Leasing has become more popular among automobile buyers in recent years, and its availability and use has continued to spread.

Leasing programs compete directly with traditional direct and indirect lending programs. Though leasing is governed by distinct laws, it is so closely related to these traditional loan products, and is such an important part of the automobile finance market, that it is critical to discuss this product to understand the trends in the market. Leasing programs are available predominantly on automobiles, although some programs are available for equipment and other durable goods. Consumers who are indifferent about whether they own or rent a product, or who may be able to realize some of the other benefits that leasing plans offer, may be persuaded to lease rather than finance a product.

Banks may offer leasing products on a direct or indirect basis. These programs are generally handled by a specialized unit due to the complexity of computing and documenting leasing transactions. However, the bank's branches and selected dealers may be relied upon to develop potential customers and service their requests.

Some of the benefits consumers perceive in leasing are attributable to how leasing arrangements are structured. They require little money down, and the monthly payments do not have to cover the estimated value of the collateral at the end of the lease term, the *residual value*. Therefore, the monthly payments on a lease are usually lower than they are on a comparable installment loan. Exhibit 5.5 illustrates these differences.

EXHIBIT 5.5   Conventional Financing vs. Leasing for an Automobile

Conventional Financing		Open-End Lease	
Purchase price	$23,000	Capitalized cost	$23,000
Sales tax & registration	+1,190	Residual value	12,700
Down payment	-4,838	Amount to be liquidated over	
Amount financed	19,352	lease term	10,300
Monthly loan payment		Monthly lease payment	
48 months at 13.5% APR	$ 523.96	over 48 months	$ 433.03
		Initial payment—one	
		month's rent	$ 433.03
Total payments	$25,150	Total payments	$20,785

Despite the apparent benefits, leasing may be more expensive to consumers in the long run. In the example, the consumer who financed the car would have paid $29,988 (total payments of $25,150 plus a down payment of $4,838) and would own an asset worth an estimated $12,700—the residual value. The net investment would be $17,288. The lease customer would have paid $20,785.44 but would not own the vehicle at the end of the lease term. On the other hand, the lease customer would have had a substantially lower down payment and would pay $90.93 less per month.

Leasing programs often offer consumers added convenience benefits and greater flexibility in financial terms. Some leasing companies take the customer's order for a car, then locate, purchase, and deliver it to the customer's door. They may also structure the lease to fit the consumer's particular needs. For example, consumers looking for the lowest monthly payment might be offered a five-year lease, while another person who likes to trade cars every two years would be set up with a two-year lease.

The attractiveness of leasing programs to lessors (banks and other financial institutions) has centered on the potential profits and the growing level of consumer acceptance. In the past, lessors have been able to take advantage of favorable tax laws. Those laws, generally limited to business-use vehicles, allowed lessors to reduce their taxes by using accelerated depreciation and then take investment tax credits on the vehicles they leased. These tax features enhanced the yield from a lease portfolio, making it a very attractive product line.

Tax reform in 1986 reduced some of the tax advantages for lessors. This forced financial institutions involved in leasing programs to reevaluate the product. As a result, some banks have curtailed their leasing programs, while others have continued to expand their leasing operation in response to profit opportunities and local market conditions.

Summary

Indirect lending programs involve the use of dealers in the development and closing of retail loan requests from their customers. Dealers can develop a significant volume of consumer loans, while performing a number of loan processing services for the bank. Dealers are compensated for their services by sharing in the interest income generated by indirect loans and by the sale of credit related services such as credit insurance.

Banks may profit from handling the dealer's retail loan needs and from providing other services to the dealer. Floorplanning is a particularly important credit service since it ties the dealer closely to the bank and produces an additional source of income. The bank may also provide dealers with checking and savings account services, investment services, capital and other loans, and credit card merchant accounts.

The indirect lending market, particularly the automobile segment, has changed in recent years due to shrinking profit margins. Because of the decline in profitability, many banks have withdrawn from indirect lending. Dealer business is now concentrated with a smaller group of banks. The growing availability and acceptance of leasing programs has also decreased the demand for indirect loans.

Review Questions

1. Name the parties to agreements or contracts under an indirect loan arrangement.
2. In what ways can a bank reduce its risk on an indirect loan? Define the various options.
3. Do dealers benefit financially from an indirect loan, other than being able to make the sale? Explain.
4. Do most banks offer identical credit terms on their direct and indirect loans? Why?
5. Give two reasons why an indirect loan to purchase a new car might not be the best loan alternative for a customer.

6. What is the connection between an indirect lending relationship and a floorplan financing plan? Describe generally the floorplanning process.

Optional Research

1. Find out whether your bank offers indirect loans and leasing programs. Notice the different types and sizes of dealers and make some observations about the scope of the indirect lending program. If your bank does not offer indirect loans, talk to your consumer credit manager and ask why.
2. Find out some facts about your bank's floorplan financing program, for example, how many accounts are active, what are the maximum credit limits, whether the bank uses outside services for inspections, and so on. Is this product handled by the consumer credit department or a commercial loan group?
3. If you have ever bought a car, boat, or similar item from a dealer, try to recall how they handled the subject of financing. How would you describe your experience?

6 Open-End/Revolving Credit Products

After reading this chapter, you will be able to

❏ list the characteristics of open-end, revolving credit accounts that differentiate them from closed-end loans

❏ identify four types of open-end credit products and describe their general characteristics

❏ describe the benefits revolving credit products offer to lenders and consumers

❏ list some of the problems or challenges that lenders must confront when offering open-end credit products

❏ list the four sources of income from a typical credit card program and identify which is the most important and why

Introduction

Open-end credit products have been the fastest growing type of lending to consumers since the mid-1970s. First credit cards then home equity credit lines emerged as new products with very high growth rates and huge market potential. Their growth was spurred by both the high degree of acceptance by consumers and increased product availability from lenders. Legislative changes have allowed the industry to be more innovative in the development and marketing of new products. Lines of credit give consumers far greater control over their use of credit—and they like it.

Retail store and gasoline company credit accounts were the first forms of open-end credit. The programs were developed to help increase the sale of goods and services and encourage consumers to shop in their stores and at their gas stations. However, as American society became more mobile and the number of retail stores proliferated, the need for more versatile credit services developed. National credit cards first appeared in the late 1950s, and they gained rapid acceptance. Financial institutions continued expanding their open-end product lines to include check overdraft lines, unsecured revolving lines, and home equity lines of credit. The newer programs expanded both the borrowing power of consumers and convenience of the credit services available.

Characteristics of Open-End Credit

Open-end credit accounts, also commonly referred to as revolving credit accounts, are established with the intention that they will remain open as long as the customer handles the account in an acceptable manner and the lender wishes to offer the product. While bank credit cards usually have an expiration date, the overwhelming majority are renewed automatically. The expiration date provides some credit control to reduce unauthorized use and also provides a logical point for increasing credit limits and introducing other marketing efforts. Many banks have also built periodic reconfirmation features—requiring updating of financial information and a review of the customer's credit file—into home equity and other line of credit programs. The intention is to keep the account open, but at the same time help manage credit risk more effectively and identify additional marketing opportunities.

Most open-end credit accounts have a specific *credit limit,* a maximum amount that can be outstanding at any time. The bank establishes the customer's credit limit at the time the account is opened and bases the amount on the type of product and the customer's credit capacity. For example, the credit limits on a regular VISA card may range from $500 to $5,000, a premium or "gold" VISA may range from $3,000 to $25,000, and a home equity line from $5,000 to $100,000 or more.

The credit limit on unsecured lines and credit cards can be increased easily at the bank's option or in response to a customer's request. In fact, banks often aggressively increase credit limits for "good" customers to encourage them to use their credit services rather than a competitor's. Credit limit increases on home equity and other secured lines require that new disclosures be made and new documents signed, and thus are more involved.

Once an open-end account is established, credit can be easily accessed. The consumer has substantial freedom and control to use the line of credit as he or she wishes, up to the maximum of the line. No waiting is required for loan approvals, and no one needs to know the customer is borrowing money. As payments are made, the amount of credit available under the line is replenished. The amount of this available credit represents future borrowing power for the consumer. It should be noted that some open-end credit programs do not have a revolving feature, though these are increasingly rare.

Types of Open-End Credit Products

The open-end credit product line includes credit cards, check overdraft lines, unsecured lines (such as professional/executive lines) and secured lines—primarily home equity plans. Credit cards constitute the largest share of the market, though home equity lines have been the fastest growing product in recent years. Each product has a unique role in the overall consumer credit market.

Credit Cards

Consumers use a wide variety of plastic cards, including retailer and national and international bank cards, travel and entertainment cards, private brand cards, and debit cards. Each has unique characteristics and markets.

Retailer Credit Plans

Many retailers offer proprietary credit plans to their customers. The availability of credit not only enables the retailer's customers to purchase more goods, it also helps tie them more closely to the store. Major retailers such as Sears, J.C. Penney, and Montgomery Ward maintain large credit card customer bases. Many regional department store chains and specialty stores also maintain their own credit programs sometimes issuing cards and maintaining store accounts. These retailers place a high value on building a customer franchise base, and they use their credit programs to increase customer loyalty to purchases from their stores.

National/International Credit Cards

Two major credit card systems, VISA and MasterCard, trace their roots to the 1950s, though they did not experience major growth until the late 1960s. Mass marketing of both cards began in the mid-1960s as many banks, recognizing the significant potential of credit cards, rushed to gain a competitive advantage in what was to be a high-growth, high-profit new product.

The national credit card systems have continued to evolve as highly efficient systems capable of handling extremely high volumes of activity. Data furnished by MasterCard International and VISA U.S.A., Inc., reveal that in 1991 over 166.5 million accounts were open and that the two systems handled sales slips worth nearly $270 billion in sales volume.

While many people feel that the credit card market is saturated, a very strong rate of growth has been maintained in recent years. Further, AT&T, which began issuing credit cards in 1990, astonished many by signing up over 7 million customers in its first year. Nonbanks now offer a major competitive challenge to the banking industry's share of this maturing market with 8 nonbanks among the top 20 credit card issuers in 1990. Among these was Greenwood Trust, the Sears unit which offers the Discover Card. Discover Cards were held by an estimated 20 million consumers in 1990. Other top twenty issuers were Household Bank; MBNA, a former bank subsidiary that became independent in 1990; and General Electric Capital Corporation's Monogram Bank.

The national credit card programs were further segmented when prestige versions, such as gold and premium, were introduced. Premium cards are positioned to compete against travel and entertainment cards. They are targeted to higher income and higher net worth customers and offer product features such as larger credit limits, travel services, free travel accident insurance and product warranties. Extra features like these enhance the perceived value of the cards, which, it is hoped, encourage customers to use the cards more often and enable lenders to generate higher annual fees.

Travel and Entertainment Cards

Travel and entertainment (T&E) cards are different from credit cards; they are viewed primarily as transaction cards, in that they serve as an alternative to cash and personal checks. Cardholders use a T&E card to purchase goods and services, which they are then billed for during the next billing cycle. The balance is usually due in full and is not subject to finance charges if paid by the due date. Some T&E cards now permit customers to repay the balance over a number of months under given circumstances.

Cards that fall into the T&E category include American Express, Carte Blanche, and Diners Club, and cards issued by airlines and other travel-related companies. Some T&E cards impose membership fees and offer several different membership levels. American Express, for example, offers green, gold, and platinum cards. A characteristic of these programs is the packaging of travel-related services with the basic product. These services range from discounts on rental cars to admittance to luxury clubs and exclusive golf courses.

T&E cards are generally directed toward consumers in high socioeconomic groups. They rarely have stated credit limits. Marketing themes, annual fees, and product features for the prestige cards all tend to create an image of exclusivity and high value. For example, Diners Club, which is owned by Citicorp, offers such features as a club chauffeur program, club workout centers, and club meeting rooms in selected hotels.

Debit Cards

Debit cards are closely associated with open-end credit products. Some debit cards simply allow consumers to withdraw cash or conduct other business at an automated teller machine. Other debit card plans such as VISA debit cards may be used to purchase goods and services in the same manner as a VISA credit card. However, unlike a credit card sale, a debit card transaction draws funds directly from the consumer's checking account rather than creating a credit account balance. When used in this way, the debit card is a convenient transaction device which simply replaces a standard check.

Many banks provide a direct link between their debit card programs and a line of credit. For example, consumers are often sold a VISA or MasterCard debit card as part of their checking account with the bank. Under this arrangement, if customers attempt debit card transactions that would overdraw their checking accounts, the transaction could be approved up to their credit limit. Funds will be taken first from the money that remains in their checking account, with the additional funds drawn against the line of credit.

Check Overdraft Programs

One of the first forms of revolving credit offered by banks was the check overdraft program. This program provides a bank's qualified checking account customers with a line of credit that can be used at their discretion. Overdraft lines offer customers protection against overdraft charges and help avoid the embarrassment and inconvenience associated with checks that are returned unpaid.

Overdraft plans are typically cross-sold to consumers opening new checking accounts, or to existing checking account customers through special marketing programs and branch sales efforts. If approved, the customer is given a specific credit limit which may be accessed simply by writing a check in an amount greater than the checking account balance. Some banks provide special checks that will directly access the credit account without affecting the customer's checking account balance.

These simple line of credit programs offer economic and psychological benefits to customers; however, as a source of business they are relatively limited. One reason is that the credit limits on overdraft lines are generally small, ranging from $300 to $10,000, with most lines under $2,000. This restricts their use to relatively small credit needs and short-term cash flow requirements, such as borrowing money until payday. Check overdraft loan programs also experience relatively low use levels, reflecting the fact that most consumers do not use them as a primary source of credit. Generally, dollar usage is less than 35 percent of the available credit, with fewer than half of the accounts having a balance during the month.

Unsecured Lines of Credit

The popularity of revolving credit programs spread rapidly and encouraged banks to develop and market accounts that would have greater value to customers as an alternative method of borrowing. Banks seeking to reach beyond their own checking account customer base to attract highly desirable segments of the consumer market began offering stand-alone unsecured lines of credit to a much broader base of potential borrowers. While some of these programs are marketed directly and exclusively to executive and professional people, others are marketed as an alternative to closed-end loans and made available to any consumer who meets the bank's borrowing requirements.

To enhance the value of these accounts as an alternative loan source, credit limits are generally high. For example, one large money center bank offers credit limits from $3,000 to $25,000 through a Delaware banking subsidiary. A similar program offered by a large west coast bank offers a similar program with lending limits up to $100,000 for qualified consumers. These high limits open up many additional borrowing uses and make the programs more attractive.

Customers who qualify can use the line to buy a car, make major home improvements, or handle other large borrowing needs.

Based on survey data gathered by the American Bankers Association, executive and professional unsecured line of credit programs typically experience a high amount of dollars in use, high average loan balances, and relatively low delinquency levels. The percentage of accounts in use is typically above 50 percent, while the dollar amount of available credit is closer to the 60 percent level. These high transaction levels reflect the value these products have as a source of credit for the consumer.

Secured Lines of Credit

Secured lines of credit were not offered by banks to any significant degree until the early 1980s. Home equity lines, in fact, were not permitted under most state laws prior to that time. However, since their introduction, home equity loans have consistently been one of the fastest growing forms of consumer credit.

Most secured line of credit programs are based upon appreciating value collateral, usually the borrower's primary residence. The credit limits on these lines tend to be the highest of any type of consumer loan. Some secured line of credit programs rely on fluctuating value collateral, primarily stocks and bonds. These programs require sophisticated operational support to continually monitor the value of the collateral. While lines secured by fluctuating value collateral are relatively limited now, they represent a market niche that could become increasingly attractive in the future.

Home Equity Lines of Credit

Home equity lines have become the most common form of secured revolving credit programs. The size of the credit line depends upon the market value of the home and the consumer's ability to handle the debt repayment required by the line. Many banks offer programs that allow consumers to establish a credit line for up to 80 percent of the equity in their home. For example,

$150,000	appraised value of residence
× .80	80% loan to value ratio (determined by bank policy)
$120,000	maximum mortgage credit
−50,000	amount owing on first mortgage
$ 70,000	maximum amount for home equity line

Obviously, credit lines of this size can accommodate virtually any type of borrowing need a customer might encounter. In fact, the line can serve as a replacement for most other consumer credit products.

Home equity line programs generally are characterized by high credit limits, higher than average loan size, high levels of account and dollar use, and low levels of delinquency and loss. Some banks report the percentage of accounts in use to be as high as 80 percent, with dollars outstanding of available credit close to 70 percent of the total amount committed. The high average loan balance, in many cases over $30,000, illustrates that consumers use this line to cover major expenses.

Home equity line accounts are the most exciting new consumer credit product since national credit cards appeared. They offer significant benefits to both consumers and banks. Consumers gain all the benefits of revolving credit products, plus access to substantial amounts of credit, possible tax deductibility, and generally lower rates than those available on other consumer credit products. Banks can attract a base of consumers who have better than average credit characteristics, and secure the loans with collateral that is generally sound. Through home equity lines of credit, banks can optimize profits and achieve operational efficiencies associated with revolving accounts and large loan amounts.

There are some special concerns with this type of credit. If the market value of a home declines, the customer may end up with no equity, or, in severe cases, customers may lose the home. Also, undisciplined or irresponsible credit use can place a significant strain on family budgets. While these problems cannot be eliminated, they can be minimized by sound credit policies and customer education.

CONSUMER CREDIT AT WORK
The Home Equity Loan Market

The autumn of 1986 ushered in a frenzy of activity in the consumer credit market. Congress had recently approved tax legislation that would phase out the deduction for interest paid on most consumer loans. The interest deduction on most loans secured by the borrower's residence was preserved, however. The media attention given this change in income tax rules, combined with aggressive bank promotional campaigns that stressed the attractiveness of home equity lines of credit, set off a new wave of consumer interest.

Banks began to form their strategies as details of the new tax law emerged. Those already offering home equity loan programs considered more aggressive promotional efforts, while those banks that did not offer the product quickly developed plans to enter the market. Participants in the market—real estate appraisers, title search companies, and bank lending personnel—all began to gear up for the anticipated rush of activity.

Typically, the opening round of competition began when one of the largest banks in a city offered an introductory rate of 7.5 percent—the prime rate at the time—until the end of the year for all new home equity line customers. Other banks quickly followed by matching the rate, while some became even more aggressive, reducing rates as low as 5.9 percent or extending the introductory rate period from three to six months.

Round two of the competitive battle began when another large bank offered to pay all closing costs—typically $250 to $500—for customers opening a new account. The program was announced in full-page newspaper advertisements, on the radio, and in other media. Closing costs had been a barrier to many customers, preventing them from opening an equity line account or from moving an account to another bank. Once banks began absorbing closing costs, consumers could not only open a new equity line account but also move their credit line from one lender to another without incurring additional expense.

The closing cost issue became the focal point for other marketing programs. Some banks introduced a rebate program, promising to reimburse customers for closing costs up to the amount of interest paid on the account during its first year. Thus, if the closing costs were $300 and a customer paid at least $300 in interest on the account during the first year, they would receive a full rebate. If the interest paid was less than $300, the customer would receive only the amount of interest paid. This creative twist was designed not only to encourage consumers to open an equity line account, but also to use the account thereby earning the full closing cost rebate.

The rate war prompted one banker to label the free closing cost and rebate programs as "kamikaze pricing." Other bankers felt that, since consumers could have only one home equity line account, it was important to attract as many customers as possible. The long-term earnings potential on these accounts would, they reasoned, compensate for the short-term marketing costs associated with offering an aggressive introductory program.

In addition to the rate competition, many banks encouraged consumers to apply for equity line accounts by telephone or by completing a coupon included in a newspaper advertisement. Management trainees and other employees were brought in to help handle the crunch of applications, which seemed to be coming from all directions.

A month or two after the tax revisions were enacted, many banks were overwhelmed with equity line applications. The workload was stretching the capacity of bank staff to the breaking point, and some support organizations, particularly appraisers and title search firms, developed lengthy backlogs. Customer service became a major problem for some lenders, particularly those who had promised quick approvals.

Despite the problems, the results were very impressive and important. Consumers opened thousands of equity line accounts with millions of dollars in credit lines. These new accounts signaled a significant shift in the way many consumers will meet their future credit needs.

The Open-End Credit Process

Consumers may apply for an open-end credit account in the same manner in which they apply for a closed-end loan. They can complete the bank's loan application form and wait for a credit decision. This is the most common process for selling home equity lines and check overdraft lines. In many cases, applicants apply for a closed-end loan but are sold an open-end credit account by an employee trained to sell the best loan for the customer and the bank.

Another common way in which consumers obtain an open-end credit account is to accept a preapproved credit offer in which the lender makes a commitment to extend a specified amount of credit under a credit plan upon receipt of a properly executed "acceptance agreement." Preapproved credit offerings begin inside the bank. Lists of prospects are obtained from selected lists and then run against credit bureau files to identify consumers who meet the bank's criteria. Consumers who pass this screening may then receive a preapproved credit offering. The consumer need only sign the acceptance form and complete some basic information, such as current employer, income, and address verification, and return it to the bank to open the account. This approach is commonly used for marketing credit cards.

A variation of this prescreening process involves the extension of credit that is not preapproved and requires the consumer to complete a lengthier application. This credit is offered subject to some back-end investigation. This second type of prescreening process allows lenders to further investigate consumers and subsequently deny the credit offering to respondents who do not meet the bank's qualifications.

In 1990, the Federal Trade Commission (FTC) reinterpreted the Fair Credit Reporting Act. Although the FTC has no jurisdiction over the banking industry, their commentary had a significant impact on the way banks extend preapproved credit. The FTC commented that it is inappropriate to conduct a back-end investigation if an offer for preapproved credit has been made. The FTC also strongly discouraged reducing the offer extended (granting classic instead of gold cards, or $500 instead of $2,500 line of credit). As a result, credit card issuers, such as banks, have tightened their prescreening criteria and are conducting more upfront research. Now a much more carefully researched group of consumers is offered either preapproved credit, or credit contingent upon completion of a more detailed application.

EXHIBIT 6.1 Credit Line Access Devices

Once the customer's application is approved, appropriate legal documents are signed, the account is opened, and the consumer receives access devices for the credit line. The most common access devices (see exhibit 6.1) are a plastic card, for use at merchant locations and automated teller machines (ATMs), and special checks. The access devices given to the customer and the restrictions placed upon their use are matters of bank policy, state law, and the type of account opened. For example, some states allow consumers to access a home equity line with a credit card, while others prohibit the practice.

Once the line is established and the access devices have been delivered, the customer has control over how the credit is used, as long as the account is handled in a satisfactory manner.

The Truth in Lending Act requires that lenders send a monthly statement for all revolving credit accounts that have a balance at the end of the billing cycle or on which there has been any activity during the billing cycle. The statement provides information about all activity on the account. The customer can pay the minimum payment due or any additional amount up to the balance on the account.

The popularity of revolving credit products and their increased availability in the market indicate that these products offer significant opportunities—and challenges—for both consumers and lenders.

The Bank's Perspective

Revolving credit accounts are attractive to banks because they can increase profits, broaden the bank's market area, have a high level of customer acceptance, tie in with technological developments, and offer operational efficiencies, and are often highly liquid portfolios.

The profitability of revolving loan products varies, depending upon state law, the type of product, competitive conditions, loan quality, loan volume and outstandings, and the efficiency of the operation. Banks have generally been able to market these products in such a way as to achieve desired profit levels. In fact, credit card programs contributed substantially to the banking industry's profits during most of the 1980s and continue to provide substantial income for many banks.

The attractiveness of revolving loan products is enhanced by the fact that they generally can be marketed outside the bank's geographic market area. Credit cards, for example, are routinely marketed on a national basis by many banks and nonbanks. During the 1980s, states such as Delaware and South Dakota became havens for credit card-issuing subsidiaries of many lenders from all over the country due to favorable usury limits, fee structures, and tax provisions in their laws. Consumers generally showed little concern for where their credit cards came from as long as the rates, terms, and credit limits were acceptable.

Unsecured lines of credit may also be offered beyond the bank's primary market area and state borders. This is particularly valuable when the bank is looking to open a new market or reach attractive loan markets beyond those served by its branch and indirect dealer network. While these programs are often targeted to the bank's current customers, direct mail can be used to market such lines to a broader prospect base.

Secured lines of credit, particularly home equity line programs, are generally limited to the bank's primary market area. These loans are usually opened at bank branches and they require a network of appraisers and other support personnel to process the applications. Some banks have opened specialty lending offices in other states to market these loans; nevertheless, a branch location and state lending powers are required.

The high level of customer acceptance has been the driving force behind the expansion of revolving credit products. If anything, the growth of open-end credit has probably been hampered by the reluctance of many lenders to offer these products and the lack of provisions in state loan laws to permit some types of revolving loan products. Customers have accepted these products because they are flexible, convenient, and offer personal credit control. Indeed, much of the future growth of credit cards is likely to come from opening new markets for accepting the card for payment. Grocery stores, doctors' offices, movie theaters, governments (e.g., tax payments), and many more either have been or will be added to the list of approved merchants in coming years.

The flexible nature of open-end credit programs gives them a natural tie-in with the industry's efforts to expand its automated teller programs, merchant payment systems, and in-home banking products. Credit lines can be packaged with other consumer banking products to create unique product offerings targeted to selected market segments. For example, some banks offer cash management accounts that tie together deposit, loan, and brokerage services for qualified customers.

Open-end credit products also offer significant operational efficiencies when compared with traditional closed-end loan programs. First, it is only necessary to go through the application and documentation process once. Second, applications are frequently handled by mail, saving the bank the relatively high cost of conducting in-person loan interviews. Third, open-end credit products lend themselves to centralized processing. Centralization is often helpful in handling high-volume products, such as credit cards, or products requiring specialized market knowledge, such as home equity loans, which require knowledge of appraisals, property reports, and similar specialized information. In these cases, centralization may improve productivity and credit quality. Banks have been able to achieve economies of scale as they develop some very large credit card portfolios.

Liquidity, which is essentially how quickly an asset can be converted to cash, is vitally important to banks, particularly in a dynamic and troubled economic environment. Revolving credit portfolios, particularly credit cards, have proven to be very attractive from this perspective. Here are two strategies for raising cash from revolving credit portfolios:

❏ **Selling the portfolio** Some banks put their entire portfolio, or large portions of it, up for sale to the highest bidder. Depending on market conditions and the quality of the portfolio, the bank may be able to obtain a premium of 20 percent or more. For example, a $100 million dollar portfolio with a 20% premium will gross the seller $120 million.

❏ **Securitization** This involves creating an investment portfolio of accounts to be sold to investors at a specified yield. The portfolio is usually removed from the bank's balance sheet, though the accounts are usually still serviced by the bank. Earnings from the portfolio go to pay the investor's yield and provide servicing income to the bank.

Problems/Challenges

Since consumers have more control over how they use credit with revolving credit products, there has been a need to continually refine credit controls. Unsecured revolving products particularly credit cards, have historically been associated with higher levels of losses than traditional closed-end loan products. New control programs directed at detecting fraud, reviewing accounts, and handling exceptions (e.g., delinquencies, deteriorating credit conditions, and overlimits) offer methods for decreasing losses.

The aggressive manner in which many open-end credit products have been marketed has contributed to a higher level of credit risk. As banks developed preapproved solicitations and expanded their market areas far beyond their traditional boundaries their control over their risk declined. Nevertheless, banks may be able to justify higher losses because of the higher gross yields and economies of scale available on some types of open-end credit accounts.

The need to balance aggressive marketing with prudent credit judgment has given rise to new services designed to help banks achieve these sometimes divergent objectives. Credit bureaus and credit scoring vendors, working with banks, have developed new control tools. For example, Equifax developed SAFESCAN, a "red flag" system designed to alert lenders to unusual variations in addresses, Social Security numbers, names, and other personal information that may indicate fraudulent applications. TRW Credit Data's Asset Control Technique (ACT) service provides a menu of programs to help manage risk in existing credit portfolios. Their Signal, Quest, and Alert products can help lenders respond quickly to developing credit problems. Another important tool is bankruptcy predictor models developed by vendors such as Fair, Isaac and Company, Inc. These programs can be used before a credit offer is extended, or on an existing portfolio to identify consumers with characteristics that usually flag future bankruptcy filings. High-risk customers can be closely monitored, eliminated from new credit offerings, or be offered reduced credit lines.

The unsecured feature of most open-end products increases credit risk. Credit card and unsecured line of credit programs tend to rank lower on the typical customer's list of bills needing to be paid, especially when they encounter financial problems.

A typical priority list for bills paid by a person having financial difficulties is

- mortgage or rent payment
- home equity/second mortgage
- car loan
- other secured loans
- credit cards
- unsecured loans

This general tendency results in higher delinquencies and losses on credit cards and other unsecured lines. Home equity lines, because they are secured by the borrower's home, do not present the same risk.

Fraud is another major area of risk posed by revolving credit products, particularly credit card programs. Potential sources of fraud are

- lost and stolen credit cards or credit access checks
- counterfeit cards
- dishonest merchants, cardholders, and bank employees

In recent years, credit card fraud has become a major business for organized crime and a popular activity for drug abusers.

The fraud menace is being addressed in a number of ways. First, VISA and MasterCard are sponsoring national efforts to reduce fraud through a variety of detection and prevention programs. Second, credit card providers are refining operations to improve credit card security at the point of purchase. They are committing significant resources to bring about technological changes, such as *holograms* on cards and *point-of-sale verification terminals,* which verify every credit card transaction, making fraud more difficult. Third, credit approval and account opening procedures are being refined to detect fraudulent applications. As noted earlier, credit reporting agencies are developing increasingly sophisticated systems for catching fake addresses, mail drop locations, inaccurate Social Security numbers, and the use of a deceased person's name and credit file. Finally, efforts are being made to catch fraud soon after accounts have been opened by distributing data on stolen cards more regularly and monitoring unusual activity levels on accounts.

The Consumer's Perspective

In a society that places a high value on material goods and services associated with the "good life," anything that makes it easier to purchase such goods and services is likely to be well received by consumers. Consumers have eagerly embraced revolving credit products because having credit readily available allows them to make impulse purchases, take advantage of unexpected opportunities, and make planned purchases with relative ease. The vast majority of merchants accept credit cards and checks, giving consumers a great deal of flexibility in making purchases.

Most people want to feel they are in control of their lives and their finances. For example, a car gives consumers control over where, when, and how they travel, while a VCR allows us control over what we see on television and when we see it. Likewise, revolving credit products give consumers control over when, where, and for what purposes they use credit. They may be used to meet short-term cash flow needs. For example, products such as *check overdraft lines* help consumers avoid the risk of an embarrassing and expensive overdraft. Large credit lines may allow consumers to reduce the number of credit accounts they use and, in some cases, to reduce the amount of interest and monthly payments on their debts.

The flexibility of payment options is also attractive. Most open-end credit lines give the account holder the option of

- paying a minimum monthly payment
- paying more than the minimum, with the excess going to reduce the *principal balance*
- or paying the balance in full

As the balance is reduced, the consumer is, in effect, rebuilding the available credit for future use. The available credit becomes immediately accessible and does not require any additional action on the customer's part.

Finally, the required monthly billing statement provides the consumer with a ready history of the account activity. This information can be helpful in managing one's financial affairs.

On the negative side, some consumers have great difficulty controlling their use of revolving credit accounts. Lack of financial discipline can become a very serious problem when an individual has access to too much credit. These consumers often can be identified by looking at their credit reports. Typically, they have a large number of credit lines available, use most of the accounts, and are near or over the credit limits available to them. Exhibit 6.2 shows sample credit information for a consumer in this situation. Of $14,500 in credit lines available, $11,492 has been borrowed. Two credit lines are over their limits, and three lines are very close to their limits. Recent late payments show the customer is beginning to have trouble meeting payments, though most of the accounts shown are current. This person could easily go deeper in debt and is likely to experience some significant payment problems in the future.

It is often necessary to rescue overextended customers by consolidating their loans into a closed-end loan, preferably one that is secured by available collateral. However, this approach has the effect of opening up all of the customer's available credit again unless steps are taken to close the revolving accounts. Although this is a difficult task, and far from foolproof, failure to limit a careless customer's access to credit could mean more serious problems in the future.

EXHIBIT 6.2   Sample Credit Bureau Data on an Overextended Customer

Creditor	Status	Credit Limit	Balance
State bank	Current	$ 3,700	$ 3,256
Regional bank	30 days P/D	1,500	1,556
Community bank	Current	2,700	2,477
First Bank	30 days P/D	2,500	2,516
J. C. Penney	Current	400	112
Sears	Current	1,500	1,415
Ward's	Current	500	0
Jewelry store	Current	1,100	40
Department store	Current	200	81
Retail store	Current	400	39
Total		$14,500	$11,492

Sources of Income from Credit Card Programs

Lenders may derive income in a variety of ways from a credit card program.

❏ **Finance charge**   The largest portion of income from a credit card program is interest; however, several other potential sources are worth noting:

❏ **Interchange fees**   These fees are charged by the national credit card companies and member banks for using a credit card network. A bank receives fee income when cardholders with accounts at other banks purchase goods and services from its merchants; similarly, the bank is charged a fee when its own cardholders purchase goods and services from another bank's merchants. The interchange income and expense fees are netted out to determine whether the bank has earned income or incurred an expense in this category.

❏ **Annual fees and transaction fees** The increasing need to develop noninterest income led banks to begin charging for services provided. The most common fee is the annual fee, which allows banks to recoup some of the cost of servicing and renewing accounts, especially those of occasional users and convenience users (those who use the account and pay the balance in full each month, thereby avoiding finance charges).

❏ **Merchant discount fees** Banks charge merchants a fee for processing their credit card sales slips which covers the cost of handling the account and generates a profit for the bank. The fee (or discount) charged varies from merchant to merchant and is based primarily upon the merchant's monthly sales volume and the average ticket price. A sample discount schedule is shown in exhibit 6.3.

Merchants generating less than $1,000 in volume per month and having an average sales draft under $17 would be subject to a discount fee of 4 percent in the sample schedule; those generating $10,000 in monthly sales volume and an average sales draft of $80 would only be subject to a 2 percent discount.

Generally speaking, the discount rate declines as sales volume increases, reflecting the importance to the bank of high volume merchants. The discount rate also declines as the average ticket size increases, the rationale being that less effort is involved in servicing an account that generates a $1,000 average

EXHIBIT 6.3   Sample Merchant Discount Rate Schedule

Monthly Bank Card Volume	Average Sales Draft				
	Under $17	$17–$35	$35–$50	$50–$80	$80+
Under $1,000	4.0%	3.75%	3.25%	3.0%	2.75%
$1,000–$2,999	3.75	3.5	3.0	2.75	2.5
$3,000–$9,999	3.5	3.25	2.75	2.5	2.25
$10,000–$49,999	3.25	3.0	2.5	2.25	2.0
$50,000 and up	3.0	2.5	2.25	2.0	2.0

ticket, in contrast to one that generates a $15 average ticket. For example, a retail drug store chain generates a much lower average ticket than a fashionable women's clothing store, with the result that many more transactions must be processed. However, the drug store may very well generate a higher monthly sales volume.

In recent years, with profit margins thinning, many banks chose to leave the merchant side of the business, and sold their operations to other banks or companies specializing in this business.

Other fees charged by banks include late charges, overlimit charges, and transaction fees. These fees are designed to offset specific actions by an account holder that result in an expense to the bank. State law governs the fees permitted on a credit card account.

Summary

The popularity of open-end or revolving credit products with consumers and bankers has continued to grow steadily throughout the 1970s and 1980s. This growth has been aided by new lending laws that enable banks to offer new products designed to more effectively and efficiently meet the borrowing public's borrowing needs.

Credit cards are the most widely used revolving credit products, while home equity line accounts have become one of the fastest growing products. Along with check overdraft and stand-alone unsecured line of credit accounts, these products have given banks a vehicle for reaching beyond their traditional markets to serve additional, attractive consumer market segments. They also have given consumers alternatives to traditional closed-end credit products. Simply stated, open-end credit has changed the way in which consumers meet their borrowing needs as well as how lenders serve the market.

Review Questions

1. What characteristics differentiate an open-end revolving credit product from a closed-end loan product?
2. List four different types of open-end credit products and describe their general characteristics.

3. Distinguish between a prescreened and a preapproved open-end credit offering. Why are banks making such offerings?
4. Why are some home equity accounts classified as open-end credit products? What primary advantages do home equity lines offer to banks in today's consumer credit environment? To customers?
5. Name three different types of credit cards typically used by consumers. How are they different?
6. Briefly explain the various types of income a bank can derive from a credit card program. Which is the most important source of income from these products?
7. Why have open-end credit products had the highest rate of growth of any form of consumer credit in recent years?

Optional Research

1. What steps does your bank take to monitor the creditworthiness of its open-end credit accounts? Ask your credit card or consumer credit manager to find out.
2. If your bank participates in one or both of the national credit card systems, find out some of the pertinent details like how many active accounts there are, what are the bank's outstandings, earnings, and losses, and how the bank markets its cards. Write a summary of your findings.

The consumer lending process comprises a series of logical steps, beginning with the generation of applications. Sometimes, the loan process is stopped short when an application must be declined, usually after the credit investigation reveals it to be a poor risk. Other times, the application proceeds through the investigative and decision-making stages and goes on to be approved, documented, closed, and booked.

The vast majority of loans are successfully repaid, and the bank gains from its investment. Unfortunately, though, some loans go into delinquency and the lending process must therefore have sound collection and recovery operations in place.

Despite the differences in individual bank procedures, it is useful to study the general processes involved in a consumer loan transaction. Related to the processes are techniques—like loan structuring and selling, pricing, and profitability analysis—that, together with the bank's policies and procedures, define how a loan transaction works, beginning to end. Part III of *Consumer Lending* ties together all the stages of the consumer lending process.

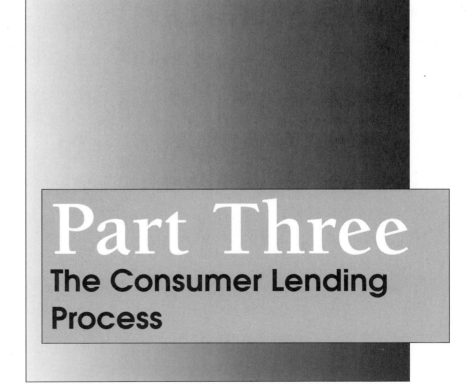

Part Three
The Consumer Lending Process

7

Developing and Taking Loan Applications

After reading this chapter, you will be able to

- ❏ list the five primary objectives of the loan application process
- ❏ discuss how the bank generates loans based on the type of loan being pursued
- ❏ describe the elements of a good consumer loan marketing plan and give examples of how marketing techniques are used to optimize results
- ❏ list the three ways in which loan applications are received
- ❏ describe some of the considerations involved in taking in-person loan applications

Objectives of the Application Process

One of the primary goals of a bank's consumer credit operation is generating enough applications from consumers to meet the bank's objectives for loan volume, portfolio diversification, asset quantity and quality, and profitability. As the consumer credit product line expands and becomes a more attractive asset for banks, this task has become more complex and challenging.

The bank has five primary objectives when developing consumer loan applications:

- ❏ generate a flow of consumer applications to meet the bank's consumer credit objectives
- ❏ obtain enough information to allow the bank to make the best possible credit decision
- ❏ ensure compliance with regulations

❑ ensure a timely response to the consumer's request
❑ initiate and develop the applicant's goodwill

The first challenge is generating sufficient applications across all the consumer loan products offered by the bank to meet all of its other objectives volume—loan outstandings, loan quality, and profitability. New loans must be generated to replace loans that are being paid off and to contribute to the bank's growth goals.

Making the task more difficult is the fact the bank must not only attract applicants, but specifically those who can be approved for a loan. Few other businesses face the dilemma of selling a potential consumer on buying their product (applying for a loan) and then having to turn around and refuse to sell it (denying a loan request). In fact, loan approval ratios can vary greatly and in some cases the lender may turn down more applicants than are approved. Thus, to get 50 new loans, the bank may need to generate 100 or more applications. A high ratio of denials may signal a problem with the marketing program for a particular product and a bank might need to alter its approach in an effort to increase the number of approved loans.

Once a consumer requests a loan, the bank must obtain sufficient information to make a sound credit decision. This involves a number of trade-offs. It seems logical to state that the bank wants to get as much information about each applicant as possible. However, this desire is often tempered by the competitive market and the desire to keep the lending process as responsive and customer-oriented as possible. Balancing these divergent pressures creates a real challenge for consumer lenders. However, banks can get into trouble when they move too far away from sound lending practices, one of which is thoroughly researching an application.

The extent of information requested on loan applications varies widely today. Preapproved credit card applications, for example, take only a moment or two to complete and ask for general information such as name, home and business addresses and telephone numbers, and yearly income. An application for a direct loan, on the other hand, requests detailed information on the applicant's financial condition, employment, and residence histories. Generally speaking, lenders have learned to be comfortable with less information. The use of credit-scoring programs and the success of prescreening techniques have switched the emphasis from quantity to quality of information. Some customer information simply is not consistently predictive of loan performance; thus, there seems little need to ask consumers to supply extensive information if it is not required for sound credit decisions.

The application generation process must conform to federal laws and regulations. A number of laws are concerned with the manner in which applications are generated. The Truth in Lending Act (Regulation Z) lists the type of disclosures that lenders must make in advertising programs and at the time a loan application is taken. The Equal Credit Opportunity Act (Regulation B) is concerned with the types of information that may and may not be asked for on applications. And the Community Reinvestment Act is concerned with the extent to which the bank serves the legitimate borrowing needs of consumers residing in its primary market area.

The bank's application process must also meet customer expectations and needs for a timely decision. While different products have different timing requirements, the guiding principle should be to reach and communicate the decision as rapidly as possible. Technology makes it possible to render a decision within minutes of receiving a completed application. Timely decisions help convert applications into loans; delayed decisions result in good applications being lost to more responsive competitors.

Finally, the application process must initiate and develop the customer's goodwill. The programs used to generate applications must attract potential borrowers by offering something of value. Furthermore, they must create interest in the bank's products and motivate consumers to respond. As part of its effort to foster customer goodwill, the bank should be attentive to the convenience aspects of the application process. If, for example, the bank does not take applications over the phone, but requires the applicant to make a trip to the bank to fill out an application form, it may lose some consumers who are looking for a more convenient loan source—and there are probably many of them available.

Product Line Considerations

The bank's efforts to develop credit applications will be different for each type of consumer credit product offered. Here are the key product line considerations.

Direct Loans

The location of a bank or branch office has a great deal of influence at the potential level of success in generating direct consumer loans. Many consumers place a high value on convenience and are unlikely to go very far out of their way for a loan. Banks located in communities with a high percentage of consumers in their peak borrowing years or with strong credit quality characteristics will naturally generate more consumer loans than those located in commercial areas, communities heavily populated by senior citizens, or sparsely populated rural markets. Even hours of operation can affect the number of loans a bank generates. Some banks have expanded their working hours to better accommodate customer needs.

Another major factor in generating direct consumer loans is the quality of the personal relationships developed with customers. Some loan officers develop a loyal following of customers who not only rely on the officer for their borrowing needs but also refer many other prospective customers through word-of-mouth advertising. Such referrals are very helpful in building a direct consumer loan base.

Personal selling by bank employees is a key element in direct loan production. Bank employees can benefit greatly from good training in product knowledge, customer service, and sales. The knowledge they gain gives them the confidence to deal professionally with all types of customers and to build good customer relationships for their branch.

Employees who are trained to hear potential borrowing needs expressed by consumers, or are aware of certain types of transactions that trigger an opportunity to sell a loan, can help generate applications. Examples of transactions that take place every day in a bank's offices and which could open up an opportunity to make a loan include

- withdrawals from savings accounts
- requests for certified checks or large money orders
- overdrafts
- payments on loans or requests for loan pay off information
- requests for general information about loans
- comments made in general conversation (kids starting college, thinking of remodeling, needs a new car)

Responding proactively to such cues can help the bank sell loans. In today's environment, it is not enough to just sit back and wait for loan applicants to come to the bank. At the same time, the bank must have established some basic fundamentals if it is going to build a direct loan portfolio. These include

- building a consumer franchise—current bank customers are the best source of prospects for consumer credit products
- letting consumers know the bank makes and wants consumer loans
- offering competitive rates, terms, and products
- maintaining sound and efficient systems for processing applications
- establishing the bank's image, awareness levels, and market share in the community
- training staff in product knowledge, customer service, and sales

Applications for some types of direct loan products may be developed in unique ways:

Type of Loan	Possible Application Sources
Student	College fairs, college financial aid personnel, state guarantee agencies
Boat and other recreational vehicle	Boat & RV shows, marine loan brokers
Home equity	Home improvement contractors, accountants, home shows, community leaders—particularly in less economically advantaged areas
Automobile	Trade shows, co-op sales, or direct marketing programs
General	Trust and commercial loan officers, attorneys, accountants
All types	A loan application for another purpose

The loan application itself is a particularly good resource for developing further business and should be used to cross-sell other bank products. For example, a customer who has qualified for a $15,000 auto loan may also qualify for a check overdraft line and/or a credit card. When notifying that customer that the auto loan is approved, the banker can say, "You know, you have also qualified for overdraft protection on your checking account with us and for a credit card as well. Are you interested in learning more about these services?"

Indirect Loans

As noted in our chapter on indirect loans, the key to developing these loan applications is the development of a dealer network. The dealer base will vary depending on the type of loan—automobile, boat, etc.—and volume desired. Managers of indirect sales must diligently monitor the volume and quality of applications developed from each dealer. Some lenders call their dealers each morning to "ask" for business, and they carefully monitor competitors to make sure the bank's plan remains attractive to the dealer.

Once an application is received from a dealer, a speedy decision is of the essence. While a consumer normally submits only one application for a direct loan, a dealer can take each indirect application and channel it to a number of prospective lenders. Which institution gets the loan depends on competitive forces including rates, terms, and speed of decision.

Revolving Credit Products

Applications for these products are obtained in a variety of ways. Most banks market credit cards, unsecured line of credit products, and their home equity line program just as they do closed-end direct loan products. Thus, applications are generated by the bank's branches in the normal course of activities. General customer characteristics can determine the most appropriate loan products.

Product	Customer Characteristics
Check overdraft line of credit	• Current checking account customers • Customers opening checking accounts • Customers who accidentally overdrew their accounts

Product	Customer Characteristics
Home equity line of credit	• Customers applying for any type of loan who - own or are buying their home - have equity to qualify - may have future borrowing needs • Any retail customer with the characteristics noted above
Credit cards	• Any consumer likely to meet minimum requirements
Executive/professional line of credit	• Established professionals

Credit card and unsecured line of credit programs may be offered to a much broader consumer market than those products closely tied to a branch distribution system. While small and regional banks may limit sales of these products to their local markets, many large banks and nonbank lenders such as AT&T and Sears seek to develop national markets. As a bank broadens its market area, additional advertising media—TV, radio, or national magazines—may supplement direct mail, telemarketing, and local advertising efforts. It is rare that a consumer does not receive at least one credit card offer in the mail per month, while being exposed to credit offers in a wide variety of print media.

Marketing Programs

Good marketing programs can generate applications even in what seems to be a saturated market. Banks offer a variety of incentives to attract new credit customers. For example, banks may

- advertise special loan sales, with lower rates during the month of July
- offer special rates and terms at consumer-oriented trade shows, for example, boat, RV, auto, and home shows
- offer closing cost rebates on home equity credit lines
- waive credit card fees for the first year

- allow one month when no payment is due (payment holidays)
- guarantee replacement of lost or stolen merchandise purchased with the credit card

Many banks, both large and small, can point to their own successful consumer credit marketing campaigns as the reason for their successful sales ratios. In this section, we will look at the process for developing strategies and tactics designed to generate loan applications.

Define Objectives

A clear set of objectives is essential to the development of a high quality marketing program. The objectives should define

- products to be promoted
- number of applications, loans, and dollar volume to be generated
- quantifiable loan quality goals

Select Target Markets

The products to be promoted will help narrow and define the target market. In many cases, prime prospects can be further narrowed using more sophisticated tools such as a marketing central information file (MCIF). Assuming the bank wants to develop home equity loans, the target market may be selected using the following process:

- Identify the characteristics of customers currently using this product—age, income, geographic location, credit characteristics. Home ownership is clearly a prerequisite.
- Determine which characteristics are most highly correlated with demand for the product, such as older neighborhoods where consumers are likely to have more equity in the home and which may also need home improvements, and families with children of college age.

The bank may find that its current home equity customers are concentrated in the 30- to 45-year-old age group, have incomes from $30,000 to $55,000, and have been in their homes for five or more years. Having defined the primary target group characteristics, the bank can use its customer information files (CIF), and other geodemographic tools to identify specific prospect names. For example, the bank may work with an outside vendor who can help define which areas of a city, county, or state have the highest concentrations of people with the desired characteristics. Lists of names may then be developed for direct mail, telephone, or other marketing tactics.

Develop a Promotional Plan

The bank now needs to evaluate alternative promotional strategies. This would include an evaluation of direct mail, telemarketing, in-bank, and general advertising.

- ❏ **Direct mail**   This medium has been heavily used to promote credit card and home equity loan products. Direct mail programs have become highly refined and targeted in order to control marketing costs and optimize response rates. Banks also use direct mail sales materials in regular correspondence with customers—account statements, etc.—to promote their services.

  One technique used to enhance the effectiveness of direct mail is the prescreening of names against credit bureau files. This technique eliminates consumers who would not meet the bank's credit requirements. Preapproved credit offers, used almost solely for credit cards, generally draw high response rates. All the consumer has to do is return the application form, after completing some basic information, and the bank **must** open an account. (Refer to chapter 6 for a more detailed explanation of prescreening and preapproved credit offers.)

- ❏ **Telemarketing**   Banks have increasingly turned to proactive telephone sales to generate a wide range of retail business. Working from targeted prospect lists, and a flexible sales script, telemarketing sales representatives extend credit offers on a range of products. Telephone follow-up is often used in conjunction with a direct mail program to increase sales results.

  Branches may use telemarketing to develop loan applications from current and former customers. Sometimes simply calling good customers and asking if they could use help with a current borrowing need or reminding them to think of the bank if they have a need in the future, can generate applications. If the bank employee handles the call well, it will also produce goodwill for the bank.

❏ **In-bank** There is an array of promotional strategies designed to motivate employees to sell loans and to motivate consumers to apply. It begins with merchandising in branch offices, using signs, branch displays, or kiosks that invite consumers to apply for loans. Some banks have installed private areas in which consumers can complete a loan application on a personal computer.

Incentive programs are frequently used to motivate employees to generate loan applications. Employees may receive cash or other awards for each application taken or for meeting branch consumer credit objectives. Including consumer credit objectives in the evaluation and reward systems for branch employees is a sure way to emphasize the importance of these products.

A note of caution: incentive programs that emphasize loan volume can encourage employees to "bend the rules" to make marginal loans, which means bad loans can be made. This problem can be minimized by focusing on developing loan applications in combination with the use of loan quality measures, such as delinquency and minimization of losses.

Implementation

Once the promotional program is fully developed, all employees who work in related areas should be fully informed. It is critical that employees know about the promotional program before consumers start responding. The implementation process should be thoroughly planned. For example, the bank must be able to effectively handle the level of response generated. Many programs that successfully generate application volume fail because the bank can not efficiently handle the heavy response. Promotions should be staggered or contingency plans developed to handle these marketing successes.

Measuring Results

It is essential to measure the results of marketing programs to determine the effectiveness of the materials, the targeted mailing lists, the product offering, and the timing. Only by monitoring and measuring the success of a marketing program can banks effectively improve their marketing campaigns in the future.

Successful marketing programs can generate enough new applications to meet loan volume objectives, and the quality of loan applicant desired by the lender. It is important to meet these goals at the lowest possible cost if the bank is to achieve the most profitable level of business.

Handling the Application

Applications are received in three basic ways: in-person, by telephone, and by mail. In-person and telephone applications involve personal contact between the consumer and a bank employee, while mail-in applications do not normally involve any personal contact.

In-Person Applications

Many lenders prefer to take applications face-to-face with consumers because they believe this gives them the best opportunity to obtain complete information about the applicant. The lender can make certain that all necessary information is supplied on the application form and get a complete picture of the customer's situation. For example, the lender can ask follow-up questions and fill in gaps not covered specifically on the application form.

Sometimes, it is difficult for a branch to fit taking loan applications into a busy work day. Occasionally, consumer credit is a low priority and generating loans is secondary to an employee's other duties. Suppose an applicant comes in seeking a loan at peak banking hours and no one has the time necessary to take the loan application in the desired manner. One common solution is to give the customer an application form and ask him or her to fill it out at home and return it to the bank. This approach may be acceptable to some customers, though it is far less personal and informative than a direct interview. It also decreases the chances that the bank will receive a completed application. Many customers leave if a bank employee cannot meet with them, never to be heard from again.

Taking loan applications ideally involves the following techniques:

❑ **Create a comfortable environment**   Applications are best taken in a setting that gives the customer some feeling of privacy. The customer is asked a lot of personal questions and may be understandably reluctant to share this information within earshot of customers in the teller lines or at neighboring desks. Privacy requires reasonable spacing, appropriate voice levels, and the projection of a feeling of confidentiality.

❑ **Smile and greet the customer**   A smile projects many things to people. It can communicate friendliness, warmth, confidence, and caring. A smile can help convey a good first impression, not only of the employee but also of the bank. Bankers often impress this on tellers but forget to give it equal emphasis when training loan interviewers.

❑ **Determine the customer's name and use it**   Calling the customer by name helps create a personal touch, although it should be maintained at the proper level of formality for the situation. Some people want to be called by their first name, while others would prefer a more formal "Mr. Jones" or "Ms. White." The safe rule is not to use a first name unless requested to do so or until you have asked the person's permission.

❑ **Set the customer at ease**   Although applicants do not consider the loan application meeting to be a social event, it is not always desirable to plunge right into the business of filling out the forms. Some general conversation is almost always helpful before beginning more formal application steps. The loan interviewer should be well-organized and project a high level of competence. If the employee cannot find the application forms and otherwise appears hurried or disorganized, the interview is off to a bad start.

Empathy with the customer during the loan interview is also important. Some customers are shy or restrained and need to be reassured, while others are cocky and demanding and need to be heard. Many customers fear rejection and are apprehensive. It is up to the loan interviewer to establish a relaxed, positive approach and to soothe these anxieties.

❑ **Use a conversational approach**   Once the loan interviewer begins to take the application, the questioning should proceed smoothly. A conversational approach is usually the most effective in meeting the objectives of gathering enough information to facilitate a sound credit decision and develop the customer's goodwill.

The conversational approach involves asking questions and responding to the customer as one would during a normal discussion. Avoid making the applicant feel as if he or she is being interrogated. You should also avoid a "fill-in-the-blanks" style interview often used by inexperienced employees.

A central issue during the question-and-answer stage is who will actually fill in the application. Some banks prefer that the customer fill in the form and then have a loan interviewer review it for completeness and clarity. Other banks prefer to have the interviewer fill in the form and then have the customer review and sign it. The preferred method is a matter of individual bank choice, and many banks use both approaches, depending upon the situation.

❑ **Practice active listening**   Listening well is not an inherent skill in everyone; it is a developed skill. Tuning in to what the customer is really saying involves paying close attention and giving proper feedback. A good listener is generally skilled at asking questions. When a customer is willing to talk freely, the interviewer may rely upon unstructured or open-ended questions which will not limit the way the customer responds. The following are examples of unstructured questions:

■ "Tell me something about your job."
■ "What credit experience do you have?"

These questions allow customers latitude for their responses. Some customers give lengthy answers to unstructured questions, while others give only limited information. The interviewer may need to switch to structured or closed-ended questions if the customer is uncommunicative and does not divulge sufficient information to complete the application. The following are examples of structured questions:

■ "Where do you work?"
■ "How long have you worked for that company?"
■ "Do you have any credit card accounts in your name?"
■ "Have you ever had a loan with our bank?"

- "Do you want a home equity line of credit or an unsecured line?"

Structured questions are also useful toward the end of an interview to steer the conversation into specific areas. Occasionally it is necessary to use more skilled probing techniques with reluctant customers. Four basic approaches that can be used to probe for essential information:

- ❏ **Brief assertion of understanding** Acknowledge that you are listening to the customer without interrupting what is being said. In a face-to-face interview, this probing technique may take the form of body language, such as a quizzical look, a nod, raised eyebrows, or simply saying "uh-huh." These verbal and nonverbal messages tell the customer to keep on talking.

- ❏ **Neutral phrases** Neutral phrases do encourage the customer to clarify a statement, such as "What do you mean by that?" or "I'm not sure I know what you mean; could you elaborate a little?"

- ❏ **Silence** This is a powerful but somewhat risky approach. It may be used after the customer has made a comment that the interviewer feels needs more explanation. Silence should not last longer than 10 seconds in a loan interview since it tends to produce anxiety, often making the rest of the interview more difficult.

- ❏ **Echo** Repeat something the customer has said in a manner that asks for more information. For example, in response to the statement, "I want a loan with the lowest rate possible," the interviewer might say, "The lowest rate possible?" The intent of echoing is to encourage the customer to elaborate, in this case, to say what they think the lowest rate possible is.

Having developed questioning and probing skills, the loan interviewer should have little trouble conducting thorough, pleasant loan interviews. The interviewer should always remember to vary the types of questions and probes used to keep the interview as relaxed as possible.

Close by telling the customer exactly when he or she will know what the decision is. Customers should leave the interview knowing when the bank will contact them with a decision. If any additional information is needed, such as the applicant must provide a copy of a recent pay stub to verify income, make sure the applicant clearly understands what is required. The bank should initiate the next contact with the customer. Instead of saying, "Get in touch sometime next week and we'll have an answer for you," it is far better to say, "Where can I reach you this afternoon with our decision?"

Telephone Applications

Taking applications over the telephone can be an efficient and effective approach for both the consumer and the bank employee. Telephone applications can take less time to handle than direct interviews, do not require the customer to be present, and can be fit into the day's schedule by arranging to call the customer back after hours or during slow traffic periods. There are some significant advantages to taking applications over the telephone. Many banks even set up a specific area in the building to handle and service telephone applications. Many banks recognize, however, there is a greater risk of fraud or gathering incorrect or inadequate information over the telephone and therefore do not accept telephone applications.

Mail-In Applications

Mail-in applications have risen in importance as some banks try to offer increased convenience to consumers. The two biggest concerns with mail-in applications are the absence of direct customer contact and missing information. Customer contact may or may not be important to an individual credit decision, but it clearly does provide the opportunity for the bank to interview and cross-sell the consumer. Since bank employees don't meet the mail-in applicants, there may be restricted cross-selling opportunities as well as less information available for the credit decision.

Mail-in applications are generally less complex than in-person loan applications. Brevity and simplicity encourage consumers to complete the form. Still, many applications are returned only partially completed. Banks have different policies regarding how incomplete applications should be handled. Some banks return the application to the customer, while other banks have loan personnel call the customer to obtain the missing information. A third approach is simply to reject the application, although this approach is clearly the least customer-oriented.

Simply rejecting the application because of missing information is not a good idea for two reasons. First, the Equal Credit Opportunity Act states that creditors must be "reasonably diligent" in collecting information to complete the application. Second, a phone call to complete the missing information presents an opportunity for loan personnel to cross-sell other bank products. Such calling programs can result in additional product sales for the bank provided staff has received appropriate sales-oriented training.

Application Problems

Some applicants are more difficult to deal with than others. The overbearing customer is easy to recognize by his attitude: he has a right to credit and is going to let you know it. He wants a credit decision on the spot and does not want to be bothered filling out an application. Be careful: fraud artists often use this approach.

It is essential to stick to the bank's requirements. Any sign of hesitation on the part of the loan employee will be interpreted as a willingness to compromise. Often, it is necessary to explain, in no uncertain terms, why procedures are in place and cannot be circumvented.

The shy customer is one who is easily intimidated by situations that are new to him. This type of customer does not offer a lot of information, so the loan interviewer may need to resort to structured questions and probing techniques to get the information needed for a loan decision.

Shy customers need to be put at ease. Spend more time making them comfortable with the process. It is usually helpful to explain the whole process in advance and to use positive terms. The easiest way to achieve a positive approach is to assume that the bank will be able to make the loan to the customer (this approach may be used with all customers).

Another application problem to be wary of is the "present customer known" syndrome. Many lenders are tempted to compromise their application and credit investigation processes for customers they know. While this may seem reasonable, the lender runs the risk that something may have changed for the customer and he may not be quite as good a credit risk as he was in the past. In fact, we know that people lose their jobs, become overly indebted, and develop personal problems that may change their behavior patterns on credit accounts. Therefore, it is always a good idea to follow the bank's lending procedures in full every time a customer requests a loan.

Summary

Generating consumer loan applications in an increasingly competitive environment presents a major challenge. In recent years, competition has motivated banks to pursue different product line strategies and develop new ways of promoting loan products. Banks have continued to sharpen their skills in order to attract loan applications from a broad cross-section of consumers.

Banks have become more aggressive in their efforts to develop loan applications. The judicious use of prescreening and preapproved credit offerings with targeted direct mail programs is designed to reach selected customer groups in a more effective manner. To complement the growing number of direct mail campaigns, many banks have placed an increased emphasis on improving the communication and selling skills of their employees so they can better serve potential new customers. These skills help employees identify lending opportunities and lead to the development of more loan applications.

Review Questions

1. What five primary objectives does the bank seek to achieve when generating loan applications?
2. Does the type of loans being pursued by the bank have any effect on the effort to generate loans? Discuss how this affects direct, indirect, or open-end loans.
3. Describe the elements of a sound consumer loan marketing plan and give examples of how marketing techniques are used to optimize results.
4. There has been a general shift among banks toward shorter loan applications. Why? Does less information necessarily compromise the decision-making process?
5. At the beginning of a loan interview, how might one go about setting a customer at ease?
6. List three ways in which loan applications are received. What benefits and challenges do telephone and mail-in applications offer over traditional in-person applications?

Optional Research

1. Look at various loan application forms your bank uses. Compare them with applications you receive in the mail. Note the differences in the information requested, appearance, and procedure for applying.
2. Find an advertisement for loan services that a local bank—preferably your bank—has placed in a newspaper, and evaluate its contents. What is the promotional theme? Do you think it is likely that the ad will be effective in bringing in loan business?

8 Credit Investigation

After reading this chapter, you will be able to

- ❏ list the primary objectives of the credit investigation process
- ❏ name the four primary sources of credit information
- ❏ describe the steps taken in the credit verification process and explain why they are arranged in a particular order
- ❏ identify red flags that may appear during the credit investigation and describe ways of dealing with them
- ❏ list the items normally investigated as part of the credit process and describe the best method for verifying their accuracy

Introduction

Credit investigation practices have changed significantly over the years. Closed-end loan applications are investigated at the time received, while open-end credit applicants may be investigated before they apply (prescreen), when they apply, or periodically during the life of the account (account monitoring). Before 1960, it was common practice to conduct investigations using the mail to verify applicant information—a practice still common on first mortgage loans. As consumer lending became more competitive, banks abandoned mail investigations in favor of telephone references to expedite loan processing. Since 1980, the burgeoning market for credit cards, home equity, and other revolving credit products has resulted in varying levels of banks investigation throughout the life of the account.

The credit investigation process is structured in a manner that allows data to be gathered quickly and at the least possible expense. Lenders rely on a variety of direct and indirect sources to verify applicant information. These include the bank's own account records, other creditors, credit reporting agencies, and employers. The extent of the investigation depends on the type of credit requested, the bank's loan policies, and the individual characteristics of each application.

Since the early 1900s, credit reporting agencies have been an important source of credit information providing a highly efficient means of exchanging information about a consumer's credit history. Credit bureaus streamlined banks' lending process by eliminating the need to directly contact each of the applicant's credit references. The bureaus also made it possible for lenders to conduct more effective investigations by providing a central source to help uncover information concerning the consumer that may not have been disclosed in the application.

Sound credit investigations can help the bank make sound loans, avoid weak or marginal credit-risk consumers, and take proactive steps to limit open-end credit use by people having financial difficulties.

Objectives of the Investigation Process

The primary objectives of the credit investigation process are to

- ❏ verify the accuracy and completeness of the data supplied on the application
- ❏ develop enough information to make a sound credit decision
- ❏ conduct the investigation in an efficient, cost-effective manner
- ❏ identify negative trends or potential problems that may affect the continued creditworthiness of a current open-end credit customer

The bank's loan policy should clearly identify the information to be verified. Some data are customarily accepted as given by the applicant, while other data are too important to the process of making a sound decision to be left unverified. Examples of data that are often accepted as given are

- time at address
- number of dependents
- previous address
- previous job
- other bank checking/savings account information

Data customarily verified by the credit investigator include

- current employer
- income—amount/frequency/type (salary, commission)
- other sources of income (source and amount)
- credit references
- home address
- value of collateral to secure the loan

It is neither necessary nor desirable to investigate and verify all data on the application. Experience has shown that most people are honest. Therefore, the investigator can focus on key data and not worry about trying to verify everything. If the investigation uncovers information that is inconsistent, inaccurate, or cannot be verified by a reliable source, the bank will investigate more thoroughly. These incidents raise red flags that may or may not indicate a problem, but warrant further investigation.

Credit decisions can only be sound if they are based upon factual information. Lenders must be able to rely on the information obtained on the application and verified during the investigation being as accurate and as complete as possible. Missing or inaccurate information can result in making loans that do not meet the bank's lending requirements. A sound investigation process will either substantiate the applicant's creditworthiness or indicate problems or factors that may represent an unacceptable level of risk.

The credit investigation process should obtain verified data quickly and at the least possible cost. The following step-by-step approach may be used:

Step 1: Receive application and review for information that might warrant its immediate rejection.

The object of this step is to eliminate from further processing any application that will not meet the bank's policy requirements. For example, if the applicant requests a car loan with no down payment, and the bank's policy states that such loans may be made only with a 20 percent down payment, the application may be rejected without further delay or expense. Likewise, if the applicant does not meet the bank's minimum income requirement or is not of legal borrowing age, the process ends there.

Step 2: Check the bank's credit files to verify whether the applicant has current or closed accounts with the bank.

If the bank has had any unsatisfactory credit experience with the customer, the application may be declined at this point. On the other hand, if the customer has a satisfactory account relationship or no experience with the bank, the investigation can proceed to the next step.

Step 3: Obtain report from credit reporting agency.

Credit reports contain information that the consumer's creditors furnish to a particular credit bureau. Obtaining a credit report is often the final step in the investigation process, though some banks choose to take this action much earlier. In fact, some lenders limit their entire investigation to this one source. The cost of most reports is small and, with automated equipment, reports can be obtained in a matter of seconds. Thus, a bank may decide that examining only credit reports is the most efficient, and least costly, process.

Step 4: Directly contact employers and other creditors for references.

Direct references may be necessary for some items of information and may be requested at this point. In many cases, employers and creditors refuse to give direct references, forcing the investigator to rely on indirect sources. If unfavorable information is discovered at this stage, such as finding out that the applicant has just been fired, the application can be declined without further action.

Step 5: Verify collateral value.

Collateral values must be verified as part of the investigation process. The following chart shows sources commonly used to verify the value of collateral:

Collateral	Valuation Source
New car, boat, RV	Dealer invoice or new product price guides
Used car	Physical inspection by authorized person or by NADA or Blue Book Valuation Guides
Used boats	Marine Survey, BUC Book
Stocks, bonds	Current stock quote from broker or newspaper such as *Wall Street Journal*

Collateral	Valuation Source
Savings accounts	Current account statement
Home	Certified real estate appraiser

This stage in the investigation process may cause the greatest delay, particularly when outside appraisals are required. Banks will usually inform consumers that their loan request is approved subject to the determination of collateral value, rather than holding off further communication until this step is completed.

Once the investigation process is complete, the applicant's file is given to the loan officer or other decision-maker for the final credit decision. In some cases, the loan might be approved provided the consumer verifies certain data that the bank could not verify directly. For example, the lender may require that the applicant bring a recent pay stub to verify income and employment to the loan closing.

Many banks establish timeframes for completing the credit investigation process. These objectives are typically set at the product line level because of the unique character of each loan type. For example, a three-hour turnaround, from receipt of an application to final credit decision, might be established for indirect loans, while a seven-day timeframe might be used for home equity line of credit applications. The longer time period takes into account the fact that external elements, such as appraisals and property reports, may be required to complete the investigation process.

What Should Be Investigated and How

The investigation is generally confined to six basic areas

- the applicant's identity
- credit history
- income
- employment
- residence
- collateral

While *direct verification* is preferable to *indirect verification,* the credit investigator usually relies on indirect sources.

Applicant's Identity

Proper identification of the applicant is an essential part of the investigation process. It is critical to have an accurate Social Security number, date of birth, and residence to request valid credit reports. Most identification problems arise because the bank did not obtain the correct identification information from the application. Some banks require a driver's license or other valid photo ID to verify the applicant's identity.

Consumers occasionally obtain credit under a variety of names. One common example of this is a married woman who maintains credit in both her married and maiden names. Another example is inconsistency in the use of initials. For example, J. Donald Jones, Joseph D. Jones, and J.D. Jones may all be the same person. These situations can make it difficult to verify the customer's identity. Likewise, generation designations (such as Sr. and Jr.) often cause considerable confusion in the investigation process. Some application forms specifically ask applicants to list all names in which they have obtained credit in an effort to catch those situations in which variations on a name have been used.

Social Security numbers are commonly used to identify people. Some credit bureaus use this number to identify matches within their report files, and some banks use it as the customer's account number. Variations in social security numbers are usually flagged in credit bureau files. They might be simply typographical errors, or they might indicate fraud. Fraud artists often use the identity of a deceased person to obtain credit—credit bureaus now attempt to flag Social Security numbers for deceased persons in their reports.

Credit History

Credit history is one of the most important decision-making variables. In evaluating a credit history, the lender wants to know

- who the applicant has borrowed from
- what type of accounts the customer has used and now has available
- how long accounts have been opened

- how credit bills have been paid
- current obligations and *exposure* (available credit on open-end credit accounts)

This information may be acquired from four primary sources:

- the bank's own internal files
- directly from other financial institutions
- credit reporting agencies
- public records

The investigator should first check the bank's own credit files. Factual data obtained from the bank's files should be the most reliable and accurate. Direct references from other lenders may also produce current and accurate credit information about the applicant, though in practice such direct references are increasingly rare.

Credit reporting agencies are the largest providers of credit information to the banking industry. Upon receiving a member company's request, they release to the bank all the information they have in their files regarding that customer. Most communities are served by more than one credit reporting agency. These agencies vary in size from large national and regional firms—such as TRW Credit Services, Equifax, The Credit Bureau, Inc., Trans Union Credit Information Services, and the Pinger System—to small, locally operated credit bureaus. Reports received from competing credit bureaus can vary because they may gather their information from different sources. It is essential that lenders evaluate the differences among the available credit bureaus, and periodically test each bureau to determine which one provides the best service and most accurate information. This may be done by requesting a credit report on a customer from each bureau serving the bank's community, then comparing reports to determine which provides the most complete information.

A common problem in attempting to investigate credit history is incomplete information. Since policies concerning submitting credit information vary, some lenders do not send their credit files to all credit bureaus in their area. Other lenders, such as credit unions, frequently do not report their loans to any bureaus, nor will they verify information directly. This makes it very difficult for the credit investigator to confirm information and also exposes the bank to higher risk. Also, if the applicant does not disclose all debts on the application, and if the undisclosed debts are not shown on the credit report, the risk on the loan might be higher than it appears.

Another problem can be the work of credit clinics, which offer help to consumers with unsatisfactory credit records. These clinics often try to pressure lenders into changing negative information on the consumer's credit report, either by threatening legal action or by offering some money on a previous loss. For example, the clinic may offer a settlement on an account that has been charged off as a loss as an inducement to get the bank to change the credit reference to a more favorable status. Credit reports that no longer reflect this type of credit history also can expose the bank to greater risk.

Another source of credit data is public records. Information on judgments, bankruptcies, and liens may be available from credit reporting agencies, but, in most cases, are obtained directly from courthouse records. Because of the time and expense involved in checking courthouse records, this is generally done only on loans secured by real property or goods recorded by filing a Uniform Commercial Code (UCC-1) financing statement.

Red Flags

Characteristics that may indicate a problem on an application are referred to as red flags, and they signal the need for special attention or extra care. Rarely does one red flag mean an application should be rejected. Rather, it should alert the credit investigator to dig more deeply or to insist on direct verification of key data instead of using indirect sources. *Red flags* commonly associated with credit report information include

- all credit history is recent
- no credit history for applicants over 21 years old
- heavy recent inquiries or applications for credit with other lenders
- all references with unknown or small companies
- all references are closed accounts
- warning flags on the credit report
- undisclosed creditors
- heavy use of open-end credit accounts

- excessive debt in relation to income
- pyramiding of debts—taking on a large amount of debt in a short period of time or steadily increasing the amounts owed

Income

Income is the principal indicator of the applicant's ability to repay the loan and a key variable in any credit evaluation process. Consumer loans are most often repaid on a monthly basis from regular, recurring income. The major elements of income that should be investigated are its source, reliability, frequency, and probable continuity over the term of the loan.

The reliability of the applicant's primary source of income is a key factor in evaluating creditworthiness. Therefore, it is desirable for lenders to know what the general market conditions and stability of at least the major employers in the market area are. The reliability of income is determined by both its source and the applicant's job history. Weakness in either area is cause for concern. For example, employees who have not been on the job long are usually riskier than those who have been employed a long time with a single company. Likewise, income that is subject to seasonal disruptions—such as in the construction industry—or that may not be guaranteed in the future—such as income from commissions and bonuses—make it more difficult to predict the reliability of the applicant's income and ability to repay debts.

Income may be verified directly by employers or indirectly by forms such as pay stubs, W-2 forms, tax returns, and legal documents. Direct references from employers are the best source of income verification; they provide the most current information and may allow the investigator to verify other data, such as type of job and time on the job. Unfortunately, many employers do not provide direct verification, or they only verify that someone is employed. In these cases, lenders must rely on indirect sources to verify income. Verifying direct payroll deposits to the customer's checking account with the bank is another direct source.

A recent pay stub may be an acceptable alternative or additional support to direct verification. A pay stub gives the lender some insight into such data as payroll deductions and overtime income, and therefore a better understanding of the applicant's net income. Closely examine the pay stub presented to ensure it is valid, is not missing information, and has not been altered; unscrupulous individuals can forge pay stubs. Also check the date on the pay stub to be sure it is recent—an old pay stub may indicate a problem.

Another source of information is a W-2 form, which offers a historical record of the applicant's annual income. An accurate W-2 form shows the name and address of the employer and the applicant, and the amount of income paid to the employee during the year covered by the form. It should be noted that a W-2 form can very easily be "dummied up," however, and should not necessarily be taken as proof of present income. Consequently, W-2s are regarded as a weak method of verification. However, if the income amount seems reasonable and it can be verified that the person is employed, most lenders are comfortable with this form of income verification.

Tax returns, like W-2 forms, relate historical, not current, income information. However, they often contain a substantial amount of information about the applicant's financial behavior. Furthermore, tax returns are generally the only reliable way to verify income for self-employed people. Lenders usually review tax returns only when they are considering large loan requests, applications from self-employed individuals, and requests for large, open-end lines of credit.

Legal documents such as divorce decrees, separation agreements, and public assistance notices are frequently necessary to verify nonwage income. Pension income receipts may also be used to verify income. It is important to review these documents carefully to determine both the amount of income and the benefit period or other limitations that may apply to these sources of income.

Employment

Employment is another key variable in assessing an applicant's stability. Major elements of employment that are frequently investigated are the type of job, time on the job, the employer's industry and stability, and the applicant's employment history.

The type of job held by the applicant gives some insight into the relative level of income, job mobility, continuity of income, and level of education. Don't be impressed by job titles alone; not all bank vice presidents are equal, and the terms "teller" and "customer service representative" may refer to the same position. It is the applicant's responsibilities and income that are important, not the job title.

Time on the job is also essential in analyzing the applicant's income stability. If the applicant's employer will not verify this information, the credit investigator will usually accept the information supplied by the applicant, assuming that the applicant's place of employment can be verified.

The final concern is the applicant's employment history. When an applicant has been at the current job only for a short time, it may be a good idea to check the previous employment. Don't overlook that a recent job change may indicate a positive change rather than a negative one. Employment history may present trade-offs that require investigation and informed consideration, especially when the applicant is a "job hopper," with many different employers and gaps in employment.

Red flags that arise in the process of verifying employment include

- home and business address the same
- addresses not consistent with local street patterns
- home or business address is a post office box or mail drop location
- home address at hotel or motel
- variations in phone numbers
- questionable persons giving references
- telephone calls answered in an unusual manner

When verifying references, investigators should not use phone numbers supplied by the applicant. Use phone directories or operator assistance before calling for employment and residence references. Variations in phone numbers may mean a third party has been positioned to give a phony reference. It is also possible that the company is out of business or that the applicant does not live or work at the address listed.

Most investigators are trained to obtain the identity of the person they contact for a reference. This helps eliminate asking an unqualified or inappropriate person for an important reference. For example, it is unusual for a secretary to be able to verify a manager's salary or for an employee to be able to verify the income of the owner of the business. While these people may be able to verify employment, it is better to verify the applicant's income using another source, such as a tax return or pay stub.

Residence

Residence information is another variable that provides evidence regarding the stability of the applicant. This information may reveal a great deal about the applicant's life-style and financial condition; however, it should serve as a general indicator of stability rather than as a major determinant of credit risk. Care must be taken to avoid discriminatory practices such as redlining, in which residents of specific geographic areas are denied access to credit solely on the basis of their location.

The applicant's residence type—own/buying, renting, living with relatives, or other—is a measure of stability and may also give some indication of financial strength. Home ownership is associated with greater stability and financial strength since the applicant has an asset of significant value and is less likely to leave the area unexpectedly. Renting and other residence statuses, such as living with parents and military housing, do not provide the same level of stability, and, therefore, may be regarded as less stable when evaluating credit risk. Despite the importance of this variable, the residence type is often accepted as given by the applicant, unless the place of residence is to be used to secure the loan. If the residence will be taken as collateral on the loan, however, it must be verified.

Time at an address is a measure of stability that should be analyzed in relation to the applicant's age and life cycle stage. Frequent changes in address are a significant negative factor, usually calling for further investigation. However, you would not expect young applicants to have lived in one place for a long time since they may have only recently established a household. Banks usually accept the information given by the applicant regarding time at address if the address can be verified.

Information regarding an applicant's previous address is usually requested, but is not often investigated. This information is helpful in obtaining accurate credit bureau reports, particularly when the customer is new to the area, and in evaluating customer stability. However, it may be expensive and difficult to verify.

Residence information may be verified directly with landlords or mortgage holders, through public records, or by credit bureau records. Although credit bureau information may not be current, it is usually enough to verify residence unless conflicting information comes up elsewhere in the investigation. For example, if the credit bureau or another lender had a different address in their records, the investigator might want to require a more direct form of verification.

If they are willing and able to provide the data on a timely basis, landlords and mortgage holders are the best sources for residence information. However, many mortgage holders will only give references in writing, making this type of verification rare on consumer loan requests; many landlords refuse to confirm residency at all.

Collateral

The credit investigator and lender are concerned with a number of issues when a secured loan is requested. These include identifying the terms on any purchase-money loans, determining the value of the collateral, and ascertaining the owners of the collateral. Determining the collateral value may be handled by the lender or in some cases by a credit investigator.

On *purchase-money secured loans*—which use the proceeds to purchase the goods securing the loan—the lender must have factual information regarding the terms of the sale in order to properly evaluate the collateral risk on the loan. A bill of sale, invoice, or purchase order should be obtained. These documents show the actual cash selling price, the amount and composition of any down payment, the amount financed, and a complete description of the collateral. This information is also essential to properly document the loan. Consumers should supply this information when they apply for a loan or when they come to the loan closing.

In analyzing the terms of a purchase, the investigator should look at the cash selling price of an item, the actual price that the consumer is paying, including the full price of the item plus any sales tax. The down payment represents the consumer's investment in the goods and is composed of actual cash paid toward the purchase of an item and the cash value of any trade-in. The amount of the down payment is then deducted from the cash selling price to determine the amount to be financed.

The amount financed should be analyzed in relation to the value of the collateral, using appropriate valuation sources as noted earlier. Simply relying on the down payment may result in advancing too much credit and increasing the risk for the lender. Therefore, the investigator should consult valuation guide books or take other steps necessary to determine the value of the collateral.

Ownership of the collateral must be verified to ensure that the bank can obtain a lien and that it can be properly perfected. For collateral presently in the customer's possession, this can be done by examining the appropriate ownership document, such as a deed or title. Ownership of goods to be purchased may be verified directly with the seller or by examining documents, such as the bill of sale.

Other Red Flags

Credit investigators should always be alert to any information that is negative or cannot be verified through normal channels. Identifying gaps in information should prompt greater care and perhaps a more extensive investigation. Many of these red flags were noted earlier in this chapter. Some other common warning signs are

❏ **Information inconsistent with applicant's age**   A strong correlation usually exists between an individual's age and life cycle stage and the characteristics that typically appear on a credit application. Indeed, lenders rely heavily on the fact that most people exhibit the same personal characteristics in the future as they have in the past, and that, as they grow older, they move toward greater stability, higher income, and the accumulation of assets.

Variations from these norms are not necessarily unacceptable or bad, but they may warrant closer investigation of the facts. They might also require an explanation by the consumer. For example, it is unusual when a 40-year-old applicant claims to have no credit experience, or when a 30-year-old person claims five different addresses in the last year.

❏ **Overly pushy or anxious applicant**   Many people have read books like *Winning through Intimidation* that emphasize getting one's way by using manipulative, pushy behavior. The danger is that a lender may, in fact, be intimidated and may compromise the investigation process, sometimes with disastrous results.

A similar dilemma is presented by customers who are intimidated by the bank and its lending process. Very few customers actually relish applying for a loan, but most come through the process without difficulty. An anxious applicant can often be made comfortable by a skilled interviewer, while an excessively anxious customer may actually be hiding something.

The inclusion of personal behavior factors on a list of red flag characteristics is risky at best. Shy people will avoid eye contact, while people experienced in borrowing or nervous about their chances of getting a loan may appear evasive or display other body language signs of uneasiness. These should not be construed as signs of a problem. Lenders must stick to facts, and avoid inappropriate personal prejudices.

❏ **Gaps in information**   The credit investigator should give the decision-maker as complete a picture of the applicant as possible, within the time constraints on the application. Gaps in key information and the inability to obtain acceptable forms of verification should be communicated to the person responsible for the decision.

Special Considerations: Revolving Credit Products

As noted earlier, the growth of revolving credit products has added some different twists to credit investigation. These include

- investigating prospects in order to extend a credit offer to a particular market known as prescreening
- investigating existing revolving credit customers to determine whether the line of credit should remain open, further borrowing be constrained, or the amount of the credit limit be changed (account monitoring)

EXHIBIT 8.1   **Prescreen/Preapproval Process**

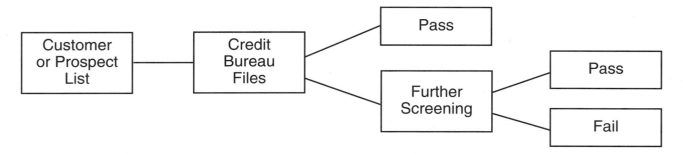

Prescreening

In the case of a prescreened loan solicitation program, the bank identifies minimum acceptable credit requirements. All potential applicants—anyone with an existing credit file with that credit reporting agency—will be run against the bank's requirements;

those who do not meet the requirements will not receive a credit offer. Customers are never aware that their names have been passed through a prescreening routine, the bank does not know the names of those consumers who fail to pass their requirements, and the information is not captured on the credit bureau files in any way. The bank will receive only the names and addresses of those consumers who meet its requirements. These individuals will then receive a credit offer directly from the bank, usually in the form of a direct mail piece.

Account Monitoring

To monitor accounts of existing credit customers, the bank runs their names against the credit bureau's files, using defined criteria. Customers who fail to pass the bank's requirements are subject to further screening. Usually, the bank will receive a printout of the credit reports for customers who did not pass the criteria. A credit analyst will then examine the report and may conduct additional investigation depending upon the circumstances. Once all required data are assembled, the credit analyst may

- continue the account under its present terms
- block the line from further use
- reduce the size of the credit limit extended to the customer

If the lender takes adverse action, such as defined in items 2 and 3, the customer must be notified of the change immediately.

Monitoring accounts is an important part of the bank's efforts to manage its loan portfolios. While state laws may modify these general procedures or require specific legal disclosures, these programs represent a responsible approach to protecting the integrity of the bank's loan assets.

Summary

The credit investigation function is an important task in the lending process. Its primary objective is to verify the accuracy of data obtained on the credit application and to develop enough supporting information to allow lenders to make the best possible credit decision. Sound investigation procedures help the bank make good loans and reject applications that represent an unacceptable level of credit risk.

Investigations must be completed within the timeframe appropriate for the type of loan product requested. The investigation process should flow in an efficient manner in order to obtain all necessary data at the least possible cost.

Finally, credit investigators always need to be alert to red flags that may signal potential problems and require a more extensive investigative effort.

Review Questions

1. What are the four primary sources of credit information?
2. Assume an employer refuses to directly verify an applicant's income. What indirect sources can lenders turn to?
3. What six basic areas are the subject of most credit investigations?
4. Why might a credit investigation begin by referring to bank files instead of credit reports or public records?
5. Name two drawbacks to the use of W-2 forms or tax returns to verify income data.
6. What data would you accept, without verification, from a loan applicant? Would the data you accept vary from one applicant to the next?

Optional Research

1. Request a copy of your credit report directly from one of the credit bureaus serving your area. (**Note: there may be a fee for this service—also do not order the report through your bank.**) What observations can you draw from your report?
2. What credit reporting agencies does your bank use?
3. Fill out a personal financial statement for your family. What does it tell you? If you do this each year, it can help you track your financial progress.

9 Credit Evaluation and Decision Making

After reading this chapter, you will be able to

- ❏ describe four primary objectives to be achieved in the credit evaluation and decision-making stage of the lending process
- ❏ discuss some of the differences in approach and operation between consumer and commercial lending
- ❏ list the five Cs of credit and give examples of the characteristics considered for each
- ❏ describe the benefits credit-scoring systems offer banks

Objectives of Credit Evaluation and Decision Making

Consistent credit evaluation and sound decision making are essential to the success of any consumer credit operation. In this stage of the lending process, the lender analyzes the application, credit investigation, and other data to reach a decision consistent with the bank's definition of acceptable credit risk.

The primary objectives of the credit evaluation and decision-making stage are to

- ❏ make the best loan for the customer and the bank
- ❏ ensure that the level of credit risk is acceptable
- ❏ ensure compliance with regulations and bank policy
- ❏ keep the goodwill of the customer

Making the best loan for the customer and the bank highlights the importance of selling in the consumer lending process. Lenders should not merely be order-takers who analyze loan applications only on the basis requested by the customer. Rather, lenders are encouraged to be active financial advisers who examine the customer's application and structure a loan that best meets both the customer's and the bank's best interests.

An example is the customer who comes in for a home improvement loan for $5,000. The easy choice would be to grant the customer a closed-end loan for 60 months, which would most likely serve the customer's current borrowing needs very well and be profitable for the bank. However, a $20,000 equity line of credit might offer even greater benefits to both parties. The customer might benefit by

- having access to loan funds in the future without needing to reapply
- being able to do more extensive home improvements for the same monthly payment
- possibly receiving a lower rate and longer term on the loan

The bank would benefit by

- having a secured loan
- enjoying operational efficiencies, particularly on future borrowings
- developing a relationship with the customer
- creating the opportunity to sell a larger loan at a good rate of return

It is essential that lenders make loans consistent with the bank's credit risk objectives. While it is difficult to be precise in defining the acceptable level of risk, consumer credit managers use several criteria to continually measure credit quality. Banks manage the levels of credit risk, delinquency, and loan loss by developing lending policies that produce consistent decisions and ensuring that customers meet defined credit standards.

Decisions must be made within regulatory guidelines. Under the Equal Credit Opportunity Act, lenders must not discriminate against applicants on any of the following bases:

- sex
- marital status
- race
- color
- religion
- national origin

- age (as long as the person is of legal age to enter into a contract)
- the fact that all or part of the applicant's income comes from a public assistance program
- the fact that the applicant has in good faith exercised any right under the Consumer Credit Protection Act

Discrimination against applicants for any of these reasons is illegal and violations can result in high penalties for lenders. Further, practices such as redlining and arbitrary discrimination against whole groups based on sex, race, marital status, etc. must absolutely be avoided. Not only is this illegal, but it is also illogical.

Decision-Making Parameters

- ❏ Consumer lending is carried out in an environment far different from commercial lending. Perhaps the biggest difference between the two types of loans is that consumer loans are made based upon the law of probability, while commercial loans are made on a "no loss anticipated" basis. Consumer lenders know that a certain percentage of loans are going to result in losses, but seek to limit the percentage of delinquencies and charge-offs to an acceptable level.

- ❏ Consumer lenders have limited information to work with when considering a loan request; they generally work with basic information about the customer's current financial condition and past credit history. More detailed analyses, such as cash flow and balance sheet analyses, are rare on customer loans, except for those involving very large dollar amounts.

- ❏ Consumer lenders rely heavily on normal individual and family life-cycle trends and past customer behavior patterns to predict whether an applicant is likely to be a good or bad credit risk. Behavioral scientists have found that human beings tend to follow certain patterns throughout their lives. Consumer lenders therefore make the assumption that customers who have been responsible about handling credit obligations in the past will continue to be responsible in the future. Also, individuals and families normally follow well-defined life-cycle patterns, which generally include steadily rising income, greater stability, and predictable credit usage. These patterns, consistently supported by practical lending experience, help consumer lenders make loans with a high level of confidence that the applicants they interview will follow these responsible patterns.

However, it is equally clear that not all people follow normal life-cycle trends. Divorce and separations cause some people to change their behavior, just as midlife crises lead some people to quit their jobs and change their lives dramatically. The hardest change to predict is job termination and layoffs, which can devastate a family's financial position and reverse all past behavior patterns. These changes are virtually impossible for consumer lenders to predict or control, yet they are often the factors that cause an otherwise good loan to result in serious delinquency, bankruptcy, or loss.

❏ Time requirements play a major role in the handling of consumer loan requests. Generally, competitive pressures require lenders to decide on direct or indirect applications the same day they are received, if not within hours or minutes of receipt. Mail-in applications and requests for credit cards, check overdraft, and other revolving credit products are generally under less time pressure; each bank sets its own standards for handling these applications. The entire loan process must be structured to meet timing pressures. In some cases, such as on home equity and boat loans, the final decision may be delayed because the collateral needs to be appraised. A good practice is to inform the applicant, as soon as possible, that the loan is approved *subject to* a satisfactory appraisal.

❏ Finally, consumer lenders rely on standardized loan policies that provide them with a sound framework on which to base consistent and timely credit decisions without being so rigid that lenders are prevented from exercising sound judgment. Making good decisions requires a process for handling applications that are deserving of an exception to the standard credit policies. For example, if an applicant fails to pass the bank's credit-scoring program, but plans to fully secure a loan with a savings account, an officer in the bank should be authorized to make an exception to the policy that all loans must exceed a specified minimum score.

Credit Evaluation Systems

Three basic systems are used for making consumer credit decisions. They are judgmental, credit-scoring, and credit-scoring with judgmental systems. These approaches involve analyzing applicant variables to determine the probability that the applicant will turn out to be a good or bad credit risk. Using these systems, the lender weighs different applicant variables and trade-offs to reach a final credit decision.

The Judgmental Approach—The Five Cs of Credit

The variables considered in the judgmental decision-making process are popularly known as the five Cs of credit. They are

- ❏ character
- ❏ capacity
- ❏ capital
- ❏ collateral
- ❏ conditions

Some lenders also consider a sixth C—"Can We"—which answers the question: Does the request conform with the bank's loan policy?

Character

Character addresses the questions: What type of person are we dealing with? Does he or she have the willingness and desire to repay the loan requested? It involves an analysis of behavior patterns as they relate to the applicant's job and residence, stability, credit history, and personal characteristics. Character is regarded by many lenders to be the most important factor in granting a loan, but it is also one that is difficult to measure precisely.

Stability is measured by the individual's time on the job, type of employment, type of residence (own/rent), previous history, time at a residence, and time within the community. Since time factors are closely related to the applicant's age, it is essential to analyze an applicant's stability with the age factor in mind. Consider the following applicant characteristics:

Applicant 1   Age 22; time on present job 1 year; prior employment college; time at address 1 year; time within community 22 years; occupation salesperson.

You would not expect someone 22 years old and recently graduated from college to exhibit long-term stability; thus, the lender would find this variable somewhat less important than other variables. On the positive side, the applicant is a college graduate, is from the local community, and has maintained the same job since graduating from college.

Applicant 2   Age 40; time on present job 2 years; prior employment 9 years; time at address 1 year, buying home; time within community 14 years; occupation manager.

By age 40, you would expect the applicant to demonstrate some stability, though some of the variables may be of short duration. In this case, the fact that the applicant's time at the present address is short is offset by the fact that the applicant is buying a home. Time at present job time is also short, the importance of this factor may be determined by considering the current employment history along with prior job history. If the applicant remained in the same industry, this may indicate that the applicant has moved to a higher paying or higher level job. This would certainly offset the relatively short employment history.

Applicant 3   Age 33; time on present job 6 months; prior employment 1 year; time at address 4 months, renting; time within community 6 months; occupation salesperson.

This applicant should certainly have more stability established than is shown by these variables. Indeed, the lack of stability that seems evident in this application may be a major negative factor. However, there may also be other positive variables that will offset this negative, resulting in loan approval.

Stability is important because consumer loans are made for extended periods of time. The lender wants to be reasonably sure that the customer will continue to be employed during the term of the loan, will continue to have regular income to service the debt, and can be found if problems develop. Job hopping, career moving from one occupation to another, and frequent changes in residence all indicate potential problems. Renting is also considered to be less stable than home buying or ownership. While all renters are certainly not high credit risks, the factor requires additional consideration.

Another primary measure of character is the applicant's credit history. A thorough analysis of credit history should take into account the following characteristics

- credit ratings
- types of credit the borrower has used
- sources of credit
- dates accounts are opened and closed
- level of debt
- credit usage patterns

Exhibit 9.1 shows the credit history for a loan applicant. Study this credit report to examine the applicant's credit history as it relates to each characteristic. This credit report contains a variety of credit ratings. Ratings such as "Curr. Acct.," an open account in good standing, and "Paid Satis.," a closed account

EXHIBIT 9.1 Sample Credit Report

Report Date: July 1992

Creditor	Status	Status Date	Date Opened	Account Type	Credit Line or Loan Amount	Balance
Chase	Curr. Acct	3-89	4-85	Revolving	$ 2,000	
Union Trust	Paid Satis.	3-88	2-84	Auto	10,900	
Union Trust	Paid Satis.	5-91	7-88	Auto	11,200	
Sovran	Curr. Acct	6-92	3-88	Credit Cd.	2,000	
United Bank	Curr. Acct	6-92	4-89	Revolving	2,600	2,570
Maryland Bank	Curr. was 90	10-89	4-89	Revolving	2,000	
Beneficial	Curr. Acct	6-92	3-87	Revolving	16,000	12,500
Union Trust	Curr. Acct	6-92	7-89	Revolving	7,500	
Sears	Curr. was 60	3-92	9-86	Revolving	1,300	
Bloomingdale's	Curr. Acct	6-92	1-84	Revolving	800	
Lord's Stores	Curr. was 30	4-92	3-85	Revolving	200	
Woodward & Loth.	Curr. was 150	7-90	10Y	Revolving	2,500	2,400
Hecht's	Curr. Acct	6-91	10Y	Revolving	800	
Dept. Store	Curr. Acct	6-87	10Y	Revolving	300	
Citicorp	Curr. Acct	8-86	10Y	Revolving	700	
HFC	Paid Satis.	9-87	6-84	Note	4,900	
Magnin	Curr. Acct	7-91	10Y	Revolving	100	
Diners Club	Paid Satis.	10-86	6-84	Revolving		
Bank of NY	Inquiry	6-92				
Bank Ohio	Inquiry	10-91				
Union Trust	Inquiry	7-92				

paid satisfactorily, are considered positive. However, the customer also has several accounts that have not been paid satisfactorily. These include Maryland Bank "Curr. was 90", Sears "Curr. was 60," Lord's Stores "Curr. was 30," and Woodward and Lothrop "Curr. was 150." These ratings indicate that the customer has been slow in paying some creditors. Thus, the credit ratings reveal a mixed picture of this customer. While some lenders would decline this applicant based upon the negative ratings, it seems appropriate to examine the report in more detail.

The report shows that most of the applicant's credit is in the form of revolving credit accounts (14 of 18 accounts are revolving accounts). Two accounts are installment automobile loans, and one is an installment loan from Household Finance. The final account is Diners Club, a travel and entertainment card calling for payments in full each month. This tells us that the customer has had experience with a variety of types of credit, and has borrowed from a variety of sources, including banks, retailers, and finance companies.

The dates that accounts are opened and closed are important to a proper evaluation of each credit reference because they identify recent credit activity and define the length of credit experience. Recent credit activity can be identified by looking down the "Date Opened" column and noting any loans opened within the past year. Assuming the sample credit report was taken in July 1992, this customer would not have any accounts in this category. However, should the applicant have a lot of recent credit activity, it could be an indication he or she is *pyramiding debts*. The danger in this situation is that the customer may be unable to adjust his or her cash flow enough to properly handle the new debt requirements. Banks have seen over the years a high percentage of loans that have been charged off deteriorated in the first year after the loan was made.

The length of credit history should also be evaluated in the context of the applicant's age. Young people cannot have long credit histories, while people 30 years and older should have established solid credit histories. The applicant whose credit report is shown in exhibit 9.1 has a credit history extending back more than 10 years.

The dates of inquiry are also important to the lender. An "inquiry" shows the applicant has applied for credit from the source indicated. Prescreening and monitoring consumer accounts does not show as an inquiry on the credit report. The credit report indicates the date that a specific status was given. For example, in evaluating the delinquent ratings on the sample credit report, it is important to note that the delinquency on the Maryland Bank account is from 10-89, and Woodward and Lothrop from 7-90, while the more recent delinquencies are on retail accounts, which now have zero balances. This indicates that the customer has not had any significant credit problems in the most recent year.

The final item on the credit report that should be analyzed is the applicant's credit usage patterns, in particular the use of revolving credit accounts. This is analyzed by looking at the total amount of open-end credit lines available and the amount owed on those accounts. In our example, the customer is a heavy user of three credit lines—United Bank, Beneficial, and Woodward and Lothrop—most of the other lines are not used at all.

How the customer uses his or her credit can have an impact upon the final credit decision. For example, if someone who constantly uses revolving credit applies for a loan to consolidate revolving account balances, the lender must be concerned with protecting the bank's interest in the event the customer begins using the accounts again after the new loan is made.

Exhibit 9.2 shows an example of a credit report on a heavy user of revolving credit. Note that this credit report shows that the customer has established many open-end credit accounts and that virtually every account is up to or over the

EXHIBIT 9.2 Sample Credit Report for a Heavy User of Revolving Credit

Report Date: July 1992

Creditor	Status	Status Date	Date Opened	Account Type	Credit Line or Loan Amount	Balance
Equitable Bk	Curr Acct	7-92	11-91	Revolving	$2,000	$1,885
Dominion Bank	Curr Acct	7-92	5-91	Revolving	2,000	1,953
Citibank VISA	Curr Acct	6-92	9-91	Revolving	1,500	1,443
JC Penney	Curr Acct	7-92	10Y	Revolving	1,700	1,496
JC Penney	Curr Acct	7-92	10Y	Revolving	1,300	1,139
Sears	Curr Acct	7-92	10Y	Revolving	3,100	3,073
Wards	Curr Acct	6-92	10Y	Revolving	3,000	1,947
Citicorp	Curr Acct	7-92	6-91	Revolving	1,000	986
Security Pac.	Curr Acct	7-92	6-91	Note	4,100	2,843
Finance Amer.	Curr Acct	6-92	3-90	Note	1,600	277
Spiegel	Curr Acct	7-92	10Y	Revolving	1,900	1,507
Firestone	Curr Acct	6-92	6-90	Revolving	900	884
GECC	Curr Acct	7-92	4-91	Revolving	1,000	1,029
Beneficial Bk	Curr Acct	7-92	5-85	Revolving	3,200	3,356

credit limit. This is a sign that the customer is so entrenched in making purchases using credit cards that it would be very difficult to change this behavior pattern. If offered another line of credit, this person would most likely accept the offer and use it fully.

Credit reports are, therefore, an essential tool in helping the lender develop a general opinion of the applicant's character. This is easy when all of the information is positive and there is no evidence of problems. However, lenders will be confronted with credit reports that contain a mixture of good and bad references, and perhaps a few red flags. The lender's ability to correctly analyze these questionable applications and arrive at sound credit decisions is critical to the success of a bank's consumer loan portfolio.

Character may also be evaluated based on variables such as type of job and personal reputation. Personal reputation undoubtedly comes into play when the applicant is known to the lender. However, care must be exercised in making credit decisions based upon such personal knowledge. In some cases, the lender may know that the applicant is related to a family that has a history of bad credit with the bank, or that the applicant is an alcoholic who is constantly getting into trouble with the law. Such intangible information must be evaluated and balanced along with more objective tangible credit criteria to make the most sound credit decision.

Many studies have demonstrated a correlation between job type and credit risk. Some credit-scoring programs assign points to job types (see exhibit 9.3), and many lenders consider this factor as part of their judgmental system.

Job rankings arise out of the fact that certain occupations are associated with higher income levels, greater employment security, and higher levels of job mobility, while others are associated with inconsistent employment, high failure rates, and short job tenures. Lenders using judgmental systems often have their own list of problem occupations. This list may be influenced by recent experiences or local economic conditions.

EXHIBIT 9.3 Sample Credit Scoring of Job Type

Occupation	Points
Professionals & officials	27
Foremen & operatives	26
Technical workers & managers	14
Clericals & salespeople	12
Service workers	5
Farm workers	3
Craftsmen & nonfarm laborers	0
Proprietors	−3

Capacity

Capacity addresses the question: Does the applicant have the ability to repay the loan and handle the proposed new level of debt? Two steps measure capacity; one determines the customer's income, the other evaluates the customer's cash flow and overall financial condition.

Determining the customer's income begins with the issue of how to treat different types of income. This is a matter of bank policy and credit regulation. The Equal Credit Opportunity Act requires lenders to count income from part-time jobs the same as income from full-time employment. In addition, if the applicant wishes, the bank must take into account any income from alimony, child support, and separate maintenance payments. To ensure consistency, the treatment of different types of income should be specified in the bank's policy. Income from investments and less predictable and consistent sources, such as commissions and bonuses, must be treated carefully.

A common but less clear-cut issue is which income to include when evaluating the credit capacity of joint or multiple applicants. For example, if two people who are not married to each other apply for a loan, should the incomes and debts be combined to evaluate capacity, or should the lender look only at the primary applicant's income? When the bank's policy calls for the lender to count both incomes for married applicants, then the lender may also combine the incomes and expenses of unmarried joint applicants. This issue becomes even more complex when the joint applicants do not live at the same address. It is not uncommon for couples who are engaged to be married or unmarried couples who live together to apply for joint accounts. The bank should structure its lending policies to recognize the realities of the social environment and provide clear and consistent policies to address these situations.

A person's capacity to handle credit obligations may be affected if the applicant will reach retirement age during the term of the loan. Retirement can mean a change in the level of income and life-style, and this should be considered when evaluating future capacity to handle debt. The lender will need to determine the postretirement level of income before reaching a decision on applicants in this category.

The other part of the capacity equation is measuring the applicant's cash flow and overall financial condition. Many lenders have made the mistake of reviewing an application from a high-income consumer and leaping to the conclusion that, because the income is high, the customer must be able to afford

EXHIBIT 9.4   Sample Debt-to-Income Calculation

Debt	Minimum Required Monthly Payment
Mortgage payment	$ 500
Auto loan	295
VISA	50
MasterCard	65
New loan request	150
Total monthly debt	$1,060
Gross monthly income	$4,000
Debt-to-income ratio	26.5%

a loan. Often overlooked is the fact that, as income rises, so generally do a customer's expenses. People in our society tend to spend what they make, and, while the amount available for discretionary spending tends to increase with income, this is not always the case.

Evaluation of cash flow is usually confined to the calculation of a debt-to-income ratio. Using this approach, the lender totals the required minimum monthly debt payments, including the payment on the proposed loan, and then relates that amount to the customer's income to determine a debt-to-income ratio. An example is presented as exhibit 9.4.

This ratio (26.5 percent) is then compared with the bank's policy to determine whether the proposed loan falls within the acceptable debt-to-income ratio standard. Exhibit 9.5 shows the amount of monthly debt payments that borrowers could have at various income levels based upon a 35 percent and 40 percent debt-to-income ratio.

The debt-to-income table can be used to help structure a loan that a customer can afford. An applicant with a gross annual income of $40,000 could afford $1,167 in monthly debt payments at the 35 percent debt-to-income ratio level. Assuming the customer currently had the following debt structure, he would not meet the bank's requirements:

Mortgage	$ 400
Auto loan	250
Finance company loan	175
VISA	75
MasterCard	50
Store account	50
Bank loan	200
New loan	150
Total Monthly Payments	$1,350

However, if the lender were to restructure the applicant's debts, and consolidate some existing loans with the new loan, the applicant could meet the bank's requirements:

EXHIBIT 9.5 Sample Debt-to-Income Table

Gross Annual Income	Maximum Monthly Debt Service 35%	Maximum Monthly Debt Service 40%
$ 10,000	$ 292	$ 333
15,000	438	500
20,000	583	666
25,000	729	833
30,000	875	1000
40,000	1167	1333
50,000	1458	1666
60,000	1750	2000
70,000	2041	2333
80,000	2333	2666
90,000	2625	3000
100,000	2917	3333

Mortgage	$400
Auto loan	250
New loan: second mortgage	325
Total Monthly Payment	$975

This illustrates how a flexible, responsive lender may be able to structure the best loan for the customer and the bank. The loan as requested requires $1,350 in monthly payments and would be rejected. However, the optional debt structure, which includes paying off five existing loans, would result in monthly payments of $975, thus bringing the request in line with the bank's debt-to-income policy.

The measurement of capacity has become more difficult with the spread of revolving credit programs. This can be illustrated by looking at our sample customer in exhibit 9.1. This customer has $17,470 in credit account balances as of the date of the report. But, the customer also has access to credit lines with an available balance of $21,330 (the difference between the line amount and any current balance due on accounts that are shown as still being open). Thus, the customer could theoretically increase his debts by $21,330 without requesting any new credit.

Another consideration is the total amount of debt in relation to the customer's income. It is possible for consumers to accumulate very high debts and still meet the bank's debt-to-income standards. When the maturity of loans is stretched out to keep monthly payments at a level consumers find attractive, monthly payments may be low, while aggregate loan amounts can be substantial.

No matter which approach is used, it is essential that the bank develop a consistent measure of capacity. It is clear that consumers get into trouble handling their debts when either their income declines or their level of debt increases beyond a certain point. Cash flow problems lead initially to slow payments, but in serious cases may result in losses and bankruptcies.

Capital

Lenders need to know whether the customer has backup capacity to pay the bank if unfavorable situations develop. Thus, the lender must analyze the relationship between the customer's assets and liabilities, generally using the customer's personal financial statement shown in exhibit 9.6. This form is most often required on large loan requests for which the issue of capital is a more critical concern. When received, it should always be properly signed, dated, and reviewed for proper completion.

Backup capacity is essentially the ability to convert assets to cash in order to meet financial obligations. Assets may be divided into several groups when examining their value as backup capacity. *Liquid assets* are readily convertible to cash to meet short-term cash needs, while *tangible assets,* such as equity in a home, are not as easily accessible but may provide more protection against serious financial problems.

Liquid assets are cash on hand and in banks; stocks, bonds, and similar investments; and the cash value of life insurance. These represent an individual's first line of defense against unexpected financial emergencies. They help the consumer meet short-term declines in income or increases in

EXHIBIT 9.6 Partial Personal Financial Statement

SECTION A – INDIVIDUAL INFORMATION		SECTION B – OTHER PARTY INFORMATION	
Name	Franklin Stone	Name	
Address	2209 Dabney Road	Address	
City, State & Zip	Ames, Iowa 56129	City, State & Zip	
Position/Occupation	Self-Employed	Position/Occupation	
Business Name	Franklin Stone, Inc.	Business Name	
Business Address	same as above	Business Address	
City, State & Zip		City, State & Zip	
Res. Phone 630-8644	Bus. Phone 630-9129	Res. Phone	Bus. Phone
Soc. Sec. No. 589-XX-XXXX	Date of Birth 10/26/48	Soc. Sec. No.	Date of Birth

SECTION C – STATEMENT OF FINANCIAL CONDITION AS OF ___December 31___ , 19 ____			
ASSETS		**LIABILITIES**	
Cash on hand and in Banks (Schedule 1)	5,700	Notes payable to banks - secured (Schedule 6)	5,000
U.S. Gov't. & Marketable Securities (Schedule 2)	9,600	Notes payable to banks - unsecured (Schedule 6)	
Cash Value of Life Insurance (Schedule 5)	2,000	Due to brokers	
SUBTOTAL LIQUID ASSETS	$17,300	Loans against Life Insurance (Schedule 5)	
		Notes payable to others - secured (Schedule 6)	
Non-Marketable Securities (Schedule 3)		Notes payable to others - unsecured (Schedule 6)	
Securities held by broker in margin accounts		Accounts and bills due	2,700
Accounts Receivable – good		Accrued taxes and interest	
? Receivable – good		Other unpaid taxes	
?? ?hedule		Rea ??? ?yable (Sch?? ? 4)	?

expenses such as medical emergencies, funeral expenses, and accidents that cause a loss of income.

Equity in a home accounts for a substantial portion of many consumers' net worth—the amount by which the value of assets exceeds their liabilities. Equity is the difference between the market value of the home and the amount owed on mortgages on the property. Exhibit 9.6 shows that the applicant's home is valued at $120,000, with a mortgage of $45,000. This means there is $75,000 of equity in the home. From the lender's viewpoint, this equity represents a significant source of backup capacity, as well as potential collateral for a loan; hence the widespread popularity of home equity and second mortgage loans.

Automobiles, boats, recreational vehicles, and other assets may also provide backup capacity for a loan. The value of these assets depends on their age, model, market demand, condition, and the amount of existing debt they already secure. If the consumer has equity built up in these assets, they can provide additional protection for lenders. However, equity in automobiles, boats, and similar assets may have deteriorated significantly by the time it is necessary to repossess them because these assets usually depreciate over time. As a result, the proceeds from the sale of assets may not even bring enough to cover the existing loan balances, much less the funds to cover other debts.

Assets such as art collections and antiques are rarely of value as backup capacity. The problems of appraising, obtaining a lien, repossessing, and selling this type of asset makes it difficult, if not impossible, to view collectibles as liquid assets.

The personal financial statement also offers insight into the consumer's debt structure. One way to determine a customer's equity position is to look at his assets in relation to the debts that they secure. Another way to measure a consumer's financial strength is by the relation of debt to net worth, known as leverage. Young customers are generally in a highly leveraged position—that is, their debts are nearly equal to or exceed their assets, and their net worth is small or nonexistent. Net worth should increase over time if the consumer practices sound financial management. In some cases, when debts actually exceed the value of the consumer's assets, the customer is insolvent and frequently will declare bankruptcy.

The importance of capital in evaluating consumer credit requests has been increasing in recent years because of the increased use of open-end credit programs. The accessibility of an open-end line exposes the bank to loss over a much longer period of time than a normal closed-end loan. Therefore, in analyzing requests for large open-end lines of credit, and when reconfirming a line of credit as part of a periodic review, lenders are emphasizing the evaluation of capital. Some banks require consumers to submit financial statements at regular intervals so they can identify any questionable trends—as well as any marketing opportunities.

Another reason for the increased use of analytical tools to evaluate capital is the increasing size of some consumer loans. Closed-end loans for boats, airplanes, and second mortgages range up to $200,000 and more. As the size of the loan increases, the level and extent of required credit analysis also increases. Backup capacity becomes a critical issue, and the size of the loan dictates that more time be spent analyzing the proposed credit extension.

Collateral

When considering a loan request, lenders may ask whether there is a readily available secondary source of repayment—collateral—on the loan. The analysis of collateral differs from the analysis of capital in that it evaluates a specific asset that is actually pledged to secure the loan.

The primary source of repayment on consumer loans is the customer's regular income. When something happens to diminish the customer's income, the bank will claim the collateral pledged against the loan to supply the funds necessary to pay off the loan balance. This is not to say that it is necessary or even possible to take collateral on every loan. Sound unsecured lending is a part of virtually every successful consumer credit program. The lender relies on the customer's character and capacity when lending on an unsecured basis.

Collateral protects the bank to the extent that it can be sold for more than the costs of repossessing or otherwise taking physical possession of it. More often than not, the forced sale of collateral results in a loss or deficiency balance in which money is still owed the bank after the collateral has been repossessed, sold, and the proceeds applied to the account.

For example:

Amount owed on loan	$7500
Car repossessed and sold at auction for	$5000
Less: repossession expenses	−350
Amount applied to loan	$4650
Deficiency balance	$2850

Therefore, it is not a sound practice to make a loan simply because it appears that the bank will have a good collateral position. All too often the bank may still take a loss or incur very high expenses in trying to collect loans from borrowers who should not have been granted a loan in the first place. While collateral can make up for minor weaknesses and allow longer repayment schedules, it must not replace character, credit, or the capacity to handle the debt level. The evaluation of collateral includes

- the value of the collateral
- the behavior pattern of the collateral's value—depreciating, appreciating, stable, or fluctuating
- the ease of collateral possession
- the marketability of the collateral
- ownership of the collateral

Collateral becomes more important as the size of the loan or credit line increases. Lending personnel should know how to evaluate various types of collateral, and the bank's loan policies should clearly define acceptable collateral. Ideally, collateral should be viewed as a means of strengthening a loan; it should not be a substitute for the bank's other credit requirements. This philosophy is evident in the use of 100 percent automobile finance programs. Less emphasis is placed upon equity and collateral and more upon the customer's character and ability to pay.

Conditions

Conditions concern any relevant outside influences that will affect the risk level on the loan. Outside influences include changes in the economy, social environment, government regulation, or the condition of the bank itself. Consider the following examples:

- ❏ You receive an application from an individual who works for a firm that has recently announced it is going to close its local plant and lay off all its employees.
- ❏ You receive an application from an individual who is an alien resident with a temporary visa.
- ❏ Your bank is experiencing severe earnings problems and is reducing the consumer credit staff.

- The latest economic forecast calls for rising interest rates, growing unemployment, and declining residential property values.
- Your bank recently became the target of a women's activist group, which is charging that the bank has discriminated against women in employment and in the granting of credit. You are currently considering an application from a member of the protest group.
- Several local industries are expecting to lay off portions of their work forces due to seasonal declines in sales. You are considering applications from a number of consumers who are employed by those firms.

In cases such as these, outside factors may have a pivotal effect on the ultimate credit decision. Often, only individual credit requests are affected; in other cases, the bank may alter its lending policy so that all customers are affected equally. In 1990, for example, many banks tightened their credit criteria in response to widespread regional recessions and rising consumer credit delinquency and loss ratios.

Changes in the external environment are often reflected in changes to the bank's lending policies. New government regulations become an immediate part of lending policy, while changes in the social environment tend to take much longer to be reflected in lending practices. Economic trends affect banks in widely different ways. Small banks are much more susceptible to economic problems in their primary market area than are larger banks, which operate in more diverse market areas. As a result, small banks may need to make more frequent changes in their lending policies in response to fluctuating local conditions. It is essential that each bank monitor the external environment so that it can effectively respond to changing conditions.

Evaluating Variable Rate Debt

Before 1980, the overwhelming majority of consumer loans had fixed rates. Since then, many banks have placed increased emphasis upon the development of variable rate portfolios. Variable rates help maintain the bank's interest margins by preserving the spread between the bank's cost of funds and the rate charge to loan customers. On the other hand, variable rates can have a negative impact on the credit risk of some accounts. For example, if changes in the rate are passed on in the form of changes in the consumer's monthly payment, a rise in the interest rate translates into higher monthly payments, quite possibly driving up the customer's monthly debt-to-income ratio from an acceptable level to a precarious one. Thus, in a rising interest rate environment, the customer may be squeezed without taking on any additional debt.

On the other hand, if rate increases are passed on in the form of extended payment schedules, the result could be negative amortization, a situation in which the minimum monthly payment is not sufficient to cover the interest due. The shortfall may be added to the consumer's balance to be paid later. If this were to continue for very long, the consumer could lose any equity position he may have had in the collateral securing the loan, thereby increasing the level of credit risk and damaging the bank's position.

Making a Judgmental Decision

In a judgmental system, the final credit decision rests upon an analysis of the individual applicant's strengths and weaknesses. Factors are weighed against each other to form an overall opinion and reach a final decision.

On most consumer loan requests, the primary emphasis is on the character and capacity of the applicant. Collateral will be factored in as a means to further strengthen the loan.

In a judgmental system, lenders also base the decision on their experience and their "feel" for the customer and the loan requested. The art of lending lies in being able to balance all the variables and, using experience as a guide, make the best possible credit decision.

The Credit-Scoring Approach

Credit-scoring systems are an attempt to quantify—that is, reduce to numbers—the pluses and minuses of the judgmental system. Variables are numerically weighted based on the bank's historical experience on consumer loans to predict the probability that the customer will repay the loan in a satisfactory manner. Credit-scoring systems approach lending as a science, using sophisticated mathematical analysis to help define the level of risk on a given application, rather than as an art.

Scoring systems are developed using the same logic as a judgmental system. The five Cs of credit are analyzed in an attempt to identify which combination of variables is most predictive of the level of credit risk. A typical score card usually has from 6 to 12 variables. Each variable has an assigned point value based upon the bank's previous experience with a large base of customers. Because of the unique characteristics of different types of loans, the bank may develop different score cards for direct loans, indirect loans, credit cards, and other major product lines. The development process results in a decision-making system similar to the one in exhibit 9.7.

The lender first tabulates the applicant's score for each personal characteristic. Assuming the applicant's total score exceeds a predetermined minimum requirement, the lender then proceeds to the next step, which is to obtain a credit bureau report or credit references. Elements on the credit report are scored and added to the total to arrive at a grand total. If the applicant does not achieve the minimum score requirement, the loan is usually rejected at this point, eliminating the need to spend time and money conducting a thorough credit investigation. If the customer meets the minimum scoring requirement, the lender may then proceed with other steps in the process, including verifying income and employment and calculating debt-to-income ratios.

The credit-scoring approach offers the following advantages:

❏ **Increased management control**   An effective credit-scoring system ensures consistent decision making. All loans that comply with the bank's loan policy and meet the scoring requirements will be made, while loans not meeting those requirements will be rejected. Furthermore, credit requirements can be raised or lowered simply by adjusting the minimum acceptable score.

❏ **Reduced loan processing costs**   Consideration of a loan can be terminated whenever the applicant fails to meet minimum requirements. It is possible to eliminate the need to obtain credit reports or conduct investigations on loans that are below cutoff scores. Further, automated credit-scoring systems can substantially reduce the time it takes to reach a credit decision and enable banks to centralize the decision-making process.

❏ **More legally defensible system**   Empirically derived, statistically sound credit-scoring systems are recognized by the Equal Credit Opportunity Act. They help lenders make more consistent decisions and control the variables used in arriving at a final decision.

Consequently, there is no opportunity to unfairly discriminate based upon a prohibited variable.

❏ **Easier training of new lenders** Banks with large lending staffs often find it a challenge to maintain a high level of lending skills. Credit scoring makes it far easier to train new lenders and get consistent decisions. Credit scoring shifts the role of the lender from one who evaluates the relative level of credit risk to one who markets and is responsible for structuring loans and selling other bank services.

❏ **Facilitates data gathering** Good system design allows the bank to constantly monitor the loan portfolio to ensure that the system is functioning properly. Management is better able to monitor trends in the ranges of credit risk for the entire portfolio or, if desired, the portfolio can be subdivided into smaller units, such as branch offices or product categories.

Credit scoring may not be for every bank. Many banks are simply too small to justify the expense of developing a system although in recent years vendors, such as Fair, Isaac and Company, Inc., have developed affordable personal computer based software programs that extend the benefits of scoring to a much larger number of banks. In many cases, banks are fully satisfied with their judgmental system and, as long as the results are in line with management's portfolio objectives, there is little need or motivation to change. Other banks, particularly large branch banking systems, have much to gain by using credit scoring. In fact, some banks have managed to automate the process to the point where it is possible for customers to sit down at a computer terminal, type in their applications, and have the system score the request and give a conditional approval on the spot. This use of credit scoring shows just how far the "lending is a science" philosophy has developed.

Credit Scoring with Judgmental Elements

Many banks that use credit-scoring systems also use judgmental variables to reach final decisions. For example, the bank may grant senior lenders the authority to make exceptions, allowing them to turn down loans which meet the score requirements or to approve loans below the minimum score. These exceptions are carefully documented, monitored, and controlled to preserve the integrity of the system.

EXHIBIT 9.7   Hypothetical Credit-Scoring System

Applicant Characteristics	Points
Home Phone	
Yes	36
No	0
Housing Status	
Own or buying	34
Rent	15
Other	5
Applicant Occupation	
Professional & official	27
Foreman & operative	26
Technical & managers	14
Clerical & sales	12
Service worker	5
Farm worker	3
Craftsman & nonfarm laborer	0
Proprietor	-3
Finance Company Reference	
Yes	-12
No	0
Applicant Age	
30 or less	6
30+ to 40	8
40+ to 50	11
Over 50	16
Time on Job	
Under 1 year	0
1 to 5 years	8
5+ to 10 years	12
Over 10 years	20
Total Score	_____
Credit References	
All references good (3 or more)	20
At least 2 good references & no negatives	15
No references	0
Some minor derogatory references	-5
Major derogatory information— judgments, repossessions, bankruptcy	-15
Credit Inquiries	
None	8
1 to 3 in last 6 months	2
More than 3	-5
Grand Total	_____

Another judgmental feature that is frequently used in addition to credit scoring is a debt-to-income formula. Thus, an applicant who meets the bank's score requirements, but does not pass the debt-to-income ratio policy may be declined.

In analyzing credit, it is important to know whether the applicant has any variable rate loans and, if so, how changes in the interest rate will affect the applicant's ability to repay debt. In response to this situation, many banks have changed their formulas for calculating capacity to allow for an increase in the level of monthly payments on variable rate loans. For example, if a customer had variable rate loan payments of $300, the bank may figure in an increase of 15 percent—$45—before calculating the debt-to-income ratio. This approach provides an extra measure of protection and caution in the decision-making process.

Declining a Loan

Not all loan applicants end up with an approved loan. The percentage of loan applications that are declined ranges widely from bank to bank and from product to product. On average, 20 to 50 percent of all loan applications are rejected. These decisions must be properly documented to ensure compliance with the provisions of the Fair Credit Reporting Act and the Equal Credit Opportunity Act.

The loan officer has two primary objectives in informing the customer of an adverse loan decision: maintaining the customer's goodwill and complying with all regulations regarding adverse action. One way of preserving goodwill is to offer financial counseling. When consumers are aware of the factors the lender considers in evaluating creditworthiness, they may be able to take positive steps to qualify for credit in the future. For example, many loans are rejected because a borrower is overextended on existing credit accounts and simply does not have the income to support additional debt. The lender may be able to suggest ways that the consumer can get his debts under control and reduce the level of monthly payments to an acceptable level.

Although many consumers know in advance that they may not qualify for a loan, this does not stop them from applying. What they may not know is how to correct the problem. This lack of knowledge gives the lending officer a chance to provide some valuable counseling and to send the consumer away with a positive impression of the bank.

The second objective, ensuring regulatory compliance, is an equally important consideration when dealing with rejected loan applications. Consumers must receive notice of an adverse action within 30 days from the time the application was made. These notices must be prepared in accordance with the Equal Credit Opportunity Act and accurately reflect the reasons for the adverse decision.

Summary

The credit evaluation and decision-making process requires that lenders evaluate the relative importance of many variables in order to arrive at a final decision that will best serve the needs of the customer and the bank. Credit analysis involves weighing trade-offs and balancing key decision variables to determine which are most important in any given situation.

Consumer loans are analyzed based on the five Cs of credit: character, capacity, capital, collateral, and conditions. Judgmental and credit-scoring systems are used to evaluate the information that was gathered on the application and verified by the credit investigation, thus enabling the lender to reach a final credit decision.

Credit analysis has become more complex in recent years. New products, higher average loan amounts, expanded use of revolving credit, and the introduction of variable rate loans have introduced new considerations into the decision-making process.

Review Questions

1. How does the law of probability enter into the consumer credit decision-making process?
2. What principle of human behavior helps the credit analyst in making assumptions about an applicant's future creditworthiness?
3. What elements of the applicant's "character" are judged during the credit evaluation process?
4. Name the five Cs of credit and give an example of what information the credit analyst examines regarding each.

5. Describe some of the differences in approach and operation between consumer and commercial lending.
6. What effect does the borrower's personal assets have on the evaluation of creditworthiness?
7. Name several assets that have value as backup capacity for a loan. Name several with little real value as backup capacity.
8. What benefits are offered by credit-scoring systems?

Optional Research

1. What is your bank's debt-to-income ratio (if it has one) for personal, unsecured loans? Make an appointment to ask your consumer credit manager if the ratio is standard for the bank's market area or whether it is on the liberal or conservative side. Finally, is it rigidly applied or relatively flexible, depending on other facts indicative of the applicant's capacity?
2. Does your bank use a credit-scoring or a judgmental approach to credit evaluation? Or are both used, each for different types of credit? If your bank uses a credit-scoring system, was it developed internally? If it uses a judgmental system, who has final authority for the decisions?

10 Credit Math, Loan Pricing, and Profitability

After reading this chapter, you will be able to

❑ list six types of rates frequently referred to by consumer lenders and explain how they differ

❑ describe the four major factors affecting consumer loan pricing

❑ describe the effect that changes in loan terms have on the profitability and other features of a consumer loan

❑ discuss the four cost categories for consumer loans and the trends for each group

❑ discuss the differences between variable and fixed-rate lending and describe how each type affects overall profitability

Credit Math

Managing a profitable consumer credit operation has become more challenging in recent years due to the deregulation of banking and intensified competition for consumer loans. Deregulation has led to greater uncertainties in the market, affecting the price and behavior pattern of deposits and the rates and manner of pricing loan products. To meet the challenge of these new uncertainties, consumer lenders have changed their traditional product lines and have become more astute managers of their operations.

Since rate books and computers have become available, computing the terms of a loan has been made much easier. Essentially, lenders need only understand how to use these resources in order to answer consumers' questions about the cost of borrowing money and the relative costs of one type of loan over another. Banks have expanded their use of computer technology to provide better service to customers and more support to the bank's selling effort, so lenders can quickly give consumers information regarding loan options. However, all lenders should understand the basic elements of credit math including the different types of rates quoted in the market and the relationship of the various elements that make up the terms of the loan.

Types of Rates

Six types of rates are frequently referred to by consumer lenders:

- ❏ simple interest rate
- ❏ annual percentage rate (APR)
- ❏ add-on rate
- ❏ discount rate
- ❏ fixed rate
- ❏ variable rate

The first four rates are methods of calculating the interest on a loan, while the last two describe the behavior of the loan rate (does it change or stay the same) during the term of the loan. First, we will discuss the methods of calculating interest, and save the discussion of fixed and variable rate loan features for later in this chapter.

Simple Interest

Simple interest is a method of computing and quoting interest rates based on applying an interest rate to the average daily loan balance outstanding during a specific period of time. The rate is generally expressed as an annual rate; however, it also may be shown as a daily periodic rate on open-end credit accounts. For example, if the simple interest rate is 12 percent, the daily periodic rate is .032876 percent—that is, the annual rate divided by 365 days. Some states stipulate using 360 days in this formula. The average daily balance is determined by adding the balance for each day in the billing cycle and then dividing by the number of days in the cycle. This number is multiplied by the number of days the loan was outstanding and then by the daily periodic rate to yield the interest for any given period. For example,

$ 1,294.89   average daily loan balance
<u>   29</u>   days
$37,551.81
<u>×   .032876</u>   (daily periodic rate)
      $12.35   interest

Annual Percentage Rate (APR)

The Truth in Lending Act requires that the APR be disclosed for all consumer loans. The APR is the finance charge on a loan expressed as an annualized percentage. The act details precise formulas that must be used to calculate the APR under a wide variety of loan terms. The annual percentage rate will be different from the simple interest rate on the loan if the loan includes certain fees that are considered by the Truth in Lending Act to be part of the finance charge. For example, if the bank charges points, loan fees, or similar charges, the simple interest rate on a loan might be 12 percent, but the APR could be 12.25 percent because the fees must be added to the interest charge before calculating the APR. The finance charge is equal to the interest **plus** any other charges deemed by the act to be part of the cost of credit.

Add-On Interest

Before the Truth in Lending Act was ratified, add-on interest was the most commonly used method of calculating and disclosing installment loan interest rates. Add-on interest is calculated by applying a rate to the original principal amount of the loan and multiplying it by the number of years in the loan period. For example, interest on a $2,000 loan at 10 percent add-on, for two years, would be calculated as follows:

$2,000   Principal
<u>×   .10</u>   Add-on rate
   $200   per year
<u>   2</u>   years
<u> $400</u>   Total interest

Principal $2000 + Interest $400 = Total of note $2,400

Add-on rates result in higher APRs than simple interest rate loans at the same absolute level because they disregard the fact that the principal will be reduced during the term of the loan as payments are made. The APR equivalents for selected add-on rates are shown in exhibit 10.1.

Add-on rates may not be quoted to consumers because they do not allow the consumer to make meaningful comparisons with other rates. However, banks sometimes calculate loan rates using add-on rates, which they must then quote as APRs, and in indirect lending programs such as bank retention or buy rates. Therefore, bankers who make these types of loans should fully understand how these rates work.

EXHIBIT 10.1   Comparison of Annual Percentage Rates and Add-On Rates

	Annual Percentage Rate				
Add-on rate	12 Mos.	24 Mos.	36 Mos.	60 Mos.	120 Mos.
6.00%	10.89%	11.12%	11.08%	10.84%	10.21%
9.00%	16.21%	16.42%	16.24%	15.71%	14.50%
12.00%	21.45%	21.57%	21.20%	20.31%	18.48%

Discount Rates

Discount rates, like add-on rates, were commonly used before the Truth in Lending Act. The terms of a loan using a discount rate is determined as follows:

$2,000	Amount of note
−200	Interest at 10% for 1 year
$1,800	Principal amount given to borrower

The use of discount rates for consumer loan disclosures is prohibited by the Truth in Lending Act on all loans it covers. As discount rates may still be used in commercial transactions, lenders should be aware these rates exist so that they may intelligently discuss them with consumers.

Calculation of Loan Terms

As noted earlier, lenders are rarely called upon to manually calculate the terms of a loan. Rate books, payment charts, and computer programs allow lenders to quickly and accurately determine all of the terms for a given loan.

Basically, you must understand four elements to calculate the interest charges and monthly payment on a loan:

- *principal*—the total amount of money that will be loaned to the borrower, including any fees or insurance premiums that are to be financed
- *rate*—the interest rate applicable to the loan requested
- *time*—the proposed term of the loan or time the money will be used
- *frequency*—the timing of loan payments, monthly, quarterly, etc.

The interest on the loan is calculated by multiplying

$$Principal \times Rate \times Time = Interest$$

For example, the calculation of interest on a 30-day single payment loan in the amount of $1,000 at a rate of 12 percent simple interest, would be as follows:

$$\$1,000 \times .12 = \$120 \times \frac{30}{360} = \$10 \text{ interest (based on 360-day factor)}$$

Thus, at the end of 30 days, the customer would pay back a total of $1,010. Some states require that a 365-day factor be used for such calculations. If 365 days is used, the interest will be lower—$9.86 in this sample.

Credit Insurance

Often, credit insurance protection is sold as part of a consumer loan. Lenders have offered different forms of credit insurance protection throughout much of the industry's history. Today, customers are typically able to buy the following types of credit protection:

- Credit life insurance
  Single—covers the primary borrower
  Joint—covers the primary borrower and spouse (other co-borrowers in some states)
- Credit accident and health/disability insurance
- Credit unemployment insurance

Generally speaking, credit life insurance will pay off the balance due on the loan if a covered borrower dies. This relieves the family and the estate of the financial burden. Credit accident and health, and credit unemployment insurance will make the monthly payments on the loan until the insured returns to gainful employment—subject to the provisions of the policy—thus relieving the family of this financial burden during periods of reduced income *and* preserving the customer's credit standing.

The chart below shows the various loan elements for a $4,500 loan for 36 months at a 15 percent rate.

Advance	Finance Charge	Total Note	Monthly Payment
$4500	$1115.64	$5615.64	$155.99

Insurance coverage increases the amount financed, since the lender loans the customer the amount of the insurance premium. This, in turn, increases the monthly payment, the finance charges, and the total amount of the loan. The overall effect is shown below.

Advance	Life Ins.	A&H Ins.	Fin. Chg.	Note	Mo. Pay
$4500	$90.66	$206.54	$1188.88	$5986.08	$166.28

Adding the insurance coverage to our sample $4,500 loan increases the finance charge by $73.24 (from $1,115.64 to $1,188.88), the note amount by $370.44 (from $5,615.64 to $5,986.08), and the monthly payment by $10.29 (from $155.99 to $166.28).

Selling insurance not only generates additional interest income, because the premiums are financed, it also increases noninterest income, since the bank usually receives a commission on any insurance sold.

EXHIBIT 10.2 **Effect of Loan Maturities on Monthly Payments**

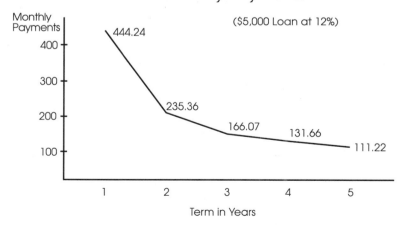

Loan Maturities

The term of the loan can have a significant impact on the monthly payment. Exhibit 10.2 shows the effect that increasing the term of the loan has on the monthly payment of a $5,000 loan at 12 percent APR. In this example, extending the loan from two to three years results in a reduction of $69.29 in the monthly payment. The importance of the monthly payment in selling consumer loans should not be underestimated. In fact, many consumers make their borrowing decision based more upon the affordability of the monthly payment than upon the interest rate on the loan. The size of the monthly payment is also an extremely important variable in evaluating credit risk and measuring the customer's ability to repay the loan. Thus, structuring the loan term and the monthly payment to fit the borrower's capacity are critical elements for both the lender and the customer.

Maturities on closed-end loans are generally set by the bank's policy based on the type of collateral securing the loan. Open-end accounts, on the other hand, generally have no set maturity. Instead, the bank establishes a monthly payment based on a specified percentage of the outstanding balance being repaid each month. Credit card programs may require the borrower to repay a minimum of 5 percent of the outstanding balance per month, while home equity lines may require a minimum payment of 2 percent or less of the outstanding balance per month. The actual percentages depend upon product design and bank policy. The lower the required minimum monthly payment percentage, the longer the anticipated payback maturity will be. It must be noted that if customers actively borrow against a credit line, the account balance must be paid off in full before the account can be closed.

Competitive pressures since the 1960s have led to a reduction in the minimum monthly payment requirements on open-end credit products of all types. This has enabled consumers to take on more debt for the same monthly payment, while increasing bank income by slowing the rate at which consumers reduce their outstanding balances.

Loan Pricing

Loan pricing is affected by four major factors

- ❏ the legal environment
- ❏ the competitive environment
- ❏ general economic conditions
- ❏ the bank's internal environment (costs, objectives, strategies, and financial condition)

Legal Environment

The legal environment has a significant impact on the prices that lenders can charge. State laws govern the rates and fees lenders can charge for consumer loans. Consequently, states exhibit considerable rate variation ranging from the extremely low rates allowed by the state of Arkansas (5 percent over the Federal Reserve discount rate) to the virtually uncapped rates allowed in Delaware. Broadly speaking, rate structures permitted by state laws have much to do with the kind of loan products offered by banks, the availability of credit, and the level of credit risk that banks are willing to accept. Banks will offer only those loan products on which they can earn a fair return on their investment. If profit margins are squeezed because of high deposit costs, for example, and the bank is unable to preserve its profit margin, it will typically limit the extension of credit to its best and most creditworthy customers.

Federal law currently does not restrict the rates charged on consumer credit. However, the federal government periodically threatens to impose a national maximum rate on selected consumer credit products. Credit card programs have come under attack in the past, particularly when the spread between the rate charged on fixed-rate credit card programs and the rates for variable rate money market instruments widens. Credit card lenders particularly have been subjected to criticism due to what observers believe to be unfairly high rates. Critics argue that credit card rates should be brought down when prevailing market rates decline. Those arguments overlook three significant problems:

- ■ Most credit card plans used fixed-rate pricing, which produces larger net interest margins when deposit rates decline, but are also subject to narrowing margins when rates rise. Margins did narrow in the early 1980s, when many credit card plans lost money.

- Rate adjustments on fixed-rate, open-end products, while possible in most states, are difficult to change and may only be extended to an account if the consumer accepts the change in terms.

- The same soft economic conditions that lead to low rates often are accompanied by higher delinquencies and loan losses.

One possible solution to high credit card rates is to place credit card plans on a variable rate pricing basis. Such plans have become increasingly available and it is likely that competitive pressures may result in making them more common in the future.

Competitive Environment

Competition for consumer credit has increased in recent years as new participants have entered the market and as banks have expanded their lending operations beyond their traditional target market areas. Lenders must closely monitor their competitors' rates to stay in a position to attract the level of business desired.

Closed-end credit pricing typically changes more frequently than open-end rates and, therefore, requires closer monitoring. Information about competitors' rates and products is easily obtained by following media advertisements. Ads not only give information about the competition's prices, they also give a clear indication of the kinds of loan products the competition is trying to sell. Competitor information can also be obtained simply by "shopping" the competition. A designated shopper may call competitors and request information about their loans and loan pricing. This allows the bank to assess not only the rates offered by the competition, but also the quality of their service and sales efforts.

Another approach to evaluating the competition's products and prices is to question dealer personnel. Keep in mind, though, that dealers are quick to let the bank know when competitors reduce rates but are unlikely to let them know about rate increases.

It is impossible to continually monitor all competitors. Smart bankers focus on competitors that are the price leaders by virtue of their share of the market or their aggressiveness in marketing products. Major banks, finance companies, and thrifts are the usual targets of monitoring efforts.

Economic Environment

General economic conditions also have a bearing on pricing decisions. Deposit market rates, the level of demand for credit, and overall economic conditions in the bank's market areas are all reflected in the bank's pricing of its consumer loan products. Fluctuations in deposit market rates are reflected quickly in the bank's cost of funds. Thus, as the cost of deposits and other bank liabilities rise and fall, they have immediate implications for the cost of consumer credit. Rising market rates mean that the costs of funding the loan portfolio go up. The bank may react by raising rates (this occurs automatically with variable rate loans) or it may elect to hold rates at the current level. Raising rates on new loans helps preserve profit margins; holding rates at the current level narrows short-term profit margins, but may result in a higher market share if competitors raise their rates. Declines in market rates generally result in price reductions, which tend to stimulate demand for consumer credit and increase the level of activity in credit markets.

The relative level of demand for consumer credit influences pricing decisions. Several indexes are monitored to assess the level of demand. Measures of retail sales, consumer buying intentions, consumer confidence, and direct measures of lending activity itself indicate the relative strength of demand. All things being equal, loan prices tend to rise or hold firm when demand is strong; they decline when demand softens. Economic conditions in the bank's market area also influence loan pricing to some extent. Weak economic conditions, evidenced by high unemployment and low retail sales, may result in some rate reductions as a response to low demand.

Bank's Internal Environment

The bank's internal environment, including its costs, objectives, and strategies, has an impact on its loan pricing patterns. Since objectives and strategies are generally set at the product line level, pricing tends to vary from product to product. If the bank has set aggressive growth plans for a product, it will tend to price at the low end of the available rate range. If growth goals are modest, and if other goals are more important for a given product line—increased profitability, for example—rates will be set more toward the middle to upper end of the competitive price range.

Each bank's financial condition has some impact on its loan pricing. In an increasingly competitive, deregulated environment, financial institutions that can deliver loan products at the lowest cost have a significant advantage over competitors. This is not to say that loan rates can be set simply by looking at the bank's cost structure and adding the desired profit margin. Rather, the lowest cost providers will be better able to price their loan products at the lower end of the prevailing rate scale and still achieve desired profit margins.

Pricing Patterns

Loan pricing is no longer regarded as simply an issue of rates. All of the following are elements of contemporary loan pricing decisions:

- annual percentage rate
- monthly payment
- credit insurance charges
- fee structure—fees such as late charges, overlimit fees, returned check charges, application fees, annual account fees, and credit report fees

Each of these elements represents an opportunity for the bank to increase its income and provides a basis for competing in the marketplace.

Although pricing of loan products varies significantly from market to market, some practices are common. For example, many lenders vary loan rates based upon the type of loan and the collateral securing the loan. Exhibit 10.3 reflects the relative level of risk associated with various types of collateral. Rates may also vary for given products based on the term of the loan, the customer's credit strength, and the size of the loan.

EXHIBIT 10.3   Sample Pricing Schedules

Variations based on loan term

New automobile loans	36 months	10.00%
	48 months	10.25%
	60 months	10.50%

Variations based on size of loan

New boat loans	$5,000-$24,999	12.00%
	$25,000 and up	11.50%
Unsecured loans	Up to $3,499	18.00%
	$3,500 and up	16.00%

Variations based on level of credit risk

Credit score	180-200 points	11.50%
	201-225 points	11.25%
	226-250 points	11.00%

These examples illustrate the concepts that

- risk increases as the term of the loan increases, therefore justifying a higher rate
- larger loans offer some efficiencies that could be reflected in lower rates
- good customers—those representing less credit risk—could be rewarded with lower rates

Loan Cost Factors

Consumer credit managers must have a sound understanding of the cost factors affecting their portfolio and the behavior pattern of these costs. Much effort has gone into developing more reliable accounting and control systems designed to identify and properly allocate costs to different areas of the bank. In addition to the bank's own systems, the Federal Reserve has developed a cost analysis for key banking products. This tool can be made a part of the bank's system to help identify cost trends and patterns and to facilitate making policy decisions regarding loan pricing.

Federal Reserve Functional Cost Analysis

The Federal Reserve publishes an annual functional cost analysis for most bank products. It identifies four primary cost categories for consumer loans

- acquisition costs (cost to make a loan)
- maintenance and liquidation costs (cost to collect a payment)
- loan loss rate (three-year average)
- cost of funds

Acquisition costs include all expenses that are incurred in generating loan applications, processing them through to the final decision, and either documenting the approved loans or processing adverse action documentation. These expenses include

- advertising and sales promotion expenses
- personnel costs for handling loan applications at all stages of the lending process
- related legal expenses

- credit-scoring program expenses
- miscellaneous supply costs
- communications costs

#3   Acquisition costs have risen steadily over time. Banks have responded to this trend by placing greater emphasis on improving operating efficiency and on directing loan business to more cost-efficient products (such as open-end loans) that eliminate the need to go through the full application and documentation process each time the consumer needs to borrow. Operational efficiencies have also been achieved by automating portions of the lending process and developing larger loans. Automated application tracking systems, credit scoring, and automated document preparation are examples of practices that help control costs and also improve performance.

#3   *Maintenance* and *liquidation costs* include expenses related to servicing loan accounts once the loan has been made:

- coupon books and billing statements
- processing payments through the bank's accounting system
- servicing, collecting, and recovering loans

A major portion is personnel expenses, computer hardware and software expenses, and related communication costs, including maintaining the database and preparing reports.

When banks began using automation, they first targeted reducing maintenance and liquidation costs. Banks have now extended their efforts from the accounting department to areas such as the central file department, customer service, and, finally, to the collection and recovery departments. Still, this cost category has experienced a gradually rising cost pattern.

#3   The *loan loss rate* represents the bank's loss experience on its consumer credit products over time. Loans that are charged to loss represent an expense because they are assets that will not be recovered by the bank. This factor varies widely from bank to bank, but it usually follows a fairly consistent pattern and range within a given bank. Loan losses tend to fluctuate with general economic conditions, the extent of risk taken by the bank, and

#3   the mix of consumer loans in the overall portfolio.

The final factor—the cost of funds—is the most important of all of the cost elements. This factor represents the price that the bank must pay for the money it loans to consumers. Banks have little money (capital) of their own to lend. They must attract deposits and borrow money to generate the funds needed for their lending activities. Increased competition in the financial services industry has had a significant impact on the cost of funds. Sources can command widely varying rates for funds based on availability and demand for those funds. These unpredictable fluctuations can result in loans becoming unprofitable or their profit margins being eroded. Consumer credit managers do not have control over the cost of funds whereas they do have some control over other expenses.

The cost of funds fluctuates over time, which affects not only loan pricing, but also the bank's product strategy, credit policies, and, in some cases, growth objectives. Because cost of funds is the largest single item of expense on most loans, it is essential that the bank plan for fluctuations in this category.

The trends and behavior patterns in recent years of average acquisition costs, maintenance and liquidation expenses, loan loss rates, and cost of funds for banks with over $200 million in deposits, is shown in exhibit 10.4.

EXHIBIT 10.4   Functional Cost Analysis Trends

	Banks over $200m in deposits			
Cost Factor	1976	1981	1985	1990
Cost to make a loan	$56.72	$97.54	$85.67	$160.60
Cost to collect payment	$ 3.17	$ 5.17	$ 5.67	$5.50
Loan loss rate	.55%	.65%	.30%	.46%
Cost of funds	4.60%	9.13%	7.42%	6.92%

Source: Federal Reserve: Functional Cost and Profit Analysis 1991 National Average Report—Commercial Banks

Average vs. Marginal Cost Analysis

From an economics perspective, there are two primary methods of analyzing loan costs—either on an average or marginal basis. The average cost approach breaks down the consumer credit department's total expenses based on the number of accounts in the loan portfolio. In many cases, a bank can reduce its average costs simply by putting more accounts on the books. This is particularly true if the bank does not incur a significant amount of fixed costs as it adds to its account base, but rather incurs only variable costs associated with making the additional loan. However, if the bank must add to its staff, buy office equipment, and incur other fixed costs to handle additional volume, this may increase the average cost.

The variable costs associated with each additional loan are also known as marginal costs. Economic theory states that the loan should be made as long as the income from the loan exceeds the marginal cost of making and servicing the loan. Thus, if it will cost $100 to make the next loan, the loan should be made if it will produce at least $101 in interest income. While the theory seems relatively simple in concept, it is far more difficult to implement. However, the concept does point out a weakness in making pricing and policy decisions solely on the basis of average cost numbers, or on the more widely used basis of pricing to meet competition.

Loan Profitability

Banks are intended to be profit-making institutions—to generate an acceptable level of profit for their shareholders. In recent years, banks have become more skilled at evaluating profitability, not only of their entire portfolio, but also of individual products and accounts. Let's consider profitability at the individual account level first and then examine how income is recognized and how loan yields are calculated.

The examples in exhibits 10.5 and 10.6 are based on the Federal Reserve's Functional Cost Analysis, and modified to reflect the true loss rates and cost of funds.

Using data from the functional cost analysis, the profitability of individual accounts can be evaluated and applied to establishing reasonable loan pricing and policies. Exhibit 10.5 shows the effect that the term of the loan has on loan profitability. Notice that the net income changes significantly as a result of the change in term. Although the acquisition costs do not change as the term of the loan increases, the maintenance costs do increase because more payments must be processed. The cost of funds also increases because the loan is outstanding for a longer period of time. The loan loss rate is based upon the size and type of loan, so it does not change in this case. Clearly, it is advantageous from a profitability standpoint to extend the term of this loan.

EXHIBIT 10.5 Profitability Analysis—Term Change

Cost Category	$3,000 Loan—18% APR	
	12-month loan	36-month loan
Cost to make a loan	$160.60	$160.60
Cost to collect payments	66.00	198.00
Cost of funds	115.52	347.71
Loan loss rate (three-year average)	7.68	23.11
Total costs	$349.80	$729.42
Finance charge	300.48	904.46
Net income	($49.32)	$175.04
Monthly payment	$275.04	$103.59

Increasing the rate on a loan also has a significant positive effect (see exhibit 10.6). For example, a 150 basis point increase in the rate (from 11.5 percent to 13 percent) results in an increase in income of $340.04 over the term of the loan. This example is designed simply to illustrate the impact of a rate increase on profitability of an individual loan, and not to speculate on the impact the rate increase would have on overall marketing efforts.

EXHIBIT 10.6   Profitability Analysis—Rate Change

	$10,000 loan—48 months	
Cost Category	11.50% APR	13% APR
Cost to make a loan	$160.60	$160.60
Cost to collect payments	264.00	264.00
Cost of funds	1518.02	1531.56
Loan loss rate (three-year average)	100.91	101.81
Total costs	$2043.53	$2057.97
Finance charge	2522.72	2877.20
Net Income	$479.19	$819.23
Monthly payment	$260.89	$268.27

The functional cost analysis can also help determine minimum loan rates and terms for the bank to break even on a loan assuming a specified cost of funds (see exhibit 10.7). If, for example, the cost of funds is 6.92 percent, then to break even on an 11 percent four-year loan, the bank needs to lend no less than $4,739. This is a handy tool for setting the bank's overall policy regarding minimum loan size, pricing, and term combinations.

Income from individual accounts may also be analyzed by running a loan amortization schedule like the one shown in exhibit 10.8. The amortization schedule shows the distribution of the payment between interest and principal, and the remaining balance on the loan. The actual loan amortization depends on the method used to compute interest on the loan. Three primary methods are used to recognize interest earned on consumer loans

- simple interest
- actuarial interest
- rule of 78s

EXHIBIT 10.7   Break-Even Loan Size

Based on a 6.92% Cost of Funds

Maturity in Years	7.50%	9.00%	11.00%	12.75%	14.50%	16.25%	18.00%
			Annual Percentage Rates (Monthly Payments Presumed)				
1	******	24,077	11,016	7,456	5,629	4,516	3,768
2	******	15,007	7,026	4,778	3,611	2,896	2,414
3	******	11,597	5,542	3,784	2,863	2,296	1,912
4	43,330	9,721	4,739	3,243	2,456	1,969	1,639
5	33,695	8,493	4,201	2,891	2,191	1,757	1,461
6	27,497	7,607	3,819	2,637	2,001	1,604	1,331
7	23,198	6,928	3,525	2,441	1,855	1,487	1,236
8	20,050	6,384	3,288	2,284	1,737	1,394	1,158
9	17,651	5,935	3,092	2,154	1,640	1,316	1,094
10	15,766	5,557	2,926	2,044	1,558	1,251	1,040

Simple interest calculations are used on all open-end credit accounts, all variable rate loans, and many closed-end loans. A simple interest loan is calculated based upon when payments are actually received. For example, if an account has a balance of $10,000 at a rate of 13 percent and payments were received on different dates of the month, the amount of interest would vary. Sample figures are shown in exhibit 10.9.

Thus, on a simple interest loan, the customer can reduce the actual interest costs by paying before the scheduled due date, but the bank will realize higher interest income on late payments. The customer may also reduce interest costs on a simple interest loan by paying more than the minimum monthly payment since this will result in a greater reduction in the unpaid balance.

Actuarial and rule of 78s interest methods work differently. These approaches, used only on closed-end loans and in states that permit their use, assume that a payment has been made every 30 days, whether it has been or not. Further, when computing interest due, they do not take into account any excess amount paid on the account by the borrower.

For example, if a customer has a 36-month loan, and wants to pay the loan off at the end of 12 months, they would receive a refund of 45.05 percent of the original interest precomputed for the loan. Thus, on a $3,000 loan at 18 percent, with a total of $904.20 in finance charges, the bank would earn

EXHIBIT 10.8   Partial Loan Amortization Schedule (60 Month Loan)

$10,500 loan—7.00% APR
Monthly Payments $207.92

Payment Number	Payment on Interest	Principal	Balance of Loan
1	61.25	146.67	10,353.33
2	60.39	147.53	10,205.80
3	59.53	148.39	10,057.41
4	58.67	149.25	9,908.16
5	57.80	150.12	9,758.04
6	56.92	151.00	9,607.04
7	56.04	151.88	9,455.16
8	55.16	152.76	9,302.40
9	54.26	153.66	9,148.74
10	53.37	154.55	8,994.19
11	52.47	155.45	8,838.74
12	51.56	156.36	8,682.38
13	50.65	157.27	8,525.11
14	49.73	158.19	8,366.92
15	48.81	159.11	8,207.81
16	47.88	160.04	8,047.77
17	46.95	160.97	7,886.80
18	46.01	161.91	7,724.89
19	56.06	162.86	7,562.03
20	44.11	163.81	7,398.22
21	43.16	164.76	7,233.46
22	42.20	165.72	7,067.74
23	41.23	166.69	6,901.05
24	40.26	167.66	6,733.39
25	39.28	168.64	6,564.75
26	38.29	169.63	6,395.12
27	37.30	170.62	6,224.50
28	36.31	171.61	6,052.89
29	35.31	172.61	5,880.28
30	34.30	173.62	5,706.66
31	33.29	174.63	5,532.03
32	32.27	175.65	5,356.38
33	31.25	176.67	5,179.71
34	30.21	177.71	5,002.00
35	29.18	178.74	4,823.26
36	28.14	179.78	4,643.48

$496.86, and the customer would receive a credit for unearned income in the amount of $407.34. The customer receives no benefit from paying early or for paying more than the minimum monthly payment on these loans. If, on the other hand, a customer made all 36 payments on time each month, he would pay exactly the same amount of interest, regardless of whether

EXHIBIT 10.9 Interest Accrual on Simple Interest Loans

$10,000 balance—13% APR

Date payment received	Number of days balance open	Interest
5 days before due date	25	$89.00
On due date	30	$106.80
5 days after due date	35	$124.60

EXHIBIT 10.10 Product Line Profitability Structures

	Bank Card	Auto Loan	Second Mortgage
Portfolio yield	17.00%	12.50%	13.00%
Cost of funds	−7.50	−7.50	−7.50
Net yield	9.50	5.00	5.50
Other income	+4.00	+.25	+.25
Operating expenses	−5.00	−3.00	−2.00
Loan losses	−3.00	− .50	− .15
Net pretax yield	5.50%	1.75%	3.60%

they had a simple interest or rule of 78s loan.

The refund methods under the rule of 78s and actuarial approaches have been widely criticized by consumers and consumer advocates for many years. Most states prohibit both approaches, and many lenders have voluntarily switched to the simple interest method to avoid customer relations problems and to receive interest on delinquent amounts.

Product Line Profitability

Each consumer credit product has unique profitability characteristics. These characteristics reflect varying levels of risk, differing cost structures, and variations in the interest rates. It is possible and desirable to construct a profitability analysis for consumer credit products, as in exhibit 10.10. Credit cards have high gross yields and many fee income sources to offset high operating costs and loan loss expenses. Auto loans have much lower yields, but also may offer lower operating expenses and loan losses. Second mortgage loans offer even lower operating expenses and losses to go with a yield that is often higher than that for auto loans.

Indirect loans present some unique profitability considerations because the bank generally must pay a dealer a percentage of the finance charge. In addition to serving as a financial incentive, it also compensates the dealer for handling the application and loan closing. Two examples of dealer earnings on typical retail contracts follow.

Example 1

Amount financed	$15,079.90	Term 36 months
Bank buy rate	10.00%	
Customer rate	16.00%	
Total finance charge	$4,005.86	
Bank interest retention	$2,437.34	
Dealer reserve	$1,568.52	

Example 2

Amount financed	$8,873.07	Term 48 months
Bank buy rate	9.50%	
Customer rate	12.50%	
Total finance charge	$2,447.73	
Bank interest retention	$1,827.09	
Dealer reserve	$ 620.64	

The dealer can also increase the income on a retail transaction by selling credit life, accident and health insurance, and warranty policies. Referring to example 2, if the dealer sold all of these policies, the income would increase as follows:

Source	Premium	Dealer Income	
Life Insurance	$255.41	$85.14	33% commission
A & H Insurance	$651.07	$217.02	33% commission
Warranty Policy	$885.00	$435.00	Excess over $450 cost to dealer

Total Fee Income	=	$737.16
+ Dealer Reserve	=	620.64
Total Dealer Income	=	$1357.80

Fixed Rate vs. Variable Rate Lending

Until 1981, virtually all consumer loans were made on a fixed-rate basis. This was possible because the cost of funds did not fluctuate rapidly in the highly regulated deposit rate structures. However, with deposit deregulation, lenders were forced to balance the pricing patterns of their loans with the more volatile rate patterns of the newly deregulated deposits.

Asset and liability management became even more important than it had previously been. In response, banks established asset-liability committees to manage the risk which develops when deposits and loans reprice at different times. The clearest example of this risk is what happened to the savings and loan (S&L) industry in the 1980s. S&Ls had large portfolios of fixed-rate, long-term, mortgage loans, but they were faced with funding those portfolios with shorter term and more volatile deposits. The dilemma is shown in exhibit 10.11. As deposit rates rose, the S&Ls were unable to raise their loan rates. This squeezed their net interest margins and in extreme cases resulted in heavy losses. This was not the only problem that

EXHIBIT 10.11   **Fixed-Rate Loan Portfolio—**
                 Yield Characteristics

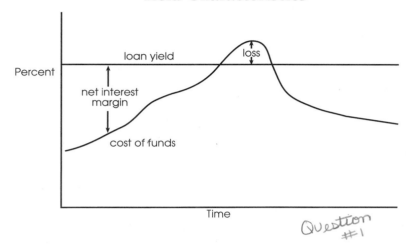

Question #1

EXHIBIT 10.12   **Variable Rate Loan Portfolio—**
                 Yield Characteristics

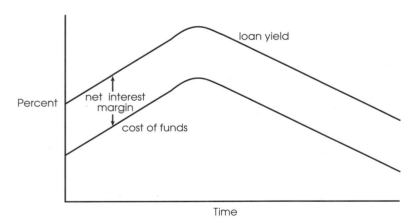

produced the S&L crisis, but it was a major contributor.

Fixed-rate loan portfolios clearly expose lenders to a high level of interest rate risk. In response, most financial institutions added variable rate loans to their consumer credit portfolios during the 1980s. They are now a permanent part of consumer credit pricing. Variable rate loans allow the lender to pass on to customers changes in the cost of funds. Variable rate portfolios have a behavior pattern similar to that shown in exhibit 10.12. The variable rate feature minimizes the interest rate risk, though it may increase credit and collateral risk.

With fixed-rate loans, the interest rate does not change during the entire term of the loan. The use of a fixed interest rate on a closed-end loan means that the customer will have the same monthly payment as long as the account is repaid in a satisfactory manner. Minor adjustments may be required in the final monthly payment to reflect early or late payments received on simple interest loans. If the customer makes payments after scheduled due dates, he or she may end up paying more in finance charges. On open-end credit accounts, a fixed-rate means that the creditor cannot change the rate without the customer agreeing to accept the new rate. Consumers in most states may avoid rate increases on fixed rate, open-end accounts simply by not using the account after receiving notification of a rate change.

The interest rate charged on variable rate loans is tied to a preselected index rate, such as the prime rate or the 90-day Treasury bill rate. As the index changes, either up or down, so does the rate on variable loans. Increases may be passed on to the consumer in the form of higher monthly payments or they may result in an increase in the number of payments required to pay off the loan. Decreases may result in lower monthly payments, fewer monthly payments, or a smaller final payment.

Most consumer credit portfolios contain a blend of fixed and variable rate loans. Fixed rates tend to be concentrated in high gross yield products, such as credit card and check overdraft programs, and in traditional markets such as automobile loans. Variable rates are increasingly used on open-end credit accounts, boat loans, and second mortgage loans. These blended portfolios appear to offer a sound middle ground in the effort to optimize profits.

Variable Rate Program Structure

Many considerations go into establishing a variable rate loan program. These include

- selecting an index rate
- determining pricing policy and strategy
- determining frequency of pricing changes
- rate floors and caps
- evaluating the effect on credit and collateral risk

Many banks have elected to use the prime rate or a U.S. Treasury bill rate as their index. An external index—one that is not controlled by the bank—is easier to defend against criticism than an internal index—one that is controlled by the bank. Many state laws stipulate that the bank must use an external index. Ideally, the index selected should follow the behavior pattern of the bank's cost of funds. However, since customers need to accept and understand the index, a readily available and understandable index should be chosen.

One strategy for marketing variable rate closed-end loans is to offer them side-by-side with fixed rates, with the variable rate loan priced somewhat below that of the comparable fixed-rate loan. This gives the customer an incentive to take the variable rate, with its lower monthly payment, rather than choosing the fixed-rate loan. The gap between the fixed and variable rate tends to grow as rates rise and narrow as rates fall.

Many variable rate loan programs call for monthly changes in the rate, although some banks have used less frequent adjustment periods in an attempt to position their product differently in the market. Less frequent adjustments can help bank yields when rates are declining, but hurt them when rates are rising.

Banks use rate floors and ceilings in an effort to balance interest rate risk considerations with credit and collateral considerations. For example, a *rate cap* protects the consumer from higher monthly payments or negative amortization, while slightly limiting the bank's ability to pass on the total interest rate risk to the consumer. *Rate floors*, on the other hand, protect the bank's yield during periods of falling prices and help to preserve a targeted gross yield objective.

Summary

The profitability of consumer loans is affected by the bank's pricing policies and practices and the cost structure of its operation. Consumer credit costs fall into four categories—acquisition expenses, maintenance and liquidation costs, loan losses, and the cost of funds. The cost of funds is the largest single expense and is also the one that consumer credit managers have the least control over.

Loan pricing is affected by regulation, competition, general economic conditions, and the bank's objectives, strategies, and financial condition. While price has a bearing on the bank's loan volume, it is also a feature that can be matched or beaten by competitors in a very short time. Thus, it is difficult to achieve a pricing advantage for very long.

Individual account profitability is affected by the method used to rebate interest or recognize income on the loan, the term of the loan, its rate, whether or not other services, such as credit insurance, are included, and any fees that may be charged on the loan. Lenders should be aware of how each of these factors affect profitability, and they should understand the basics of calculating loan terms.

Review Questions

Final Exam Question

1. What are the differences between fixed and variable rate loans? What implications do these differences have for overall profitability? — *Pages 209-210*
2. Why is the annual percentage rate sometimes different from the interest rate on a loan? *Page 191*
3. List the four cost categories on consumer loans. What is the trend of costs in each category? *Pages 200-202*

4. Why is the amount of the monthly payment on a consumer loan such an important factor when structuring a loan? How can a loan be adjusted to lower the payment without lowering the principal or rate? — Page 195

5. When pricing the bank's loans, how might one gather information about rates offered by competitors? Page 197

6. What factors must be taken into consideration when setting the price for consumer loans? Which single factor is the most important? Why? Page 196

7. Why did consumer variable rate lending come into being? What particular profitability problem does it address? Pages 208-209

Optional Research

1. What does your bank currently charge for its consumer loans? How does this compare with its major competitors?

2. How are loan rates set in your bank? By whom? How do they determine what to charge?

11 Selling and Loan Structuring

After reading this chapter you will be able to

❑ list the four stages of the sales cycle and give examples of how each stage affects the consumer lending process

❑ discuss the implications that credit insurance programs have on the consumer credit sales effort

❑ list the objectives for emphasizing loan structuring and cross-selling by lending personnel

❑ define loan structuring and give examples of how this approach can be used to sell the best loan for the customer and the bank

❑ identify the loan structuring options that are available to lenders based on the type of product—direct, indirect, open-end—or method of application

The Sales and Service Culture

Selling bank products and services has become significantly more important as the financial services industry has been deregulated. In the past, competitive advantage was based primarily upon the convenience and number of branch locations, small differences in pricing, and the quality of service. Hence the emphasis was on building branches, price competition, and developing close relationships with consumers. These are still important aspects of competition, but with deregulation came the opportunity for innovative product development, greater pricing flexibility, and the need for more focused and creative promotional programs. Today, as a result of this new environment, traditional order-taking practices have given way to the development of the bank sales and service culture.

Before beginning, let's distinguish between the terms order-taking, selling, and cross-selling. Order-taking is a passive process in which employees give the consumer the product requested. There is usually little if any intentional attempt to inform consumers of alternatives or sell any other bank services which may meet their needs. For example, a consumer may request a $5,000 home improvement loan to put new windows and doors on her home. The order-taker would simply process this request and make a decision without regard for any other circumstances.

Selling, on the other hand, is an active approach in which employees attempt to determine the consumer's needs and then use that knowledge to offer a particular bank product or products that will meet those needs. Selling by bankers often involves financial counseling. It always involves an interest in and sensitivity to the real needs of the client. Thus, selling becomes a way of offering better customer service.

A selling approach within the consumer lending function will result in higher loan volumes, greater profitability for the bank, better loan quality, and more satisfied and loyal customers. In our example, the sales-oriented employee would consider the consumer's overall debt structure and financial position, and structure a loan proposal that would best meet the customer's needs. The lender may identify from the application that the customer has children who will begin college in a couple of years and that the family will need the flexibility of borrowing to pay college expenses. Instead of filling the customer's order for a $5,000 loan, the employee may recommend a $25,000 home equity line of credit that would not only better serve the immediate need, but also provide a sound way of preparing to meet future needs.

Question #1

Cross-selling is a form of selling in which a banker suggests related products and services that might be of interest to a customer. Cross-selling opportunities are especially abundant during the lending process. With a complete loan application, the banker has access to a wealth of information that can help assess the customer's needs for other products and services. The sales effort may lead to the recommendation of a better checking account product, an investment program, or a regular savings program to meet unexpected or planned future expenses. Effective cross-selling results in expanded account relationships with customers, enhanced customer loyalty and retention, and higher bank profits. Studies have consistently found that the more products a consumer has with the bank, the more likely they are to remain with that bank. One bank found that they retained only 20 percent of the customers with one service, but 70 percent of those with five services.

The successful financial institution in the 90s is likely to be one that can develop a sales and service culture truly focused on meeting consumers' needs and delivering quality services through qualified employees.

Establishing a Sales Culture

To be effective, a sales-oriented philosophy must be woven into the fabric of an organization. It must be constantly developed, nurtured, and renewed to maintain the best possible performance.

Developing a sales culture requires hiring the people with the right skills: for example, people who

- communicate well and easily
- are self-motivated
- enjoy the challenge of selling
- enjoy working with people
- view selling as a way of sharing needed information about worthwhile products and services

While most bank services are sold via a "soft sell" or consultative approach, some people are simply not suited to the sales role and may not necessarily want to develop the skills required. Placing people in sales positions who are energized and excited by this type of work is far more likely to be successful in building a sales culture.

❑ **Developing and maintaining selling skills**   People with basic skills and interests in sales must continuously practice and develop selling skills. The ability to identify needs, handle objections, and close a sale must be sharpened by continuous training and practice.

❑ **Motivating people to sell**   Sales-oriented businesses constantly seek to motivate their people to sell. This may be done via monetary rewards tied directly to sales goals and by a wide variety of nonmonetary incentives such as recognition awards, sales rallies, and other ego-enhancing techniques.

As financial institutions have sought to emphasize the importance of sales, many have offered monetary rewards. These incentives are tied to specific products to stimulate sales, such as paying cash awards for each new home equity loan or annuity product sold. The key to success is ensuring that these programs truly focus on meeting the consumer's needs and not simply pushing products to meet the bank's needs.

❏ **Supporting the sales force** The sales and service culture must extend to every department in the bank. The operations departments, support staffs, and technical support areas all must be focused on the consumer and on delivering good customer service. Contrary to popular belief, good customer service is not simply a matter of common sense. Comprehensive training programs, and the support of top management focusing on a sales and service culture, are increasingly important in banking.

Selling Skills

Effective selling requires the following skills

❏   establishing rapport with the customer
❏   recognizing customer needs
❏   understanding the products' features and benefits
❏   handling and overcoming objections
❏   closing the sale

Direct personal selling situations for credit products usually begin with a specific request from the borrower, for example: "I want a loan to purchase a new car." Often the request is stated as follows: "What is your rate on a car loan?" Many enthusiastic, but poorly trained lenders, might immediately respond —"Our new car rate is 10 percent!"—only to be treated to a "Thank you and goodbye." In fact, the lender's response was dead wrong—in most cases. In fact, the lender has a range of loan programs available to meet the customer's need, but determining the "best loan for the customer and the bank" is going to require more information.

Before the employee offers a direct, potentially too simple response to a loan request and plunges into completing an application form, he or she should put the customer at ease, build rapport, and gather additional information essential to respond more accurately and completely.

Identifying customer needs sounds easy, but it can actually be quite challenging. The basic need—the need for funds—is obvious, but other needs are less obvious and must be determined by talking with the borrower. Alternatively, needs can be assumed based on the data submitted on the loan application. For example, if the customer faces a series of borrowing needs in the near future, such as making major home improvements, the lender may satisfy the customer's immediate need with a closed-end loan. However, a better answer might be a line of credit that covers both the immediate and long-term needs.

A much different example of a hidden customer need is ego gratification. A basic VISA or MasterCard may satisfy the need for a convenient transaction device, but a gold MasterCard or a premier VISA may satisfy the higher priority need for ego enhancement demanded by some customers. Identifying these intangible needs helps to "sell the sizzle, not the steak," and to make the most of each selling opportunity.

Effective selling also involves matching the customer's needs with the product that best meets those needs. To do this, the salesperson must be very familiar with both the bank's and competitor's products. This is not to say that the salesperson must have an exhaustive knowledge of all aspects of every product. That is virtually impossible in today's rapidly changing banking environment. Rather, the salesperson should have a basic understanding of the key features of each product and know to whom to refer the customer for more detailed information.

Another essential skill is the ability to handle and overcome customer objections—often the difference between making or losing a sale. An objection raised by a customer can be viewed positively, in that it helps the salesperson identify the needs that seem most important to the customer. In response to an objection, the salesperson should empathize with the customer, clarify any misunderstanding, and offer a solution to the objection. Typical objections to consumer loans and some possible responses are presented below.

 Question #7

Objection: Your rate is too high.
Response: Mr. Jones, I agree that the rate is an important consideration when obtaining a loan. That is why we offer a wide range of loan products with different loan rates. You may qualify for one of our lower rate plans.

Objection: I don't want a second mortgage on my home.
Response: I understand your concern, but a home equity line of credit offers many benefits that actually help you reduce

financial risk. You will have money available to meet financial emergencies, be able to control how much credit you use, and also keep your monthly payments at a comfortable level, and may be able to deduct the interest on your tax forms.

Closing the sale has two steps. The first step is actually getting the application. The second involves turning the application into an open loan account. Skilled lenders know how to turn customer inquiries into loan applications, while less skilled employees are often unable to get past the customer's first question—"What is your rate?"

But getting the application and approving it is no guarantee that the sale will be completed. Sales are lost because the bank failed to respond quickly, the application was handled poorly, the customer found a better deal somewhere else, or the customer decided not to borrow. Lost sales are unavoidable; however, a sound consumer credit operation should minimize these missed opportunities through effective selling from start to finish.

The Selling Process

At any given time, there are a group of consumers ready, willing, and able to purchase consumer credit products. It is the bank's challenge to market its products in a manner that will attract this group. The effort begins with an understanding of the sales cycle.

The basic sales cycle for any product or service can be broken into four elements, as shown in exhibit 11.1.

EXHIBIT 11.1   Sales Cycle

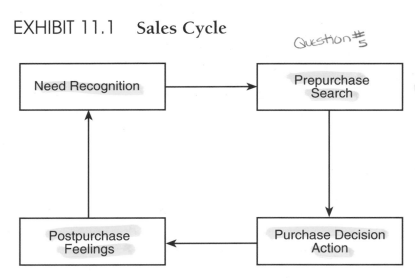

Question # 5

Need Recognition

The selling process begins when the consumer needs to borrow. The need for credit is almost always derived from the desire to satisfy some other need. For example, if a consumer's car is about ready to fall apart, he or she needs a new car, which in turn, may lead to the need for a loan. Obviously, a consumer does not need to purchase an

$85,000 car to satisfy the need for basic transportation. However, consumers have other needs, such as ego gratification or a desire to establish a certain image, both of which may result in the perceived need to purchase a luxury or particular model of car.

Prepurchase Search

Question #5

When the consumer needs funds to purchase goods or services, the process of searching for a loan source begins. This may be a very brief process or it may be quite extensive, depending on the consumer involved and the relative importance of the decision. Some consumers search no further than the car dealer's finance and insurance office. Others respond immediately to a direct mail offering or an advertisement. Still other consumers—a relatively small but highly visible group—go through an extensive process of comparing competitors to find the one with the lowest rate or the best overall product. Some consumers will shop their bank, and maybe a couple of other financial institutions, before applying for a loan, many will look no further than their primary bank, particularly if the bank's personnel have established a strong personal relationship with the consumer.

This stage is highly individualized. The factors that are important to the consumer vary greatly. The key is to identify which factors in the decision-making process are most important to the customer and then to tailor the sales effort accordingly.

If the bank's credit products are convenient and offer exceptional service, consumers may purchase them even though the bank may not offer the lowest rate in town. Skilled salespeople can also control sales and minimize "credit shopping" by consumers if they have the ability to recognize the consumer's needs and offer products that meet those needs. Another essential skill is the ability to build credibility with the consumer. Indeed, many of the finer consumer credit salespeople in the country have substantial followings by loyal customers who trust their advice and seek them out over competitors that, from a price standpoint, offer more attractive products.

Another point at which selling opportunities are created is the period between when the credit application is taken and the credit decision is made. This is unique in credit sales. In virtually every other type of retail sale, the consumer makes a decision to buy, then simply presents the necessary form of payment, and the transaction is concluded. With credit products, the customer must wait for the seller—the bank—to make a decision, "Do we want to sell our product to the customer?" It goes without saying that this decision should be made as quickly as possible, but, in the process, the lender can use the information on the application to identify possible sales opportunities.

Postpurchase Feelings

All consumers have "feelings" about the service they received and the products they purchased. If consumers are satisfied with the loan product and if the loan process was handled in an efficient and customer-oriented manner, they will probably think of the bank the next time they need another loan. They will also be more receptive to the bank's cross-selling efforts. On the other hand, if consumers had an unpleasant experience applying for a loan, found the rate was too high, or decided that the product did not perform as expected, they are going to be less receptive to future selling efforts.

Sound marketing programs continually work to make favorable impressions on potential customers. This is very important to the success of open-end credit programs. It does no good to sell a consumer a credit card unless they are going to pull it out of their wallet—ahead of their three other cards—and use it. Promotional activities emphasize the product's benefits to the consumer, introduce added features and services, and tell the customer how much the bank values his or her business.

The sales cycle should be kept in mind as the bank reviews its consumer credit products and the lending process. It is vitally important that the consumer be the focus of product design and operational procedures. These factors cannot be designed solely out of concern for the bank's needs or they will be doomed to failure in the highly competitive markets of today.

Objectives of Loan Structuring and Selling Strategies

Five broad objectives should be considered when developing the bank's sales culture as it relates to consumer loan structuring and selling

- ❏ to make the best loan for the customer and the bank
- ❏ to sell loans, not just take orders

- to optimize bank earnings by selling other bank products
- to optimize customer retention
- to minimize credit and interest rate risk

The concept of making the best loan for the customer and the bank embodies most of these objectives. The consumer is looking for a loan product that meets specific needs, is priced fairly (not necessarily the lowest rate in town), is convenient, and offers high quality customer service. The bank wants to earn an acceptable yield on its investment, limit its risk to an acceptable level, and build strong customer relationships.

For both parties to realize their overall objectives, there may be some trade-offs. For example, if the customer is charged a very high interest rate on a loan, the bank will realize higher earnings in the short run but risk losing the customer in the future. On the other hand, consumers are often willing to pay higher prices for products and services that they perceive as having added value. Convenience stores are a good example. Many consumers patronize these stores knowing that they may buy the same goods for less at the grocery store, however their convenient locations and store hours frequently offset any price disadvantage they may have.

A bank that establishes the philosophy of "making the best loan for the customer and the bank" will develop procedures that include analyzing alternative loan structures on each loan application. The nature of the structuring process varies with the type of loan product requested, manner in which the application is received, and the way the bank processes applications. We will consider these issues later in this chapter.

The opposite approach to active selling is simply to fill customer orders. The problem with this approach is that it presumes customers have full knowledge of the different loan products that are available and know the best way to manage their financial affairs. Quite often, these assumptions are false. Professional bankers, on the other hand, are up-to-date on what financial service products are available in the market and are skilled in matching customers' needs with the appropriate product.

Selling the best loan does not mean the bank should not promote individual loan products. The bank may still need to advertise credit cards, home equity lines, automobile loans, and other products in order to develop a flow of loan applications. These product promotions should generate new applicants who,

Question #2

in turn, should be evaluated for loan structuring opportunities and may be promising candidates for cross-selling other services.

Optimizing bank earnings can be viewed from either a long-term or a short-term perspective. Bank managers are usually under pressure to achieve short-term growth objectives, asset quality targets, and profit goals. At the same time, to maximize profits in the long term, the bank may price loans to meet aggressive competition to increase or preserve market share. An example of this strategy is the aggressive marketing of home equity lines of credit following passage of favorable tax legislation in 1986. Many banks offered low introductory rates or waived closing costs to encourage consumers to open an equity line account. While these introductory rates reduced loan yields in the short run, they attracted new accounts that offered significant income opportunities over the following years.

Question #3

One of the most important assets any bank has is its base of retail customers. Some bankers prefer to think of their customers as clients who are receiving professional service from the bank. These clients not only represent a current source of income, but also a source of future earnings and a high potential market for the bank's other retail services. Developing and retaining a customer base are critical to the success of any retail business. Customer retention is enhanced by consistently delivering high-quality service and selling products that meet the client's tangible and intangible needs. Products and services that have ego-enhancing benefits—gold VISA cards, affinity group credit programs, and quality service—can also go a long way to strengthen the account relationship.

Sound loan structuring goes hand-in-hand with the bank's effort to properly control credit and interest rate risk. This requires a commitment to training and using sound decision-making and lending policies. For example, a well-structured bill consolidation loan will reduce a customer's monthly payments and improve his cash flow so he can meet those payments easily. Some bill consolidation loans can be made on an unsecured basis with little risk, while others may have to be secured in some way. Collateral reduces the bank's risk, so the bank can offer borrowers lower interest rates, longer maturities, and lower monthly payments.

Loan Structuring by Product Line

A bank that embraces the philosophy of aggressive loan structuring is presented with a variety of issues depending upon the product line involved.

Direct Loans

The direct lending environment offers the bank the best opportunity for significant loan structuring and the cross-selling of other bank services. Assuming the bank's employees have developed basic selling skills, they should be able to identify customer needs, determine products that offer attractive benefits to the consumer, and present these benefits using an effective sales approach. Direct contact allows the salesperson to obtain better information and respond to concerns (objections) and questions raised by the applicant.

The credit application provides a wealth of information that can help identify potential product sales. In fact, it is absolutely the best source of consumer information available to the bank. When customers open checking or savings accounts, we know relatively little about them. When they apply for a loan, we know a lot about them. Putting this knowledge to work is the key. Exhibit 11.2 presents consumer characteristics that may be determined from a loan application and a list of potential products that could be sold.

EXHIBIT 11.2   Cross-Selling Opportunities

Customer Characteristic	Potential Products
Has only a checking account	Savings, overdraft credit line, safe deposit box, investments
Has child ready to begin college	Home-equity line of credit, guaranteed student loan, savings/investment accounts, student credit cards, ATM card
Age 22, just starting to work	Credit cards, checking, savings, ATM card
High net worth, high income	Private banking, investments, professional lines of credit, ATM card, brokerage
Homeowner	Home equity line or second mortgage, IRA, savings/investment products, ATM card
Has three dependents and little life insurance	Credit insurance protection, life insurance (where permitted)
Age 55, married	Senior citizen product package trust services
College student	Student loan, credit card, ATM card

Loan structuring should take into account

- pricing—fixed or variable rate
- type of loan—open-end or closed-end
- amount of the loan
- term of the loan
- collateral
- control of loan proceeds
- automated loan payments
- credit insurance protection

Pricing: Fixed or Variable

Some banks have elected to offer both fixed and variable rate options on at least some of their loan products. The customer may be able to choose which pricing approach they prefer. In general, consumers are more likely to opt for variable rates during periods of relatively high market rates, (hoping rates will decline) while preferring fixed rates when market rates are low. When both a fixed and variable rate loan product are offered, the consumer often elects to take the one that offers the lowest monthly payment at the time. For example, the following options may be available to a consumer purchasing a new car:

Loan Amount	Rate	Term	Monthly Payment
$10,000 w/life	13% fixed	60 months	$234.44
$10,000 w/life	12% variable	60 months	$229.20

Assuming that the bank is indifferent about which option the customer selects, the lender would simply present both options to the consumer and allow him or her to make a choice between taking the fixed-rate loan with a monthly payment that is $5.24 higher, or selecting the variable rate to gain the lower initial monthly payment (while also taking the interest rate risk). The greater the difference between the monthly payments, the more attractive the variable rate loan will appear.

The bank may elect not to give the consumer a pricing option for all loan types. This is usually controlled by lending policy. For example, the bank may not want to offer fixed rates on loans with a maturity of over 5 years, or may not want to make any variable rate loans with maturities of 36 months or less. These policy decisions will be made based on factors such as the overall competitive environment, the bank's asset-liability management philosophy, and state lending laws.

The type of loans offered to an individual consumer is a matter of growing importance to banks. In part, the decision may be based on the loan products the bank wishes to promote, but it should be driven primarily by the desire to meet each consumer's unique needs. Consider the following scenarios:

Example 1

An applicant has requested a $5,000 unsecured line of credit to be used to consolidate a number of accounts open with other banks. The lender notes that the applicant now has three open lines of credit and that the balance on two of them is up to the limit, and the applicant is over the credit card limit. The applicant has a good credit history and each of the accounts is rated "as agreed." The lender is concerned that the applicant would resume borrowing on the other accounts if the balances were to be consolidated and then be unable to handle the added debt burden.

Lender	Loan Type	Credit limit	Balance
Bank A	Credit card	$1500	$1595
Bank B	Unsecured line	$1500	$1500
Bank C	Check overdraft	$1000	$ 990

Many lenders are reluctant to grant an additional open-end line of credit under these circumstances, and some banks even have policies prohibiting loans to consumers who have more than a specified number of revolving credit accounts. The lender may be able to structure a closed-end loan that would limit the borrower's access to further debt without reapplying. This requires paying off and closing the revolving accounts with the other lenders to give the bank more control over the borrower's future credit use. However, in today's competitive environment, it is naive to think that most consumers would not be able to reopen accounts if they so desired.

There is no universal correct answer to this request. The lender will need to carefully consider the applicant's situation and the bank's policies and reach a decision acceptable to both. This is a good example of lending as an art.

Example 2

An applicant has requested a $2,500 loan to pay the tuition for her daughter's first semester of college. Her credit history is excellent, she is a homeowner with a substantial amount of equity, and has the ability to handle a significant level of debt.

This situation is one that fits well with open-end home equity loan programs, since there is a very strong probability that the customer will be facing a series of borrowing needs. To meet the expense of future semesters, the borrower may need to incur additional debt. Rather than filling the customer's order, it would be preferable to sell her a home equity line of credit that would meet both her current and future borrowing needs, tie her to the bank, and **reduce** the bank's cost. It would also be beneficial to counsel her regarding special tuition loan opportunities, such as the Guaranteed Student Loan Program, or special college financing payment plans, which could help meet her needs at the lowest possible cost.

In our discussion of loan profitability, we noted that the size of the loan advance or credit limit has a significant impact on profitability. Selling a customer a larger loan can make the difference between a profitable and an unprofitable loan. Many banks encourage their lenders to look for ways to sell larger loans. One common practice is to set minimum loan sizes high enough to make each loan profitable. For example, a bank might set a minimum loan size of $2,000 for closed-end loans and $1,000 for a check credit plan. Assuming a larger loan could not be sold, smaller loan requests would be directed toward open-end products where they can be handled more cost efficiently.

Exhibit 11.3 shows the effect that increasing loan size has on interest income. This underscores the importance of selling each qualified applicant a larger loan whenever appropriate. This is key to improving the productivity of the

EXHIBIT 11.3   Loan Size Relative to Interest Income

Advance	Term (Months)	Rate	Interest Income
$ 1000	12	18%	$ 100.16
2000	12	18	200.32
3500	12	18	350.36
2000	36	15	495.88
3500	36	15	867.52
5000	36	15	1,239.52
5000	60	12	1,673.20
7500	60	12	2,509.80
10,000	60	12	3,346.40

consumer loan function because it drives more loan volume through the system on the same number of loans. It also increases loan profitability, because many costs are not affected by the size of the loan. For example, the cost to investigate an application is virtually the same whether the loan request is for $4,000 or $10,000.

If the lender can offer tangible benefits, the customer can often be sold a larger loan. Some possible benefits include a reduction in overall monthly debt payments as a result of paying off other obligations, reduced interest rates on at least some of the debts, a lower monthly payment as the size and term of the loan increase, or tax advantages associated with certain types of loans.

The term of the loan also is a vital consideration in structuring a closed-end loan. The term has a direct impact on the monthly payment, which is a key concern of many consumers. Some lenders argue that the amount of the monthly payment is as important as, or more important than, the APR when selling a loan. However, stretching the maturity can increase the bank's risk exposure, particularly on unsecured and declining value collateral, such as automobiles. This factor must be considered in the development of the bank's loan policies and practices.

Small differences in interest rates have little effect on monthly payments, while stretching out the loan term can dramatically lower payments. These comparisons are illustrated in exhibit 11.4.

Exhibit 11.4 gives you an insight into the potential to compete against a competitor's low interest rates by offering

EXHIBIT 11.4 Term, Rate, and Monthly Payment Comparisons

Advance	Term (months)	Rate	Monthly Payment
$ 2000	12	15%	$180.51
2000	12	16	181.46
2000	36	16	70.31
5000	30	13	196.10
5000	60	13	113.76
5000	60	14	116.34
15,000	36	2.9	435.56
15,000	60	9.9	317.96
15,000	72	10.5	281.69

longer maturities. For example, many banks attempt to compete against manufacturer interest subvention programs by emphasizing the monthly payment reductions available with longer maturities. As shown in exhibit 11.4, the monthly payment on a $15,000 loan can be lowered from $435.56 to $317.96 when the loan is financed at 9.9 percent for 60 months instead of 2.9 percent for 36 months. The lower monthly payment allows the lender to present options to price-sensitive customers and brings the loan within the reach of a broader segment of the market.

Consumers can also be sold on a higher rate loan if it can be demonstrated that such a loan will cost only slightly more per month, and that the bank's customer service is worth the additional cost—such as ease of applying, speed of making a credit decision, and convenience of branch offices to handle loan closings. Notice the very small difference that a 1 percent change in the rate makes. On a $2,000, 12-month loan, the payment on a loan at a 16 percent interest rate is only $.95 more than a loan at 15 percent.

The following examples are typical of loan structuring situations, with comments regarding some of the benefits available to consumers.

Example 1

Ms. Brown wants to borrow $2,000 for home improvements. She currently has the following debts:

Loan	Monthly Payment	Balance	Rate	Term
Car	$250	$2800	13%	36 months
VISA	50	1000	19%	Revolving
Bank loan	75	500	18%	24 months
Dept. Store	15	200	21%	Revolving
	$390	$4500		

Option A: One option would be to give her a $2,000, 24-month loan at 16 percent as follows:

	Monthly Payment	Balance	Rate	Term
New loan	$98	$2,000	16%	24 months
+ Existing debt	$390	$4,500		
Total	$488	$6,500		

Option B: An alternative would be to consolidate all the existing loans with the new loan for $6,500 as follows:

	Monthly Payment	Balance	Rate	Term
Consolidated loan	$222	$6,500	14%	36 months

Option B **benefits the customer** by

- reducing monthly debt payments by $266 (from $488 to $222)
- reducing the rate from those paid on most of the outstanding loans
- giving the customer a lower rate on the new money than she would be charged on a smaller separate loan

Option B **benefits the bank** by

- creating a new loan of $6,500, rather than $2,000, which substantially increases the loan's profit potential
- enhancing the relationship with the customer

Example 2

Mr. and Mrs. Johnson are trading in their car for a new one and need to borrow an additional $8,500, plus pay off their current balance of $1,500. They currently owe the following debts:

Loan	Monthly Payment	Balance	Rate	Term
Second Mortgage	$175	$9,000	12.5%	120 months
Boat	350	17,500	13	120 months
Car*	125	1,500	9.5	48 months
VISA	20	400	18	revolving
MasterCard	45	900	18	revolving
Dept. Store	15	300	21	revolving
Dept. Store	25	500	16	revolving
Total	$755	$30,100		

Option A: One option would be to lend the Johnsons $10,000— at the bank's current rate of 10 percent for 60 months—to finance the car purchase and pay off the remaining balance on their current car loan. The new loan, added to the remaining other debts would result in total monthly payments of $842 as follows:

	Monthly Payments	Balance
Current debts	$755	$30,100
– current car payment	$125	$ 1,500
=	$630	$28,600
+ new loan	$212	$10,000 at 10% for 60 months
Total	$842	$38,600

Option B: An alternative is to consolidate all loans except the boat loan with the new loan request. An 11 percent, 10-year second mortgage loan of $21,100 results in a total monthly payment of $640 as follows:

New second mortgage	$290	$21,100 at 11% for 120 months
+ boat	350	17,500
Total	$640	$38,600

Option B **benefits the customers** by

- reducing the monthly debt payment by $202 (from $842 to $640)
- reducing the interest rate on a significant portion of debt
- simplifying their financial management by reducing the number of open credit accounts
- consolidating a major portion of their debt into a loan secured by their residence, which may allow them a tax deduction on the interest paid

And again, the benefit to the bank is in selling a larger loan at a profitable interest rate, and covering many borrowing needs efficiently with one loan application instead of several.

These examples show the potential for loan structuring available with many consumer loan applications. Options that offer significant benefits for the customer and the bank without compromising credit quality should certainly be presented to consumers for their consideration. Any loan structuring effort should strengthen the bank's position.

The availability of collateral is obviously important to loan structuring. Normally, the greater the security that an item of collateral offers the bank, the lower the interest rate the bank may offer the consumer. Thus, stable and appreciating value collateral usually qualify the customer for lower rates than depreciating or fluctuating value collateral.

For example, selling the consumer a real-estate-secured loan rather than an unsecured loan not only gives the bank a much stronger position, it also allows access to larger loan amounts, lower rates, and longer terms for the consumer. Therefore, both parties may benefit if the loan can be secured by collateral.

However, always exercise care when considering the value of collateral on a loan. Collateral should not be used to justify selling a larger loan to a customer who does not have a sound credit history. Nevertheless, the prudent lender should request collateral to help strengthen the many loans that fall between obvious approval and obvious rejection.

When lending directly to the customer, the lender controls what the loan is used for—an important benefit of direct lending. This feature allows the lender to structure the loan knowing that the loan proceeds will be used as intended. This control is particularly important when the lender is making a marginal loan or a bill consolidation loan. On a direct loan, the lender may require that certain obligations be paid off directly by the bank. The bank prepares individual checks for each payee—the proceeds are not available for borrowers to use at their discretion. The following examples illustrate when this is desirable.

Example 1

To reduce monthly debt payments to a more manageable level, an applicant wishes to consolidate four other closed-end loans. The new loan would reduce the customer's monthly debt obligations by $150 and just satisfy the bank's debt-to-income ratio policy.

In this case, the lender wants to be sure that the existing loans are paid off. Otherwise, the borrower's debt-to-income ratio could be increased, creating an even greater strain on the family budget and weakening the bank's loan. To avoid this possibility, separate checks are made out to each creditor, and no new funds are given to the borrower.

Example 2

The applicant wishes to consolidate four open-end credit accounts in order to lower monthly payments and reduce the rate of interest currently paid. This situation poses an entirely different problem. Because the accounts to be paid off are open-end accounts, the lender faces higher credit risk and more difficulty in controlling the borrower's future credit use. Individual checks could be sent to pay off each of the accounts; however, the lines of credit would still be open and the customer could easily begin to accumulate debt once again. If that happens, the borrower's ability to pay could again be strained and the level of credit risk would be increased. Clearly, the least desirable option in this case would be to sell the customer on another open-end line of credit. Credit judgment should always take precedence over the desire to sell customers larger loans and more flexible credit arrangements.

Credit Insurance

Credit insurance protection is another important consideration in structuring and selling consumer credit products. The sale of credit life, credit accident and health, and credit unemployment insurance enhances the lender's profits and protects the consumer and the lender. Credit life insurance benefits the customer's estate by paying off the loan in the event of death, relieving the heirs of this additional financial burden. Credit disability and credit unemployment insurance usually make the payments on a loan when the borrower is unable to work for an extended period due to medical or other specifically covered reasons. The bank benefits by reducing delinquencies and losses associated with borrower death and disability. Credit insurance also helps preserve customer goodwill during difficult periods.

Insurance experts recommend two basic approaches when selling credit-related insurance services. First, minimize the use of the word insurance. The term "insurance" causes many consumers to immediately bring up many objections. Instead, use phrases such as credit protection plan. This allows the lender time to present the benefits of these products before having to address the consumer's concerns about their need for insurance. The second practice is to always quote monthly loan payments with the full credit protection package. Then, if the customer does not want some of the coverage, the result will be a lower monthly payment. Psychologically, it is easier to sell credit protection when payment quotes are not raised as insurance coverage is added. Another popular approach is to quote the cost of insurance on a daily basis. Pennies-per-day quotes attempt to refocus the customer's reference point on an easily understood and much smaller cost number.

The effect credit insurance plans have on the cost of closed-end consumer loans is shown in exhibit 11.5. Line 1

EXHIBIT 11.5   Credit Insurance Sales: Effect on Loan Payments and Bank Income

$3000 loan—36 months—16% APR

Life Premium	Disability Premium	Monthly Payments	Finance Charge
1. No insurance	No insurance	$105.47	$796.92
2. $57.79	Not included	107.50	812.21
3. 60.48	$139.74	112.51	850.14

$10,000 loan—60 months—12% APR

Life Premium	Disability Premium	Monthly Payments	Finance Charge
1. No insurance	No insurance	$222.44	$3,346.40
2. $303.97	Not included	229.20	3,448.03
3. 321.66	$582.12	242.54	3,648.62

shows the monthly payment and finance charge on the loan if the customer does not purchase any insurance. The second line shows these items, plus the cost of the life premium, assuming the customer purchases only life insurance. The third line shows the amount of each item, assuming the customer purchases both life and disability insurance

Notice that adding just single credit life coverage to a $3,000 loan, based on a premium of $.63 per $100, results in a $2.03 increase in the monthly payment and a $15.29 increase in the finance charge. Adding both credit life and disability insurance adds $7.04 and $53.22, respectively. These amounts increase significantly as the size of the loan and term increase. Full coverage on the sample $10,000 loan results in an increase of $20.10 in the monthly payment and $302.22 in the finance charge. Clearly, it is easier to sell coverage when the highest monthly payment amount is quoted and then reduced if the customer does not want certain types of insurance coverage.

Indirect Loans

Indirect loans do not provide many opportunities for bank employees to structure loans or cross-sell other bank products. Loan structuring is restricted to adjusting the terms of the loan as requested by the dealer. The bank may ask for a larger down payment, modify the term of the loan, approve a lower loan amount, require cosigners, or limit the amount of the monthly payment. With indirect lending, there is no opportunity to cross-sell other services until after the loan has been made. Once a loan is made to a new customer the bank may pursue an aggressive direct mail and telemarketing effort to sell these customers other bank services.

The lender should instruct the dealer to make credit-related sales—insurance, warranty policies, and so forth—on finance transaction commensurate with the borrower's creditworthiness and ability to pay. If the borrower will not be able to comfortably handle his or her debt load after the new loan, the lender must extend the approval on the condition of bringing the loan within acceptable bank standards. For example, if the new loan would result in a debt-to-income ratio of 45 percent, and the bank's policy standard is 40 percent, adjustments would need to be made in the loan terms to bring the ratio into line. This may be done in a number of ways:

- Extend the term of the loan, reduce the monthly payment.

- Increase the amount of the down payment, which lowers the amount financed, lowers the monthly payment, and decreases the bank's collateral risk on the loan.

- Approve the loan subject to a specific monthly payment that meets the bank's policy, which allows the dealer to restructure the components of the loan. The dealer may elect to write the loan at a lower rate, drop the sale of insurance or the warranty policy, ask for a bigger down payment, or sell a lower priced model.

From these examples, you can see that bank lenders have less control over indirect loan structuring. They are unable to do anything about the borrower's other debt obligations, nor can they truly sell the best loan for the customer and the bank. Any structuring of the customer's overall debts will need to be done in a later transaction.

A word of caution is in order at this point. Dealers count on the finance income from loans they sell to a bank. If the bank were to sell loans aggressively to the dealer's customers, and if this resulted in many of the indirect loans being consolidated into new direct loans, trouble would quickly develop since the dealer would lose finance income on accounts that were paid off early. To avoid this problem, yet still make the most of the indirect customer base, some banks follow the practice of approving indirect loan applicants for two loans. For example, they approve the indirect loan request and also qualify the customer for a credit card or unsecured line of credit. These credit products are then offered to the customer on a preapproved basis soon after the dealer loan is made.

Open-End Credit

The ability to offer loan structuring and cross-sell open-end credit applications varies with the type of product and how the application was generated. Loan structuring is an essential strategy for selling open-end home equity lines and large, unsecured professional line-of-credit products. These lines are large enough to allow the consumer to consolidate debts and to gain other advantages such as lower rates, lower monthly payments, and perhaps tax deductibility of interest; however, the complexity of the products requires a fairly high level of personal selling effort by the lender.

Loan structuring on credit card and check overdraft plans is primarily related to the establishment of a credit limit. However, in the case of credit cards, it may involve upselling consumers to "gold" or other premium card products. In practice, lenders are only able to influence the sale of these products when the customer is applying on a direct basis, as opposed to when they are responding to a specific direct mail offering. But cross-selling opportunities abound with open-end accounts. The monthly billing statement provides a convenient vehicle for cross-selling and may be used to supplement other direct mail and telemarketing efforts.

The credit limit established for an open-end credit account has a significant effect on the value of the account to the consumer. Higher line limits encourage much greater use of the account. For example, a $1,000 classic VISA places significant limitations on how and for what purposes the customer uses the line. Larger borrowing needs are automatically eliminated, as the line is practical only for small borrowing needs and purchases and short-term cash flow requirements. A $5,000 gold card, on the other hand, allows the customer to purchase higher ticket items and could also alleviate a customer's concern about going over the limit and being embarrassed at a checkout counter.

The close relationship between the size of the line and the level of account use is reflected in the lending practices of marketing-oriented banks. Some credit card lenders will establish the highest practical limit at the outset and encourage consumers to use the line to pay off their other credit card balances. Other credit card lenders set low to moderate initial credit limits, then steadily increase the size of the credit limit available to good customers. For example, a bank may decide to increase the credit limits on all of its good check overdraft or credit card customers by 15 percent. This is accomplished by calculating the new limits and informing the customer of the new limit. No action is required on the customer's part unless he or she wishes to decline the new limit and close the account. This approach can be viewed as a form of loan structuring since the bank is attempting to increase the value of the account to the customer while increasing both the level of account use and ultimately portfolio profitability.

Credit card marketing programs typically emphasize additional services and features available to their customers. These features include items such as travel discounts and special privileges, protection against damaged goods and lower prices, and other benefits that individual consumers may deem attractive. These product packages have helped to increase the perceived value of the credit products, encourage greater use, and give one competing institution an advantage over others.

Loan structuring and cross-selling efforts are enhanced when open-end applications are generated via direct personal contact or over the telephone. Direct customer contact gives the bank salesperson greater flexibility in obtaining information from the customer and tailoring the sales approach to the specific applicant. The employee is able to sell any of the bank's products using "the best loan for the customer and the bank" philosophy. This may mean that the customer will be sold a closed-end loan or an open-end product different from the one initially requested.

Summary

Selling is a vital part of a consumer credit operation. The deregulated, highly competitive financial services environment has made it essential that banks emphasize strong selling skills in their employees, and implement sales programs designed to meet the needs of both the consumer and the bank.

Consumer credit selling includes structuring loans to enhance the attractiveness of loan products to the consumer, while enabling the bank to optimize earnings, retain customers, and keep credit risk within acceptable levels. Loan structuring requires that lenders have a sound knowledge of what products the bank has to offer and how those products can fulfill the consumer's specific needs.

Finally, consumer lenders must recognize their role as full-service bankers. They must look for ways to cross-sell the full range of retail bank services and products to loan customers. These selling efforts may begin with the loan application, but they extend into sales programs designed to sell additional bank services to all of the bank's customers after loan accounts have been opened.

Review Questions

Final Exam Question

1. What is the distinction between loan structuring and cross-selling? Give an example of how each might be used. — *Page 214*
2. Explain the meaning of this statement: A consumer lender should sell loans, not just take orders. — *Page 221*
3. What difference in service is implied if you think of bank customers as clients? — *Page 222*
4. Why is a direct lending transaction more conducive to loan structuring than most other types of consumer credit transactions? — *Page 223*
5. List the four stages of the sales cycle and give an example of how they influence the consumer lending process. — *Pages 218-220*
6. What loan structuring alternatives are available to consumer lenders when selling credit card and unsecured line of credit products? — *Page 235*
7. Why are a customer's objections often a helpful element in a loan interview? — *Page 217*

Optional Research

1. Does your bank promote a sales culture by actively encouraging consumer lending personnel to sell and cross-sell bank products and services? Is selling mentioned in your bank's policy statements or procedural manual? If so, what is your bank's position on the subject?
2. Does your bank use a philosophy of loan structuring within its consumer lending operation? What specifically is done to encourage this approach?

12 Loan Documentation and Closing

After reading this chapter, you will be able to

❏ list five key objectives for the loan documentation and closing functions

❏ identify the types of documents required on consumer loans and describe their purpose

❏ describe the process for establishing a security interest on collateral

❏ discuss the functions and importance of the loan review group

❏ describe the differences associated with the closing of various types of credit products, such as credit cards, direct secured and unsecured loans, and indirect loans

Objectives of the Documentation and Closing Process

Loan documentation is the process of preparing loan papers, obtaining necessary signatures, examining executed documents for accuracy, and recording collateral documents with proper authorities. The loan closing is the part of the documentation process in which the borrower actually signs the loan papers.

Proper documentation is essential for the bank to protect its investment and ensure that customers fully understand the loan product they have selected. Failure to properly document loans can leave the bank exposed to the costs of litigation, credit losses, and costly compliance violation penalties. Financial institutions have enhanced their documentation process by developing automated systems to minimize errors and by implementing a formal loan review process to ensure that all required loan forms are properly completed.

The loan closing can be held at a variety of locations. Direct loans are closed in the bank's offices, indirect loans are closed at the dealer's place of business, and open-end lines of credit may be closed by mail or at the bank's offices. Occasionally, loans may be closed by an attorney or service company that represents the bank.

The loan closing is also a stage of the lending process that offers some significant marketing opportunities for the bank. The loan closing can be used to lay the groundwork for a future credit sale, to cross-sell other bank services, and to create a positive image of the bank and its employees.

Banks have five primary objectives during the documentation and closing process

Question #2

❏ complete all documents required by state and federal law for the type of loan being made

❏ comply with all applicable regulations and the bank's lending policy

❏ ensure that the consumer understands how the loan works

❏ create a positive image for the bank

❏ use the opportunity to sell other bank products

Let's examine how each of these objectives affect both the bank and the consumer, and ways to achieve the desired results.

Completing the Appropriate Documents

Most banks have developed loan policy and procedures manuals detailing the documents that must be completed for each type of loan and the proper means of completing those documents. For example, the bank's procedures manual may state methods for handling

- loan application
- loan note and disclosure statement
- security agreement
- insurance "loss payee" letter (sent to borrower's auto or homeowner's insurance company)
- title or other ownership documents

It is up to the lender to make sure each of these documents is obtained at the loan closing. Generally, the lender relies upon the bank's legal counsel to provide documents, which, if properly completed, will be in compliance with all applicable regulations. The lender's responsibility is to ensure that the forms are properly completed. This means

- all appropriate sections are filled in
- the numbers are entered correctly and add up properly
- the collateral description is correct (model, serial number, etc.)
- all necessary signatures are obtained where required
- signers' identities are verified

Preparing documents accurately is essential to operating an efficient consumer credit department. Automated document preparation systems are now widely used to help minimize documentation errors. Properly completed forms flow through the system without delay and without the need for expensive special handling. If, on the other hand, there are documentation errors, normal work flow is disrupted and additional time and expense must be invested to correct the problems. For example, when a branch loan officer fills in the wrong numbers for the amount of finance charges and the amount of the monthly payments, the loan has to be sent back to the branch. The branch must then contact the customer and ask that they return to the office to sign corrected documents. While most customers are cooperative, the need to correct documents does not contribute to the desired image of the bank as a quality service provider. If the documentation error goes undetected, the bank is exposed to additional credit risk and compliance violations.

Complying with Regulations

The need to comply with all applicable regulations is closely related to the objective of getting complete and accurate documents. This objective extends beyond the forms themselves to the order in which disclosures are made. For example, Regulation Z requires that federal disclosures be presented to the consumer before any documents are signed. You will violate this regulation if you have the customer sign a note—the legal agreement that contains the customer's promise to repay the loan—before executing the Truth in Lending disclosure form. It is also a violation to allow a consumer access to an open-end credit account before the necessary disclosures have been provided.

Consumers generally seem far less interested in disclosures than regulators and lenders. Many consumers are happy to be getting the loan and are more concerned with getting their check than with listening to, or reading all of, the information on the loan documents. A consumer's impatience should not, however, lull the lender into complacency regarding proper disclosures. The lender is responsible for proceeding through the loan closing in the appropriate order and for ensuring that the consumer is aware of the required disclosures. Despite these precautions, lenders and collectors are occasionally confronted by consumers who claim "I didn't know the loan was secured by my home," or "That's my husband's loan, I don't have to make payments on it!" In most cases, consumers are not interested in the fine print unless or until a problem arises. Then, they and their attorney may closely scrutinize the documents looking for errors.

Making Sure the Customer Knows What's Going On

The third objective for the loan closing is to ensure that the consumer understands how the loan product works and what rights and obligations they have with respect to the loan. To answer customers' questions in this regard, lenders must read and be thoroughly familiar with the loan documents the bank uses. Basically, the consumer needs to understand

- ❏ when payments are due and the effect late payments will have on the cost of the loan (late charges, etc.) (Depending on the circumstances, the lender may want to emphasize the importance of making payments on time to preserve a good credit rating. This is particularly desirable if the consumer has had some credit problems in the past or this is his or her first experience with credit.)
- ❏ the method of calculating earnings for the bank (simple interest, rule of 78s, etc.)
- ❏ how extra payments (amounts in excess of the minimum required monthly payment) are handled and how they affect future payments
- ❏ where and how payments may be made
- ❏ the effect any variable rate feature will have on the loan (are changes in the rate reflected by changes in the monthly payment, the term of the loan, or both)

- how to access the line of credit and any restrictions, such as a minimum check size of $100
- who to contact in case of questions or problems, such as not being able to make payments when due. (If the bank has a special customer service department the consumer should contact about any questions, this should be emphasized during the loan closing.)

If the customer understands these features from the outset, they are likely to repay his or her loan on time and fully utilize open-end credit accounts. For example, informing customers that their interest is calculated on a simple interest basis, and that they will pay more in finance charges if they pay after the due date may encourage them to pay earlier. This may also help minimize the number of loans that become delinquent in their early stages.

An old saying puts it this way: "A loan well made is half collected." In other words, a sound credit decision and a good closing can prevent problems from arising later in the loan term. Both parties tend to benefit when the consumer understands how the account works. Consumers are also less likely to have customer service questions if they understand how their loan works and who to contact if they do have a problem.

Creating the Best Image for the Bank

Question #6

The fourth objective is to create a positive image for the bank. If a loan closing is handled in a professional, consumer-oriented manner, the customer is likely to form a positive image of the company. This, in turn, is likely to increase the customer's receptivity to future marketing efforts and enhance the possibility the customer will refer other people to the bank.

Cross-Selling

Finally, the loan closing presents an excellent opportunity for the bank to sell other services. Customers are usually pleased to have been granted a loan and, if the closing is handled well, they will have a positive impression of the bank. This makes it easier for the banker to cross-sell other services that can meet the customer's needs. In fact, the loan closing is perhaps the best possible time to cross-sell targeted services to the consumer. Analyzing the credit application provides a wealth of information to guide the sales effort, and since you often have the customer right in front of you, the opportunity couldn't be better. If the customer is in a hurry, you can at least make a recommendation and give the customer sales literature. It's a good idea to follow up by phone a few days later to see whether the customer has any questions. At the least, the stage is set for a future sale.

Types of Documentation

The forms required to document a consumer credit transaction vary depending on the type of loan being made and the collateral securing the loan.

For **direct, closed-end automobile loans,** the principal documents are the

- ❏ credit application
- ❏ Truth in Lending disclosure statement (see exhibit 12.1)—this form includes all of the required federal Truth in Lending disclosures as well as some disclosures required by state law
- ❏ note—this is the borrower's promise to pay according to the terms and conditions detailed in this legal agreement
- ❏ security agreement—this document describes the security interest in goods being pledged as collateral on the loan. The security agreement precisely describes the collateral and sets forth the rights and responsibilities of each party relative to the collateral.
- ❏ insurance policy or agreement to insure—these forms are used to verify that the collateral is covered by insurance and that the bank is named as loss payee. The loss payee endorsement provides that, in the event the collateral is damaged or destroyed, the bank will be named as joint payee with the borrower on the insurance check. The proceeds may be used to repair the collateral, and thereby restore its value, or to reduce or pay off the balance on the loan.
- ❏ motor vehicle title—this is the certificate that identifies the legal owner of the vehicle

Note that several of these documents are occasionally combined into one form. Variations will occur from one institution to the next and from state to state.

EXHIBIT 12.1   Truth in Lending Disclosure Statement

DISCLOSURE STATEMENT REQUIRED BY FEDERAL LAW

This Disclosure Statement is provided in connection with my loan from _____ Bank, National Association.

In this Disclosure Statement, the words *I, me, my* and *mine* mean each and all Borrower(s) who sign below. The word *Bank* means _____ Bank, National Association.

ANNUAL PERCENTAGE RATE The cost of my credit as a yearly rate.	FINANCE CHARGE The dollar amount the credit will cost me.	Amount Financed The amount of credit provided to me or on my behalf.	Total of Payments The amount I will have paid when I have made all payments as scheduled.
%	$	$	$

My payment schedule will be:

Number of Payments	Amount of Payments	When Payments Are Due
		Monthly, Beginning / /

Security: I am giving the Bank a security interest in any monies, deposits or credits held by the Bank for or owed by the Bank to, me, and in:

☐ the goods or property being purchased   ☐ the following property:

_____

Collateral from other loans may also secure my loan.

Late Charge: If a payment is more than 15 days late, I will be charged a late charge of the larger of $2.00 or 5% of the payment.

Prepayment: If I pay off early, I will not have to pay a penalty.

(e) means an estimate

Itemization of Amount Financed of

	$ _____
Amount given to me directly	$ _____
Amount paid on my account	$ _____
Amounts paid to others on my behalf:	
To public officials for filing fees	$ _____
To Credit Life Insurance company	$ _____
To Accident and Health Insurance company	$ _____
To Vendor's Single Interest Insurance company	$ _____
To _____	$ _____
To _____	$ _____

INSURANCE

A. CREDIT LIFE AND/OR ACCIDENT AND HEALTH INSURANCE
NOTICE OF PROPOSED INSURANCE

I understand that neither Credit Life nor Credit Accident and Health Insurance is required to obtain my loan and the Bank will not provide any insurance unless I sign and agree to pay the additional cost.

Credit Life and/or Credit Accident and Health Insurance is available through the Bank with the insurer named below. If purchased, the initial amount of Credit Life Insurance is $ _____ for a total premium of $ _____ for single coverage or (if joint coverage is available) of $ _____ for joint coverage. If purchased, the monthly benefit under the Credit Accident and Health Insurance offered through the Bank is $ _____ for a total premium of $ _____ . Credit Accident and Health Insurance is not available on a joint life basis.

This insurance will cover only the person(s) signing the request below for the type(s) of insurance indicated. Subject to acceptance by the insurance company, the insurance will be effective as of the date I sign the Bank's current form of promissory note ("Note") evidencing my loan and will expire on the earlier of the scheduled maturity date of the Note or the date of discharge of my indebtedness, for any reason, prior to the scheduled maturity of the Note. All benefits and proceeds of the insurance will be payable to Equitable Bank, National Association to the extent of its interest and any balance will be payable to me or my estate. Until the insurance expires, the amount of Credit Life Insurance will be the amount repayable under the Note that is not delinquent for more than 90 days. If I am jointly obligated on the Note with my wife or husband and we have both signed the request for Credit Life Insurance, death benefits will be payable only with respect to the first one of us to die. Subject to exclusions, eliminations, or waiting periods stated in the insurance policy or certificate, Credit Accident and Health Insurance is for the monthly benefit stated above for each month of total disability as defined in the insurance policy or certificate. If the Note is prepaid in full prior to the original maturity date, any unearned insurance premium will be refunded to me in the manner prescribed by law. Within 30 days after I sign the Note, I will receive a certificate of insurance more fully describing the insurance coverage. If the insurance is not accepted by the insurance company, I will receive a refund of the insurance premiums I have paid.

Name and Home Address of Insurance Company

I want ☐ Credit Life Insurance   I want ☐ Credit Life Insurance
☐ Credit Accident and Health Insurance   ☐ Credit Accident and Health Insurance

Borrower's Signature   Borrower's Signature

B. PROPERTY INSURANCE

I understand I must maintain insurance against loss or damage to my property which is subject to the Bank's security interest, and against liability arising out of my ownership or use of such property. I have the right to choose the person through which such insurance is to be obtained, but the Bank may refuse to accept the insurer which I chose for reasonable cause. Such insurance is not available from or through the Bank. I also understand that I must maintain All Risk Physical Damage Installment Loan Insurance on my property which is subject to the Bank's security interest (called "Vendor's Single Interest Insurance" in this Disclosure Statement) but that I may choose the person through which such insurance is to be obtained. Such insurance is available through the Bank for the entire term of my loan at a cost of $ _____ .

ACKNOWLEDGEMENT

By signing below, I acknowledge full understanding and agreement to all of the provisions of this Disclosure Statement and authorize all disbursements itemized above. I also acknowledge receipt of a completely filled in copy of this Disclosure Statement prior to signing any commitment letter, deed of trust, mortgage, promissory note, contract of indebtedness or security agreement.

Executed under seal this _____ day of _____ , 19 ____ .

_____ **BANK, NATIONAL ASSOCIATION**

By: _____   _____ (SEAL)
                                                                                      (Borrower)

                                                                       _____ (SEAL)
                                                                                      (Borrower)

                                                                       _____ (SEAL)
                                                                                      (Borrower)

For **indirect automobile loans,** the principal documents are the

- ❏ credit application
- ❏ closed-end installment sales contract—this form combines the federal and state disclosures with the security agreement and the note
- ❏ agreement to insure
- ❏ copies of credit insurance and warranty policies, if applicable—banks generally require that copies of these policies be submitted with the other loan documents
- ❏ motor vehicle title

For **unsecured, open-end line of credit accounts** (such as check overdraft and professional line of credit programs, the principal documents) are the

- ❏ credit application or acceptance form—the abbreviated applications used for preapproved and prescreened credit offers
- ❏ open-end credit agreement—this agreement sets forth all of the contractual terms for the account and includes Truth in Lending disclosures. The consumer must receive the agreement before using the account, though this form generally does not have to be signed.

Documentation checklists are often included in the bank's policy manual as a reference source for lenders. Some loans, such as those secured by real estate, require even more extensive documentation, while others, such as unsecured closed-end loans, require only the Truth in Lending disclosure statement and the note. Regardless of the type of loan being made, controls must exist to ensure that the documentation is complete and accurate.

Document Preparation

Automation has helped tremendously in assuring the efficient, accurate, and professional completion of loan documents. While the documentation equipment is readily available, each institution must cost justify the expense. The benefits offered by an automated document preparation program are

- **faster document preparation**   Automation allows lenders to respond quickly to any changes which must be made to the documents at the time of the loan closing. For example, the borrowers may decide to purchase credit protection coverage as a result of the lender's sales efforts. New documents can quickly be generated, thereby removing a potential obstacle to the sale and reducing the customer's wait if a last minute change is made.

- **more accurate documents**   The potential for error still exists, but many of the more common types of errors, such as incorrect calculations, are eliminated. If a lawsuit arises, be forewarned that the borrower's attorney will ask for copies of all loan documents and will look for errors to aid in the client's claim.

- **complete documentation is enhanced**   Most systems prepare sets of documents depending on the type of loan made. This ensures that the lender does not forget to prepare a required document. Documentation checklists also help ensure all information is completed.

- **service quality is enhanced**   The benefits noted previously all contribute to building a perception of professionalism and quality service that should help build better relationships with customers.

Institutions that prepare documents manually must carefully develop their procedures and ensure the employees are well trained to meet the demands of an accurate and responsive documentation process. In either case, the lender should have post-closing procedures to ensure the accuracy and completeness of the loan documents.

Establishing a Security Interest in a Consumer Loan

Although the *Uniform Commercial Code* (UCC) was first drafted in response to the need for uniformity in handling commercial transactions, it applies to many consumer loans as well. Of particular importance to consumer lenders is *Article 9* of the UCC, which governs most loans secured by personal property; however, it does not apply to real estate transactions. The provisions of Article 9 have been adopted by every state except Louisiana.

Question #3

A lender making a secured loan covered by the UCC provisions first needs to create a valid *lien* between the lender and borrower. This is accomplished by having the borrower execute a security agreement that creates or provides for a security interest (an interest in property that will secure payment or performance of an obligation). The actual document used must meet several minimum requirements. It must

- be in writing
- provide for a security interest
- be signed by the debtor
- contain a description of the collateral

The security agreement contains numerous provisions that stipulate the creditor's and debtor's rights and duties with respect to the collateral. To create a valid security interest, the agreement must be executed by all parties with an ownership interest in the collateral. For example, if a car is owned by John and Mary Jones, both of them must sign the security agreement in order for the bank to obtain a valid lien, even if only one of them will be obligated under the note.

Most collateral taken on consumer credit transactions remains in the possession of the consumer and is available for the consumer's use, subject to limitations that may be included in the security agreement. Cars, boats, and recreational vehicles are examples, and are referred to as non-possessory collateral. On the other hand, some collateral—such as savings accounts and stock—are held by the lender and referred to as possessory collateral. Certain obligations are associated with possession, and violation of these obligations can affect the terms and status of the loan. For example, some security agreements require that the borrower keep the collateral in a specified location. If the collateral, let's say a boat, is moved from its home state, to another location, the borrower may be obligated to obtain the lender's approval before making the move. Failure to notify the lender may be a breach of contract and could result in the loan being considered in default. The lender and the customer should fully understand all requirements spelled out in the security agreement.

Question #3

Once the security agreement has been signed by all appropriate parties, and a valid lien has been created, the lender must perfect the lien. To *perfect a lien,* the lender must file documents with the appropriate legal authority so that the lien and the filing date are a matter of public record. A creditor perfects a lien by attaching its security interest to the collateral using one of the following means

- placing its lien on a title
- placing its lien on a mortgage or deed of trust
- physically taking possession of the collateral
- filing a financing statement with the proper government authority, usually the secretary of state (see exhibit 12.2)

When the lien is perfected, the lender, now a secured creditor, has priority over rights that the borrower's other creditors may have in the same collateral. Exhibit 12-3 indicates the most common method of perfecting a lien on various types of collateral.

Lien perfection procedures vary from state to state. Virtually all states have automobile title laws, while only a few have title provisions for boats. Therefore, to avoid errors in the

EXHIBIT 12.2   UCC Financing Statement

UNIFORM COMMERCIAL CODE — FINANCING STATEMENT — FORM UCC-1

INSTRUCTIONS

DISTRICT OF COLUMBIA

1. PLEASE TYPE this form. Fold only along perforation for mailing.
2. Remove Secured Party and Debtor Copies and send other 3 copies to the filing officer. Enclose filing fee.
3. When filing is to be with more than one office, Form UCC-2 may be placed over this set to avoid double typing.
4. If the space provided for any item(s) on the form is inadequate the item(s) should be continued on additional sheets, preferably 5" x 8" or 8" x 10". Only one copy of such additional sheets need be presented to the filing officer with a set of three copies of the financing statement. Long schedules of collateral, indentures, etc., may be on any size paper that is convenient for the secured party.
5. If collateral is crops or goods which are or are to become fixtures, describe generally the real estate and give name of record owner.
6. When a copy of the security agreement is used as a financing statement, it is requested that it be accompanied by a completed but unsigned set of these forms, without extra fee.
7. At the time of original filing, filing officer should return third copy as an acknowledgment. At a later time, secured party may date and sign termination legend and use third copy as a Termination Statement.

This FINANCING STATEMENT is presented to a filing officer for filing pursuant to the Uniform Commercial Code		3 Maturity date (if any):
1 Debtor(s) (Last Name First) and address(es)	2 Secured Party(ies) and address(es)	For Filing Officer (Date, Time, Number, and Filing Office)
4 This financing statement covers the following types (or items) of property:		5. Assignee(s) of Secured Party and Address(es)

Check ☒ if covered: ☐ Proceeds of Collateral are also covered   ☐ Products of Collateral are also covered. No. of additional sheets presented:

Filed with:...

By:..   By:..
    Signature(s) of Debtor(s)   Signature(s) of Secured Party(ies)

FILING OFFICER—ALPHABETICAL

STANDARD FORM — UNIFORM COMMERCIAL CODE — FORM UCC-1

REORDER FROM
Registré, Inc.
5284 TAYLOR ST. N.E.
MPLS., MINN. 55421
(612) 571-2803

EXHIBIT 12.3   Methods of Perfecting Collateral

Type of Collateral	How Perfected
Airplanes	Federal Aviation Administration title
Automobiles	Title
Boats	Financing statement title, or Coast Guard ship's mortgage
Household goods	Financing statement
Mobile homes	Title
Recreational vehicles	
Self-propelled	Title
Other	Financing statement
Real estate	Mortgage/deed of trust
Savings passbook or certificate	Possession
Stock	Possession

lien perfection process, lenders must be aware of the requirements in each state in which they do business.

A perfected interest in collateral provides the bank with a secondary source of repayment—a source of funds to help it recover its investment should the borrower be unable to repay the loan for any reason. When the bank does not properly perfect its interest in the collateral, its position can become subordinate to the security interest of other properly filed interests and the bank may lose collateral rights in the sale of that collateral to a third party.

Question #4

Special Requirements

Question #3

Three common forms of secured consumer lending require additional discussion. They are loans secured by airplanes, loans secured by boats documented with the U.S. Coast Guard, and mortgages.

Aircraft

Loans secured by aircraft must conform to the documentation requirements of the *Federal Aviation Act.* The creditor's security agreement must be recorded with the Federal Aviation Administration (FAA) office in Oklahoma City, Oklahoma. Liens perfected with the FAA provide a very strong secured position for the lender since there is little chance the aircraft could be sold without the bank first being paid. The large dollar size of most aircraft loans makes it particularly important that the bank properly perfect its security interest, using the FAA documents and processing procedures.

Boats

The *Ship Mortgage Act of 1920* established procedures for the federal documentation of vessels. Boats weighing over five net tons may be documented under the act. Vessels that will operate in international waters or in several states and which meet the Coast Guard's requirements should be federally documented in order to provide the strongest possible lien position for the bank. Federal documentation takes priority over state titles or UCC filings.

Coast Guard documentation is a long and relatively complex process. Therefore, many banks rely on outside documentation companies to handle this task for them. It can take up to nine months for the bank to receive notification that its mortgage has been recorded, so many lenders take the additional precaution of recording their lien via either a financing statement or state title to protect them during the interim period.

Real Estate

Consumer lenders may be heavily involved in mortgage lending through the offering of closed-end second mortgage loans and open-end home equity loans. Most states have distinct procedures for recording a mortgage or deed of trust in the county in which the property is located. State laws also control the types of mortgage loans that can be made and the loan provisions—rates, maturities, fees, etc.—that can be used.

While few problems exist regarding closed-end mortgages, some states have not adopted open-end mortgage provisions that fully protect the bank. For example, in Washington, D.C., if a bank grants an equity line of credit to a consumer who subsequently obtains a second mortgage, the second mortgage holder would have priority over the equity line account for all advances made after the second mortgage was made. This situation increases the bank's exposure and makes the use of open-end credit plans much riskier. Most states have now passed laws that protect lenders by establishing a priority position, up to the maximum amount of their credit line, against all subsequent lenders. It should be noted that some states, Texas, for example, still do not permit second mortgage lending.

This undoubtedly has an adverse effect on credit availability in the state.

Attorneys and service companies are frequently used by banks to handle mortgage title searches, loan closings, and mortgage recordings. The cost of outside specialists can usually be passed on to the customer. Using attorneys and service companies gives the bank extra assurance that its lien will be properly perfected, and may help in spotting documentation errors that if unnoticed would increase the bank's loan risk exposure.

Establishing the market value of real estate is a critical element in sound mortgage lending. Banks and other financial institutions are required to use certified professional appraisers for loans over $50,000, and many require such appraisals on all mortgage loans.

Despite more stringent appraisal requirements, it must be noted that there are no absolute guarantees on housing values. Many areas have experienced substantial declines in home values during the recessionary period from 1988 through the early 1990s. These declines left lenders undersecured and exposed to large loan losses. Nevertheless, a sound real estate appraisal policy is an essential element in mortgage loan documentation.

Variable Rate Loans

The documentation for fixed-rate, closed-end accounts is handled entirely at the time the loan is made. While follow-up will be required to ensure that documents are obtained from the appropriate agency for perfecting liens, there are no ongoing documentation requirements aside from insurance renewals. Variable rate loans, on the other hand, require some ongoing disclosures to the consumer after the loan has been made. Generally speaking, the lender is required to notify customers of changes in the loan rate and the effect that the changes will have on the loan payments—higher, lower, or unchanged —and the remaining loan term—extended, shortened, or remain the same. Such notifications are usually part of the monthly statement sent to the customer.

Open-End Credit Accounts

Most open-end account programs require periodic disclosures to account holders. These were discussed in the chapter on consumer loan regulations. Lenders also may, under specified conditions, make changes to the terms of their open-end credit programs. For example, many banks have reduced the minimum monthly payment requirement, or lowered rates on these plans. They may also have added new fees, such as overlimit, annual membership, and late fees. Generally speaking, the bank must send a "Notice of Change in Terms" to the customer. The changes, if unfavorable to the customer, can only be made if the customer "accepts" the change, with acceptance defined by state law. In most cases, favorable changes, such as lower monthly payment requirements, can be automatically implemented following a specified notification period, usually 30 days.

The ability to change the terms of existing credit agreements without having to completely redocument these lines has enabled lenders to continually enhance their products. At the same time, consumers who do not want to accept the new provisions may liquidate their accounts under the previously agreed terms without having to take any further action. Typically, a charge to the account after the new terms have gone into effect indicates acceptance of the revised agreement.

Loan Review

Many banks have established a formal loan review function within the consumer credit division as an additional control point in the loan documentation process. The unit performing this function plays a key role performing such tasks as

- ❏ ensuring that the loan is in compliance with all applicable regulations
- ❏ examining completed documents for accuracy, completeness, and adherence to bank lending policy
- ❏ following up to resolve documentation errors
- ❏ expediting the booking of new loans
- ❏ developing and maintaining management information regarding items such as documentation problems and lender performance

❏ maintaining follow-up for necessary lien and insurance documents

Question #5

The development of increasingly sophisticated software programs, have greatly enhanced the bank's ability to control risk with ongoing review programs. The key is to define what must be monitored and then to build the reporting system to facilitate the unit's informational needs.

Some loan review tasks should be performed before the loan is booked on the bank's application systems. Other tasks require monitoring and follow-up. For example, lien and insurance follow-up programs are essential for a bank to ensure that its collateralized loans are properly secured. The department usually maintains a checklist of all necessary forms and then records each one as it comes in from the appropriate agency—state motor vehicle department, insurance company, and so forth. Monthly reports track documents, enabling the review department to follow-up promptly when documents are not received within normal timeframes. For example, if the state motor vehicle department normally sends the bank its lien notification within 30 days, the bank would follow up only on those documents that have not been received after 30 days.

Even if the bank obtains all the documents needed to properly perfect its liens, things can still go wrong. For example, the motor vehicle department may not pick up the bank's lien and may issue a title without a lien to the borrower, or the dealer may add another name to the title, leaving the bank in the position of not having its lien properly perfected since all owners may not have signed the loan documents. These errors can be resolved with relative ease if detected early in the life of the loan.

For banks with limited resources or that elect not to establish follow-up programs, collateral insurance programs are available to protect them against the risk of having liens improperly recorded.

Management information reports developed by a loan review department can strengthen the bank's consumer lending operation. If the loan review area is able to identify problems more quickly, then the bank will be able to resolve problems before they become serious. For example, if an individual loan officer is making a lot of documentation errors, the problem can often be remedied by additional training. Likewise, if one dealer seems to be having problems preparing contracts or resolving contract errors, the bank can act quickly to remedy the problem through additional staff training or, in extreme cases, by terminating the dealer relationship.

Loan review is becoming increasingly important in monitoring the risk ratings on consumer credit products. The trend is toward systems such as those used to track credit risk on the commercial loan portfolio. As banks increase the volume of consumer loans sold to investors, and as regulators seek to better monitor the health of regulated institutions, it is likely that more sophisticated risk rating approaches will be developed. These systems will provide information needed to establish the bank's loan loss provision and to help banks be more proactive in their approach to managing consumer credit portfolios.

Question #5

Booking Loans on the Operating System

In a sound lending program, loans are booked quickly, new loan information is accurate and complete, and essential information is correctly stored for retrieval. The development of sophisticated central information systems (CIS) has improved the efficiency and quality of the booking process. The account information may be supplied directly from the loan application system to the central file, linking the new account with any other services the customer may currently use. In the best systems, key customer information, such as age, home ownership, and number of dependents is captured and stored for use in the bank's marketing efforts.

The application systems should contain all the information necessary to manage the account and monitor the overall customer relationship. The capabilities and performance of these systems will directly affect the bank's ability to provide quality service to the customer; intelligently market bank services; and optimize the productivity of the loan review, collections, and other departments servicing the account.

Summary

The loan documentation and closing process is an important element in developing a sound consumer credit portfolio. It involves the preparation and execution of loan documents that comply with all applicable regulations and provide the bank with a firm legal basis for collecting and servicing its loans.

Loan documents must be accurate and complete to establish the bank's and consumer's rights under the terms of the loan arrangement. When a loan is to be secured by collateral, the bank must establish and perfect a security interest in the collateral. This requires an understanding of specific provisions of state law regarding lien perfection, as well as special documentation requirements for real estate, aircraft, and large boats.

The loan closing offers the lender an opportunity to create a positive image for the bank, ensure that the customer fully understands the loan product purchased, and sell other bank services. If the loan closing is handled efficiently, it will help control costs while creating a positive impression of the bank.

Review Questions

1. Give three reasons why accurate document preparation is so important in a loan transaction. - Page 246-247
2. List the primary objectives of the loan documentation and closing process. - Page 240
3. What is the purpose of a UCC financing statement? Are there other ways to achieve the same purpose? What types of collateral is it used for? - Pages 248-250
4. What happens if the bank does not properly perfect its security interest on collateral pledged for a loan? - Page 250
5. What is the purpose of the loan review function? What benefits does it offer the bank? - Page 253-254
6. Give two reasons why it is important to create a positive image for the bank during a loan closing. - Page 243

Optional Research

1. Does your bank include documentation checklists in its policy manual? If so, take a look at them and note how many and what different types of forms are required for various consumer credit transactions.
2. Read your bank's disclosure forms, security agreements, and line of credit agreements. Is there anything in them that surprises you? That you don't understand? That you never realized was included?

13 Collection and Recovery

After reading this chapter, you will be able to

❑ list six objectives for the collection and recovery functions

❑ list the objectives of the Fair Debt Collections Practices Act and describe some of the practices that it prohibits

❑ identify the primary causes for consumer loan delinquencies and tools for remedying the problem

❑ describe the stages of the collection cycle and their effect has on the bank's collection and recovery departments

❑ explain the difference between Chapter 7, 11, and 13 bankruptcy filings

❑ describe how and why the recovery department functions much differently than the collection department

Objectives of Collection and Recovery

The loan collection and recovery functions are essential and inevitable elements of the consumer credit operation. The collection department is charged with collecting payments on time from consumers who are delinquent—those who make payments later than their contractual due date. The *recovery department,* also known as the *salvage department,* is responsible for collecting money still owed on accounts after they have been charged off as a loss by the bank. These functions have a key role in preserving the quality of the consumer loan portfolio and in avoiding unnecessary loss of revenue.

There are six primary objectives for the collection and recovery departments:

Question #1

- ❏ maintain delinquencies within acceptable parameters
- ❏ maintain loan losses within acceptable parameters
- ❏ generate loss recoveries at desired levels
- ❏ counsel customers experiencing difficulty handling debt
- ❏ ensure consistency with other bank objectives
- ❏ achieve collection and recovery cost efficiently

Management must decide what constitutes an acceptable delinquency rate—usually stated as the percentage of accounts 30 days or more past due—for each type of product in the consumer credit product line. These benchmarks help the bank measure the quality of its loans and evaluate the performance of the loan and collection departments. They also directly affect the bank's lending policies. Generally, the delinquency objective is defined as a maximum percentage of the portfolio that can be in default. For example, the bank may set an objective of 1.5 percent delinquency for direct closed-end loans. Lower delinquency will always be welcomed by management, while higher levels are indications of problems that require attention and possible adjustments in the bank's lending program. Portfolio delinquency objectives under 1 percent are regarded as conservative, while objectives above 3 percent are very aggressive or liberal.

Delinquencies tend to vary with the type of loan and the season (see exhibit 13.1). Of the six types of loans listed, note that revolving loans have a relatively low delinquency rate. This can be misleading because consumers experiencing financial difficulties can continue to borrow against lines of credit to make payments on loans. The result may be low past-due levels, but increased loss exposure on individual accounts. Unsecured personal loans, on the other hand, usually have the highest delinquency rates. Loans secured by the borrower's home or by savings accounts tend to have the lowest delinquency.

Seasonal factors also affect delinquency levels. Each collection manager should be aware of the seasonal delinquency patterns in the bank's market area as well as within individual products. Many banks experience rising delinquencies during the fourth quarter of the year,

EXHIBIT 13.1   Consumer Credit Delinquency

Percent Delinquent—National Averages

Type of loan	Oct.	Nov.	Dec.
Unsecured, closed-end	3.07	3.08	2.95
Automobile, direct	2.18	2.20	2.14
Automobile, indirect	2.74	2.75	2.66
Home equity, closed-end*	1.84	1.93	2.06
Credit cards	3.28	3.28	3.29
Revolving loans	2.79	2.70	2.75

*not seasonally adjusted

Source: *1991 Quarterly Delinquency Report,* American Bankers Association

as heavy retail buying during the holiday season puts a strain on family budgets. Managers who know and understand these seasonal patterns can more effectively manage the collection department.

Delinquencies can be influenced by economic conditions. Defaults and losses usually rise during recessionary or stagnant economic cycles when more people are unemployed or when inflation outstrips income. Some banks modify their delinquency objectives during these economic downturns to take into account the realities of the market. On the other hand, late payments and loss experience should improve during strong economic periods. Thus, the bank must evaluate the economy's effect to determine its impact on portfolio quality as measured by delinquency and losses. This information can then be used to set credit approval standards and justify staffing levels in the collection department.

Ideally, the bank should respond proactively to anticipated economic changes—tightening credit standards **before** a recession begins, for example—rather than chase rising delinquencies in the wake of a decline in the economy. Clearly, management must be sure that its credit and collection philosophies are sending the same signals to lenders and consumers.

Management must also set loan loss objectives at either the total portfolio level or the individual product level. Exhibit 13.2 shows the variation in loan losses for different products. The differences in loan losses reinforce the desirability of setting unique delinquency and loss objectives for each type of loan. The difference between the gross and net losses is the amount recovered from consumers after loans have been charged off. Therefore, a significant difference between gross and net losses can represent a large amount of money coming back to the bank. The amount of money collected from borrowers whose accounts have been charged off is therefore very important and provides a benchmark for measuring the performance of the recovery department and an additional measure of overall portfolio quality.

Economic conditions also affect loan losses. Losses tend to follow patterns in relation to the economy, rising during recessionary periods and falling during stronger economic cycles. Loan losses increased in the early 1980s and then again in the late

Question #1

EXHIBIT 13.2 1990 Installment Credit Dollar Losses Based on Outstandings

Type of Loan	Gross Losses	Net Losses
Unsecured, closed-end	2.04%	1.53%
Automobile, direct	.93	.67
Automobile, indirect	1.40	.98
Second mortgage	.19	.17
Small business	1.29	1.13
Unsecured, open-end*	2.98	2.57

*excludes bank card credit

Source: *1991 Installment Credit Report,* American Bankers Association

80s and early 90s when the economy slumped. Experience has shown that charge-off rates also tend to move in unison with delinquencies; thus, higher delinquencies normally result in higher losses.

While it is important to set quantifiable goals for the collection and recovery departments, it is also important to recognize the qualitative aspects of loan collection. Successful collectors are usually good salespeople and financial counselors. They can sell the customer on making a payment and can counsel the customer on how to manage his or her finances to achieve a workable repayment schedule. Collectors' sales and counseling skills can contribute to lower loss and delinquency performance over time.

Many consumer credit managers agree that loan delinquency and loss objectives should be set in conjunction with the other product line objectives. For example, if a bank is embarking on an aggressive marketing program to promote its credit cards and is liberalizing its lending policies or using aggressive marketing techniques such as preapproved mailings, it must anticipate a higher rate of loan delinquencies and losses. It is unlikely that the bank could liberalize its credit standards without having some effect on asset quality.

The final broad objective is to achieve collection and recovery in the most cost-efficient manner. Automated collection systems have helped keep collection costs under control while greatly improving the department's efficiency and the productivity of individual collectors. Automated dialing machines linked to online terminals enhance collection results by maximizing contact with delinquent customers and minimizing paper shuffling. Other techniques to increase productivity and control expenses include flextime to match collecting schedules with the times when consumers can most frequently be reached (5 p.m. to 9 p.m.) and creative organizational approaches to assigning delinquent accounts.

At the individual level, collectors must be trained to compare the anticipated costs of a collection technique to the potential for recovery. For example, the collector who spends $250 repossessing a car worth the same amount has wasted time and energy, while not reducing the amount outstanding on the loan. Similarly, it is difficult to justify the cost of attempting to recover a $250 loss from a consumer who has left the market area and has no job or assets. It may be better to discontinue any collection effort and instead concentrate on those accounts with a greater potential for recovery.

The collection department's procedures should be structured to keep costs low. Low-cost notices, such as computer-generated notices that are automatically sent to all past-due accounts, can be used to reduce the number of delinquent accounts before more expensive personal contact is initiated.

Fair Debt Collection Practices Act

The Fair Debt Collection Practices Act took effect on March 20, 1978. The act is directed primarily at independent debt collection agencies, but its provisions form a basis for identifying acceptable and unacceptable practices for bank collection departments as well. The act also serves as the basic framework for many state laws dealing with collection practices. The act's major purpose is to

- ❏ ensure the fair treatment of consumers by debt collectors
- ❏ define the rights of consumers
- ❏ eliminate abusive, deceptive, and unfair practices

When the consumer has failed to make a payment when it is due, the bank tries to protect its best interests and recover its investment. This does not pose a major concern when the customer's problem is minor, such as when someone simply forgot to make the payment or had a temporary problem that is easily resolved. The issue becomes far more difficult when it is clear the customer can no longer make any payments.

In the past, in an effort to resolve problem loans to their satisfaction, some collectors and collection agencies engaged in abusive collection practices. The Fair Debt Collection Practices Act addressed these abusive practices by stating that collectors may not

- ■ harass, oppress, or abuse any person
- ■ use any false statements
- ■ be unfair in attempting to collect any debt
- ■ threaten any action that cannot legally be taken.

Harassment and abuse include the use of obscene or profane language, advertising the consumer's debt, or repeatedly calling customers in order to annoy them. The bawlerouts of earlier days can no longer be used. These are clearly unpleasant and unethical practices, and they certainly do not belong in a responsible collection program. One specific limitation imposed by the act is to allow collection calls only between the hours of 8 a.m. and 9 p.m.

The act also requires honesty in collection practices. Implying that the caller is an attorney or a representative of a government agency, or that the customer has committed a crime and faces arrest, and misrepresenting the amount or terms of the debt are specifically prohibited.

The act also prohibits using postcards; discussing debts with neighbors, friends, or other third parties; requiring the customer to accept collect calls or pay for mail or telegrams; or depositing a postdated check prior to the date on the check.

Collectors are also prohibited from threatening to take any action to cure a default that is not specifically provided for in the loan contract. This provision makes it absolutely essential that collectors know what remedies are available to them on each type of loan they handle.

The regulation of debt collection practices has not had a major impact on responsible financial institutions. Sound debt collection practices are those that enable the collector to balance the need to collect delinquent obligations without delay while preserving the customer's goodwill. Collection efforts need not alienate customers just because they are experiencing financial difficulties. Many good customers have, at some point, experienced short-term problems. Once past their current problems, most consumers return to a healthier financial condition.

Causes of Delinquency

To have an appreciation for the collection process, it is helpful to understand what causes customers to default. The major contributors to delinquency are

 Question #2

- unexpected problems that change the customer's income or debt situation
- economic downturns
- excessive levels of debt
- poor money management
- marital problems

- carelessness
- changing attitudes toward responsible credit use
- irresponsible lending
- fraud or intentional default

Just as attitudes toward borrowing have changed, so have attitudes toward repaying loans. Some consumers and consumer advocates believe that borrowing is a right, not a privilege. Further, when they have a problem on a loan, they are quick to blame the lender or the bank for their problem. They may refuse to honor their contractual obligations and look for ways to avoid the debt. Other consumers simply do not care to repay debts, particularly if they feel they have nothing to lose. Unfortunately, this condition has been exacerbated by "credit clinics," some bankruptcy-oriented attorneys, and the aggressive lending practices in the industry. It is indeed true that people can abuse credit in many cases and still have access to more.

A major cause of delinquency is the development of unexpected problems that lead to either a decrease in income or an increase in expenses. Examples of the kinds of problems that may lead to loan delinquency include illness or physical disability, job layoff or termination, death, and unplanned major expenses. These changes may alter the customer's ability to repay the loan for either a short or long period of time. As such, a careful examination of the facts is necessary to determine the best possible remedy for the problem.

In recent years, consumers have increasingly been able to accumulate excessive debt obligations which has in turn reduced their capacity to pay. This is primarily due to the aggressive marketing of consumer credit, particularly open-end credit products. Consumers may easily acquire access to credit, which, if fully used, places severe strain on their finances. When debts become excessive, the customer may be unable to make loan payments when due. At best, the consumer may only be able to make minimum monthly payments, and eventually may need to make choices concerning which loans to pay and which not to pay.

When financial problems develop, most consumers have a priority order in which they repay loans. Debts are generally paid in the following order

- mortgage or rent
- other primary residence secured loan—equity line or second mortgage

- automobile loan
- other secured loan (boat or recreational vehicle)
- credit card account
- unsecured closed-end loan
- unsecured open-end line of credit

This order of priority has important implications for lenders and collectors, and it helps explain the variations in delinquency objectives and experiences on various loan portfolios.

Poor money management is revealed in many ways. The failure to plan for financial emergencies, establish a reasonable budget, organize finances, as well as the lack of self-control when purchasing goods can all contribute to problems. Poor financial management may be detected by examining the consumer's credit history and capacity at the time the loan is made, but, in many cases, problems do not appear until after the loan is made.

Marital breakups frequently leave both parties scrambling to get out of debt obligations. An income and debt structure that was in balance when the couple was one financial unit may be totally disrupted after the marriage breaks up. In many cases, one of the parties attempts to deny responsibility for the debts. In other cases, the marital breakup results in a reduced level of income or an increase in debts, and, consequently, the debts simply can no longer be handled.

Carelessness leads to some delinquencies. Those who can pay, but who are not strongly motivated to pay on time are careless. This type of customer can usually be identified by credit reports that show a history of delinquencies, but no reason for paying late other than sloppiness. This is evidence of weakness in handling financial responsibility.

Some loans simply should never have been made. They are the result of irresponsible lenders who compromised the bank's policies or used poor judgment. The result may be loans that will result in chronic collection problems or losses.

Fraud or intentional default is significantly different from the problems already discussed because they involve the deliberate attempt to avoid repaying an obligation. Fraud is an ongoing problem for consumer lenders. Most fraud is uncovered by the collection department after an account has been set up and the culprit has the bank's money. When they are detected, fraudulent accounts are typically removed from the mainstream collection effort and given to a specialist with the time and expertise needed to track down the responsible party.

Organization of the Collection Function

The collection function may be centralized or decentralized. The approach taken usually reflects the style, philosophy, and organization structure of the institution. In a centralized operation, collection specialists devote their full attention to the task of resolving delinquency problems. This approach allows for the development of high levels of expertise and enhances efforts to automate collection activities. Advocates of the centralized approach believe that collection specialists are more efficient and effective in handling delinquency problems.

In a decentralized environment, collection tasks may be handled by lenders and employees who also have other responsibilities. Some consumer credit managers prefer the decentralized approach because they believe lenders use more discretion in making credit decisions when they must collect their own loans, and that the lender may be more effective in collecting payments.

No matter which approach is used, the collection process must function smoothly if loan delinquencies and defaults are to be minimized. Essentials of a smooth operation are

- a highly automated system for handling early stage delinquencies
- the identification of delinquent accounts as soon as they are in default
- a system of tracking customer contacts and following up on repayment promises
- the development of enough information to allow collectors to work intelligently with delinquent customers
- the isolation of serious collection problems for handling by specialized collectors

Automation of the collection function is essential for large portfolios. Automated systems generally help speed up account handling, maximize productivity (as measured by the number of accounts handled per collector), and improve efficiency by providing more and timely information to collectors.

The Collection Cycle

The vast majority of consumer credit customers make their loan payments on time. Of those who go into default, the majority pay within 15 days of the due date. Those who do not pay within that time are the focus of most collection activity.

Stages of the Collection Cycle

Exhibit 13.3 presents the stages in the collection cycle for a typical closed-end loan product. Open-end products generally have a longer cycle and are not charged off until 180 days. Let's examine these stages and discuss the collection approaches, collection tools, and delinquency remedies that are used at each stage.

Most accounts that are in default—one day or more past due—do not pose a significant problem. The primary objective in this stage of delinquency is to eliminate as many of these accounts from a past-due status as possible before the problem becomes more acute, thus allowing more attention to be directed toward those accounts that are seriously delinquent. It is also the bank's objective to hold down the costs of this collection effort.

The distribution of accounts falling into the collection cycle is demonstrated in exhibit 13.4. The percentage of accounts entering the process may seem high, but payment is often made before the bank takes any action. Most customers respond to notices and the imposition of late charges, paying their accounts before or soon after the 15-day past-due point. Thus, by the time collectors become involved, the number of delinquent accounts has been reduced to a manageable size.

EXHIBIT 13.3   Collection Cycle

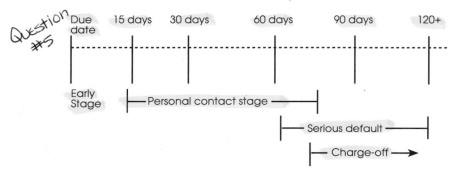

EXHIBIT 13.4   Percentage of Accounts Delinquent

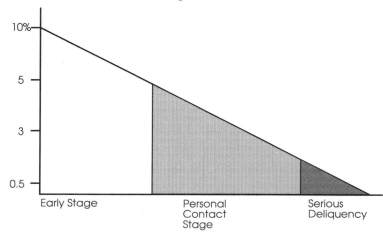

Early Stage of Delinquency

Question #5

The collection approach used in the early stage of loan delinquency is often highly automated, requiring little personal involvement. These two characteristics help to keep the costs of collections as low as possible.

The collection tools used at this early stage are letters, reminder notices, late charges, simple interest, and due date adjustments. A simple, inexpensive reminder notice is sufficient to bring in many payments. This is usually the first formal action taken by the collection department. The notice may be very low key, and may even contain a sales-oriented message.

Delinquency notices on closed-end accounts are typically mailed 10 days after the due date. For an open-end account, notices are usually included on the billing statement, advising the customer that the payment is past due.

Late charges, imposed generally 10 to 15 days after the payment due date, provide another incentive for customers to make payments on time. Simple interest also encourages customers to pay on time. If the customer understands that late payments will cost more in terms of interest, he or she may be predisposed to make payments as soon as possible.

Due date adjustments can be an effective solution to a delinquency on some loans. This remedy may be desirable on closed-end loans when the due date coincides with a monthly shortfall in the customer's cash flow. For example, if the customer gets paid twice a month, and the loan payment is due at the same time as the mortgage payment, it may be very difficult to make both payments out of the same paycheck. By changing the due date, the bank reduces its costs, and the customer avoids late notices and late charges. This problem may not be as severe on open-end accounts since the customer frequently has a period of up to 25 days in which to make payments and can time the payment to his or her cash flow.

Personal Contact Stage of Delinquency

Question #5

The collection effort becomes more intensive once an account exceeds 15 days past due. At this point, a collector becomes involved. Direct contact is needed to identify the problem and resolve it in a manner acceptable to both the lender and the customer. The personal contact then continues until the delinquency is resolved, either by bringing the account current or by charging it off.

Problem-solving is an important aspect of successful collection practices. The objective is to first identify why the customer did not make the payment on time, then to determine how and when the payment can be made. A collector using this approach might say, "Mr. Jones, I notice that the payment on your car loan is past due. Can you tell me if you are having a problem and when you will be able to make the payment?" This is preferable to such structured questions as, "When are you going to make the payment?" or "When am I going to get my money?" The first approach is customer-oriented and is likely to elicit more information than the second approach. The key is to identify the problem in order to find the best solution.

Question #6

Some remedies available to collectors attempting to resolve delinquency problems are

- payment collection
- extension
- refinancing
- new loan
- insurance claim
- right of offset
- consumer credit counseling

The overwhelming bulk of delinquencies are resolved by having the customer make the delinquent payment by some mutually agreed upon date. Collectors should attempt to establish exactly when the customer will be making the past-due payment, why the payment will be made on that date (for example, customer payday; other source of cash due), and how the payment will be made (for example, brought in to the bank; sent by mail). This information allows the collector to follow up immediately on broken promises. Consider the following example:

> Mr. Jones's loan payment is 20 days past due. When called by the bank's collector, Mr. Jones says he will make his payment on Friday. The collector asks, "Why Friday?" Mr. Jones replies, "That's when I get paid." The collector then asks, "How will you be making your payment?" To which Mr. Jones responds, "I will bring the payment in to your Main Street branch." This information seems reasonable and lets both parties

know what to expect. The collector should review the account the following Monday to ensure that the payment has been made as promised. Timely follow-up on broken promises is essential to a sound collection effort.

Another collection remedy is a loan extension, also known as *reaging an account.* This remedy allows the customer to postpone or skip a payment. On a closed-end loan, payment may be postponed until the end of the loan, usually increasing the term of the loan by one month. Thus, the customer may skip his June payment, but resume regular payments in July. On an open-end loan, it simply means the customer is allowed to miss making a payment. The customer may be charged a fee for an extension in some states. In other instances, an additional interest cost is assessed.

Granting an extension is an appropriate collection remedy when the customer has missed one or two payments but is expected to be able to resume normal payments and eventually make up the delinquent payments. For example, if a customer was temporarily laid off due to a short-term plant closing, he may not be able to meet all his debt obligations. After the layoff, he is able to make payments on time again but cannot make up the delinquent payment. Granting an extension resolves the delinquency and preserves customer goodwill.

The use of extensions must be controlled by the manager of the collection department and monitored by divisional management. This tool can be used too liberally by collectors who are looking for easy ways to resolve delinquencies and reduce the number of past due accounts. The result is that serious delinquency problems may be hidden.

Refinancing—rewriting a closed-end loan to reduce monthly payments, change interest rates, or change other terms of the loan—may be an appropriate collection remedy if the customer is facing a cash flow squeeze and needs to reduce his level of debt. Sound refinancing reduces the customer's monthly payment by extending the number of payments, while possibly strengthening the bank's credit position by allowing it to gain additional collateral on the loan. This may be an appropriate solution when a customer has changed jobs and now has less income, resulting in a high debt-to-income ratio. Assuming the customer has a good credit history, and the bank is in a position to refinance the loan and reduce the customer's monthly payments, this may be the most appropriate collection remedy.

The best solution to some collection problems may be a new loan. Not only can a new loan resolve many minor delinquency problems, it can also have a positive effect on loan volume and customer relations. Consider the following example:

Ms. Adams is 16 days late with her loan payment. In response to the collector's call, Ms. Adams says, "I'm sorry, I'll make that payment today. I just had to pay for some more car repairs; it's getting to be a real drain." The collector responds, "Ms. Adams, our new car rates are a low 9.9 percent now, why don't you consider a new car, then you won't have to keep pouring money into that old car and have it drain your finances?" Many collectors, having the tools at their disposal to make such recommendations, are trained to think positively about their customer contacts and recognize loan opportunities.

Some delinquencies may be resolved by filing credit insurance claims. Identifying insurance claims should be an easy process. If the collector asks a customer why he has not made his payment on time, and the customer states that he has been out of work due to illness or injury, the collector should check to see if the customer has credit disability insurance. If he is covered, arrangements should be made to have a claim form processed. Potential credit life insurance claims are identified and pursued in a similar manner. To preserve goodwill, it is important that collectors act with discretion and sensitivity under these circumstances.

Some loan contracts give the bank the *right of offset*. This provision allows the bank to withdraw funds the customer has on deposit with it to make delinquent payments or pay the loan in full. Because the right of offset has repercussions for the customer's other account relationships with the bank, it should be exercised only as a last resort. To avoid creating overdrafts, immediate notification should be given to the customer when this action is taken.

Another remedy is to refer customers to a qualified credit counseling agency such as Consumer Credit Counseling, which is a nonprofit organization that assists consumers who find themselves deeply in debt. The counselors work with the consumer and the lending institution to devise a payment schedule that will repay all obligations and help the consumer avoid more drastic problems like bankruptcy. While there are a number of good credit counseling agencies available, some credit clinics have begun to operate in recent years. The objectives of such firms may be quite different than the not-for-profit credit counseling firms. Care should be exercised in working with these agencies to ensure that the consumer's long term best interests are being considered.

The primary methods of communicating with customers in the personal contact stage of the collection cycle are phone calls, letters, and direct contact. Direct contact is generally preferable to letters since more information can be obtained and the collector has the opportunity to work with the customer. Many collection departments have their less experienced collectors handle accounts that are 16 to 30 days past due, with more experienced collectors having responsibility for seriously delinquent accounts. Generally speaking, the longer a loan is in default, the more time and skill are required to resolve the problem.

Serious Delinquency Stage

The serious delinquency stage may occur at any time, depending on the particular circumstances. However, most collectors feel that any account more than 60 days in default is a serious problem. Serious delinquencies most often arise when customers declare bankruptcy; move in an effort to hide from creditors; die, leaving behind uninsured debt; or simply lose all regard for their responsibilities. These events may occur at any stage of the collection cycle, and, in some cases occur before a customer is even delinquent.

Accounts in this category require special attention and are often handled by specialists in skip tracing, fraud, or bankruptcy. These trained personnel have both the time and the expertise to handle the accounts effectively, freeing the bank to address more routine collection activities. *Skip tracing* is the process of locating customers who cannot be found at the employer's or home address shown on the bank records. As with fraud and bankruptcy cases, time-consuming and structured follow-up are required before serious cases of delinquency can be resolved.

Occasionally, the bank may enlist the assistance of outside resources, for example, agencies that specialize in repossessing collateral, a task that can be dangerous and almost always unpleasant. Attorneys and collection agencies may also be used to handle customers who are not responding to the bank's own collection staff. Letters or personal contact from an attorney often have a stronger impact on the delinquent customer than the efforts of the bank's collectors.

Collection remedies for seriously delinquent accounts include

- repossession
- collection suits resulting in judgments
- foreclosure
- wage garnishment
- bankruptcy

Repossession is an appropriate collection remedy when the customer is uncooperative, and the bank stands to recover some or all of its investment by selling the collateral securing its loan. Most states have laws governing how repossessions may be carried out and the customer's rights when collateral is repossessed. The customer usually has the right to redeem the collateral by bringing the account up-to-date and paying the cost of the repossession. If the customer does not redeem the collateral, the bank may sell it and apply the proceeds to the loan balance. The customer usually remains liable for any balance owed after the sale.

Another course of action is to pursue collection through the courts. If the bank can establish its claim and prove the customer is liable for the balance due on the account, it will be granted a judgment. This allows the bank to pursue collection by placing a claim against the assets of the debtor.

Foreclosure is the forced sale of real estate in order to satisfy a debt. Because of the consequences of this action, the procedures used are regulated by state law. The proceeds from the sale of property are generally distributed based on the order of claim. First mortgages are paid in full first, then second and subsequent mortgages, and judgments last. If the proceeds cover all debts and expenses, the excess must go to the consumer. This is also true on the sale of repossessed merchandise. It must be noted that state law variations can affect this distribution process.

Wage garnishments or attachments are permitted by some states to allow lenders to recover debts. A garnishment requires the customer's employer to send a certain percentage of the employee's wages directly to the bank until the debt is paid in full. This type of arrangement provides a strong incentive for customers to work out their delinquency problems before they become this serious.

Bankruptcy

Bankruptcy is a major problem for consumer credit lenders, individual consumers, and society at large. Unfortunately, the problem is growing. According to American Bankers Association surveys, in 1990 over half of all credit card losses and nearly one-third of all installment credit losses that year were due to bankruptcy. While these results occurred during a recessionary period, they nevertheless demonstrate the magnitude of the problem.

Customers who are deeply in debt and unable to pay their debts when due may resort to filing for bankruptcy. Although it is an event to be avoided, there are occasions when, through no fault of their own, individuals find it necessary to seek protection under bankruptcy laws. Federal and state bankruptcy laws were intended to eliminate the social stigma and other destructive aspects associated with early practices such as debtor prisons. Instead, the intent was for debtors to be rehabilitated, while treating creditors fairly. Subsequent legislation has attempted to balance these two objectives, with varying levels of success. Liberalized bankruptcy legislation in 1978 and changing values and attitudes undoubtedly led to a significant increase in bankruptcy claims and to what many lenders feel are abuses of the process. These concerns resulted in revisions of the law that went into effect in 1984.

Two types of bankruptcy may be pursued by consumers: Chapter 7 and Chapter 13.

❑ **Chapter 7** is designed to discharge all of the consumer's debts. The law allows consumers to redeem property for personal, family, or household use, and state laws allow consumers to exempt many assets from distribution to creditors. Secured creditors may be protected only up to the value of the collateral as determined by the court. Thus, if the bank has a car loan with a balance of $10,000, but the car's value is determined to be $6,000, the debtor could pay $6,000 and keep the car. The bank would take a $4,000, nonrecoverable loss. Unsecured creditors are likely to suffer a total loss on their loan balances.

❑ **Chapter 13**, also known as a "wage earner plan," was developed as an alternative for consumers who sincerely wanted to repay debts, but were unable to do so under the existing contractual arrangements. At the same time, debtors may seek total discharge from specific debts.

The court will ultimately approve a plan, usually providing for significantly lower monthly payments, to enable the debtor to repay obligations from future income.

A bank may be able to recover money loaned to a customer declaring bankruptcy by filing a claim with the court and petitioning for recovery of its investment. Banks often fight bankruptcy filings when they feel the customer misrepresented his financial condition or filed a false financial statement. The court may agree to release collateral to secured lenders, allowing them to repossess and sell the goods in order to recover all or a portion of the loan balance. The court may also establish a repayment plan under Chapter 13 of the *Bankruptcy Code,* which provides for the restructuring of debts by the court in a manner that would permit creditors to be paid back over a period of time. On the other hand, the bank may be unable to recover any of its investment from a bankrupt consumer, particularly if its debt is unsecured and the customer has no assets and very limited resources.

Lenders have also taken a more proactive approach to bankruptcy. Bankruptcy predictor models and scoring systems have been developed by leading credit reporting agencies and credit-scoring providers. These systems help screen out high potential bankruptcy consumers and allow for timely action to block credit lines on a timely basis.

Charge-Offs

Charging accounts off as a loss is the final stage in the loan collection cycle. It is not, however, the end of the bank's efforts to collect.

The collection manager reviews all accounts to be charged off during the month. This review is designed to check on the progress of the collection effort, evaluate alternatives to charge-off, and inform management of the dollar amount of loans scheduled for charge-off that month. If losses are lower than projected, management may elect to recognize some other accounts as losses even though they may not be at the point for required charge-off. (The Comptroller of the Currency requires national banks to recognize accounts as a loss when closed-end accounts reach 120 days past due and open-end accounts reach 180 days.) For example, an account may be charged to loss if the collateral has been sold and there is no hope of recovering the deficiency balance even though the account is not 120 days past due. On the other hand, if losses are higher than anticipated, management may elect to hold some accounts back from charge-off.

When an account is charged off, other actions are taken to report the loss to the appropriate credit reporting agencies and to set an action plan for future recovery efforts. The collector may give some guidance to the person in the salvage/recovery department that will help that individual begin pursuing recovery as quickly and efficiently as possible.

Accounts recognized as losses are actually charged against the bank's loan loss reserve account (see exhibit 13.5). As new loans are made, a percentage of the dollar volume is set up, or added to the loan loss reserve account, based upon the bank's historical loss experience and other factors. For example, if the loan loss rate was 1 percent, the loan loss reserve account would be increased by $10 for each $1,000 in new loan volume ($1,000 X 1% = $10). The balance in the account is reduced as individual loan accounts are charged off as losses. The loan loss reserve account is shown on the bank's balance sheet as a reduction in loans receivable.

EXHIBIT 13.5   **Loan Loss Reserve Account**

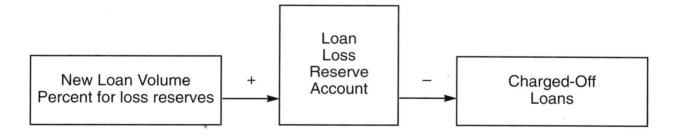

Recovery Operations

The emphasis in the recovery department is significantly different from that of the collection department. The collection department's goals are to maintain delinquencies and losses at acceptable levels, get accounts to a current status as quickly as possible, and maintain customer goodwill as much as possible. The recovery department is solely concerned with collecting as much of the money charged to loss as possible. This objective allows the recovery department to operate in very different ways from the collection department.

Charged-off accounts are reviewed to determine whether it is possible to recover any money on the account and, if so, who can best handle the recovery effort. Some accounts are abandoned and no further attempt made to recover the debt. For example, accounts are abandoned when the borrower is deceased and there is no estate, when the balance is too small to justify further recovery efforts, or when the account cannot be collected for legal reasons such as bankruptcy. If the recovery effort is to continue, the initial effort is usually handled by a bank employee. Accounts may also be referred to outside parties such as attorneys and collection agencies. These sources either charge a flat fee or work on a commission basis, keeping a certain percentage—normally one-third to one-half—of the amount collected.

The recovery collector or outside agent first attempts to work directly with the customer to arrange for repayment of the debt. In some cases, the collector settles for a lump sum that may be less than the balance owed. For example, the collector may agree to accept $750 for a $1,000 debt if the smaller amount is paid by a certain date. However, collectors generally try to recover the full amount owed.

If repayment cannot be arranged, the recovery specialist next attempts to find any assets the customer has that may be claimed to settle the debt. The initial credit application can be helpful in this regard, particularly if it includes a personal financial statement, tax returns, or other information such as the location of bank accounts. The search for assets should focus on tangibles, such as cars, homes, and boats; financial holdings, such as checking and savings accounts, stocks, and bonds; and sources of income. Any of these may provide the necessary leverage needed to collect a bad debt.

Once assets are located, collection is pursued through a combination of direct contact and legal action. Common approaches to recovery include judgments, garnishments, foreclosures, repossessions, and settlements. These strong actions can persuade customers to settle their debts, sometimes long after the loan was charged off.

The cost of recovery must always be balanced against the potential gain. It does not make sense to spend a lot of time and money on accounts when chances of recovery are slim or when the balance owed is small. Effort should be directed toward accounts that offer the best chance of recovery and the highest possible dollar value.

Summary

The collection and recovery functions are essential to the success of a sound consumer credit operation. Well-trained and motivated collectors can make the difference between retrieving a profitable bank asset and writing off an account as a loss. If the bank's loan collection and recovery departments are guided by realistic and attainable delinquency, loss, and recovery objectives, and are provided with the necessary support system, optimal results can often be achieved.

The collector has an array of collection tools at his or her disposal. The key task is to identify the customer's problem and then match it with the appropriate remedy. This must be carried out in a way that both encourages timely repayment and preserves the customer's goodwill. Serious delinquencies, on the other hand, require special skills to ensure that proper collection procedures are used and that strong action is taken as quickly as possible.

The recovery department operates in a less structured environment than the collection department. Its job is to recover as much of the bank's investment as possible, but it does not experience the time pressures and other constraints faced by those collecting active accounts. Money recovered on charged-off accounts can significantly improve the bank's charge-off record and contribute directly to overall profits.

Review Questions

Page 258-254

1. What are some of the objectives normally established for the bank's collection department? Why might different objectives be set for different loan products?

2. List some of the primary causes for consumer credit delinquencies. Is it possible to predict any or all of these at the time the loan is made? Pages 262-263

3. Give several examples of loan collection practices deemed illegal under the Fair Debt Collection Practices Act. - Page 261

4. Name an advantage of the decentralized approach to loan collection in a bank. What are the advantages of the centralized approach? Page 265

5. List the stages of the collection cycle and describe some of the characteristics of each stage. At what point in the collection cycle does a loan collector generally become involved in collecting the debt? - Pages 266-271

~ Page 268

6. Explain the problem-solving approach to loan collection.
7. What is the purpose of the loan recovery function? How does it differ from the operation of the collection department?

Optional Research

1. What are your bank's objectives for consumer loan delinquencies and losses? Are product differences taken into consideration?
2. Does your bank handle collections on a centralized or decentralized basis? Is the collection function automated or primarily manual? Is there a separate department handling the recovery function?

Consumer credit, like any other bank operation, must be steered by skillful hands if its potential for profit is to be fully realized. Now that you have learned all the basic, procedural, and technical information you need to function in a bank's consumer credit area, you are ready to explore the administrative aspects of the subject.

Part IV of *Consumer Lending* focuses on developing loan policies and managing the consumer credit area. Sound policies—if clearly stated and vigilantly enforced—give the consumer credit area its mission and character. Sound management—which involves planning, organizing, directing, and controlling—gives consumer credit policy its vitality and strength. Together, skillful policymaking and management steer the bank's consumer credit operation on the road to success.

Part Four
Consumer Credit Administration

14 Consumer Credit Policies

After reading this chapter, you will be able to

- ❏ list the objectives for the bank's formal loan policy statement
- ❏ describe the components of a sound loan policy and give examples of each component
- ❏ describe the specific elements typically included in the statement of the bank's terms and conditions for various types of loans
- ❏ discuss different approaches to granting credit authority and explain why this is a vital part of the lending policy

Purpose of a Formal Loan Policy

Question #1

The primary purpose of a consumer loan policy is to help officers make decisions in all aspects of the consumer credit operation. Informed and consistent decisions are the foundation of an efficient and effective operation. A formal loan policy enables the bank to

- ❏ serve the legitimate credit needs of the bank's market area
- ❏ establish guidelines for the bank's lending staff
- ❏ increase operational efficiency
- ❏ facilitate the accomplishment of the bank's consumer credit portfolio objectives—growth, volume, profits
- ❏ ensure compliance with applicable regulations

An effective consumer credit department depends on the development and use of a sound lending policy. A policy can be defined as a course or method of action to guide present and future credit decisions. Sound policy is developed in the context of a certain set of conditions. Therefore, credit policies should, and do, vary from one bank to the next, depending on the specific situation.

The bank's lending policy involves a dynamic, rather than static, process. Policies are not intended to be written and then forgotten. They must reflect and evolve with the bank's current philosophy and objectives and be responsive to the rapidly changing competitive environment.

Commercial banks, unlike some other financial institutions, have a legal responsibility to serve the borrowing needs of qualified customers located within their primary market areas. This is required by the Community Reinvestment Act, but it is also sound business practice.

Establishing guidelines for the bank's lending staff is vital to the development of a sound loan portfolio. In establishing guidelines, the two primary considerations are to ensure that credit decisions are made on a sound and consistent basis and that the bank develops a diverse loan portfolio that conforms with its overall goals.

The first consideration—providing guidelines that will result in consistent implementation of the bank's credit policies—can only be achieved by having a clear written policy and by maintaining a follow-up review to ensure lender compliance.

The second consideration—developing a diverse portfolio that conforms with the bank's goals—is always a concern of management. To ensure loan quality, an acceptable level of delinquency and loan losses must be defined by management. Banks with very conservative delinquency and loss goals emphasize the minimization of risk. They may require higher down payments, use lower debt-to-income ratios, and screen out even those applicants with minor derogatory information on their credit reports. In contrast, a bank with more liberal loss and delinquency goals may accept lower down payments, use higher debt-to-income ratios, and overlook minor negative information. Thus, the type of loan policy can help control the level of risk within the portfolio.

The loan policy should also indicate which types of loans the bank wishes to emphasize. Assuming the bank wants to aggressively promote its open-end credit products, it would use its loan policy to encourage lenders to sell those types of loans more aggressively than closed-end products. The bank might price its open-end products at lower rates and may even elect to use less stringent debt-to-income and credit history requirements. Achieving portfolio diversification also depends on having the bank's goals clearly communicated and supported with specific objectives at the branch or departmental level.

A clearly stated bank loan policy also helps avoid some of the following pitfalls:

❏ The lender, unsure whether a certain type of loan can be made, must either make an arbitrary decision or take time to call someone else.

❏ The lender incorrectly assumes the bank does not want a certain type of business and, therefore, refuses to take an application for a loan that the bank would accept.

❏ The lender, biased against people employed in certain jobs, rejects loan applicants simply on that basis.

❏ The lender was not informed of a recent policy change and continues to operate under the old guidelines.

These are examples of some of the problems that may occur when the bank does not have a sound and well-communicated lending policy. To avoid them, the bank should specify precise loan standards. Examples of clear lending specifications are

■ minimum down payment of 20 percent
■ maximum debt-to-income ratio of 45 percent
■ no loans to an applicant who has declared bankruptcy in the past seven years
■ no loans to an applicant living outside of the bank's trade area
■ minimum credit score of 190 points

If specifications such as these are incorporated into a bank's loan policy, the lender is spared the need to spend time on applications that do not meet the bank's credit requirements.

In contrast, the following statements exemplify unclear policy statements that are subject to interpretation:

■ Loans should not be made to applicants who have been at their address less than one year unless there are offsetting positive attributes. *This needs a definition of positive attributes.*

■ Applicants with any major derogatory credit history should be declined. *This needs a definition of major derogatory items.*

- Bill consolidation loans should not be made unless the applicant has been cross-sold on a higher loan amount. *The intent of this statement is unclear and seems arbitrary.*

The bank's loan policy should be coordinated with the bank's overall portfolio objectives. Tight credit policies do not complement an aggressive loan growth objective. Likewise, relatively lax lending policies are out of place when the bank is trying to clean up its loan portfolio or improve the quality of its asset base. For example, in an aggressive growth environment, the bank may offer 100 percent financing on cars and other depreciating value collateral, while, in a conservative environment, a 25 to 30 percent down payment may be required.

Lending policies also provide protection against regulatory violations. Sound credit policies reduce the opportunity for employees to willfully or unknowingly violate regulations. Combined with sound review procedures, they help to identify inadvertent compliance violations and ensure timely correction of errors. Indeed, when defending itself against claims of regulatory violations or when undergoing regulatory audits, the bank may offer its lending policy as evidence of its intent to comply with all regulations.

Developing a Sound Loan Policy

The bank's policy statement can be brief or it can be quite extensive depending on such factors as the size and complexity of the organization, the types of products offered, and the degree of management preference for detail. Regardless, a number of topics should be addressed to some degree in all consumer credit policy statements:

- ❏ geographic limits
- ❏ types of loans desired
- ❏ credit authority
- ❏ general terms and conditions
- ❏ compliance and loan review
- ❏ collection and charge-off

Geographic Limits

The lending policy should define the bank's primary trade area and, if appropriate, a secondary trade area. A bank's primary trade area for consumer credit products may vary with the type of product. Direct loans are generally restricted to a specific geographic area, while indirect loans and open-end products may extend over a broader geographic area.

Types of Loans Desired

The policy statement should state which types of loans the bank wishes to pursue and avoid. A clear statement should be made concerning loans to officers, directors, and employees of the bank. Federal Reserve *Regulation O* imposes restrictions on loans to the highest officers of the bank—executive vice president, president, chairman, and the board of directors—but there are generally no restrictions on loans to other bank employees. As a result, many banks view their own employees as promising candidates for loan products. When loans are made within the bank, the policy statement should define which employees are eligible, what underwriting requirements exist, and who will have the authority to approve these loan requests.

Another policy concern regarding loan types is to define undesirable loans. Management should exercise care in identifying and defining types of loans that it does not want in the bank's portfolio. Generally, loans in this category present high credit risk or are more appropriately handled by the commercial loan department. Loans fitting this description might include those for

- bill consolidations
- speculative purposes, such as investments or new businesses
- motorcycles
- corporations or partnerships
- home equity loans secured by investment properties

Credit Authority

The policy statement should set forth the bank's lending authority system and the decision-making approach to be used.

The power to grant lending authority is vested with the board of directors. As a practical matter, this authority is delegated to a senior operating officer or a committee. Those holding this authority are responsible for establishing lending limits for each lender and for monitoring the performance of the lending staff. Lenders who do not meet specific standards may lose their lending authority or have it reduced.

The policy statement should also specify the procedures for approving loans. The loan approval system may take the form of individual lending authorities, loan committees, or a combination (see exhibit 14.1). Loan committees are generally not appropriate for approving consumer loans, which usually require quick response times and involve lower dollar amounts and a high volume of applications. However, committees are often used for very large consumer loan requests such as airplane and boat loans over $200,000. The size and less urgent nature of these requests may allow time for committee consideration. Another option in handling larger or special loan requests is to allow lenders to combine their credit authorities. This ensures that at least two lenders have looked at a large loan request or have reviewed an adverse credit decision. The sample lending authority structure depicted in exhibit 14.1 provides a clear framework for handling credit decisions.

The actual decision-making system used by the bank should be described in the policy statement. Credit-scoring

EXHIBIT 14.1   Sample Consumer Loan Authority Schedule

Level	Unsecured	Secured	Minimum Qualifications
I	$2,500	$3,500	Must complete the bank's credit training program and have one year experience in handling loan applications
II	$5,000	$7,500	Must complete the bank's advanced lender training, have one year of lending experience, and have a satisfactory lending record
III	$10,000	$25,000	Must have three years of a satisfactory lending record and complete the consumer credit review course
IV	$25,000	$50,000	Reserved for senior consumer credit department officers who have proven lending records

Note: Loans over the lender's authority are referred to the regional consumer credit officer. Level III and Level IV officers may combine their authorities to approve unsecured loans up to $50,000 and secured loans up to $100,000. Loans over those amounts must be submitted to the consumer credit committee for final approval. All closed-end loan applications that are rejected must be signed off by two lenders.

systems offer a more precise approach to lending and require less explanation than judgmental systems, which are more subjective.

General Terms and Conditions

The loan policy should define how the bank measures the applicant's capacity, character (as reflected in his or her credit history), and collateral risk. As capacity is a key element in evaluating credit risk, it is critical to quantify it. For example, the applicant's debt-to-income ratio may not exceed 40 percent of gross monthly income. Thus, if the customer's gross monthly income is $2,000, the maximum amount of debt payments, including the new loan payment, would be $800.

The debt-to-income ratio can be calculated in many ways. The ratio may be based on gross or net income, and any outstanding revolving debt may be valued at current balances or as if the accounts were being fully used. Likewise, variable rate debt may be figured at its current level or at a higher level to allow for possible interest rate increases.

An applicant's credit history has been identified as one of the most important variables in predicting future behavior. However, interpreting credit history is not always a simple task. The lending policy usually focuses on what factors in the applicant's credit should be interpreted as unacceptable and therefore lead to automatic rejection of the application. Prior bankruptcies, repossessions, judgments, foreclosures, charge-offs, and installment loan accounts delinquent 90 or more days are often cited as reasons for rejecting a loan. If such conditions should lead to automatic rejection, the loan policy should clearly communicate that intent. However, if exceptions are to be made, the reasons for considering an exception should also be defined. For example, some lenders consider loans to applicants who have experienced bankruptcy if the bankruptcy was due to a medical crisis. Similarly, exceptions could be made for those who have had small judgments against them, delinquencies on department store accounts, or voluntary repossessions.

Collateral risk requirements should also be spelled out in the lending policy. The kinds of collateral that are acceptable, and the amount that may be borrowed against various collateral, should be clearly itemized. Exhibits 14.2 through 14.4 present sample loan policies that illustrate some of the detail that might be included.

Notice that the policy shown in exhibit 14.2 sets forth precise guidelines for determining acceptable collateral, the maximum loan amounts, terms, documentation, and insurance requirements. Note also that the lender has some flexibility on the down payment requirement on an automobile loan.

The policy statement shown in exhibit 14.3 is not intended to be complete, but rather illustrates a few of the unique considerations that should be taken into account when making a marine loan.

EXHIBIT 14.2 Sample Automobile Loan Policy

Automobile Loans	Maximum Advance	Maximum Term
New automobiles	100 percent of dealer invoice	Advance up to $7,500—48 months Advance over $7,500 —60 months
Used automobiles	100 percent of wholesale value	Current model—48 months 1-2 years old—36 months 3-4 years old—30 months 5-6 years old—24 months

Automobile models over six years old are not eligible. All vehicles must be covered by physical damage and liability insurance coverage with $250 maximum deductible. The bank must have first lien on all vehicle loans. The suggested down payment on all automobile loans is 20 percent; however, the lender may grant an exception as long as the total advance is less than the maximum advance as just defined. Required documents:

- consumer credit note and disclosure statement
- security agreement
- copy of insurance policy naming bank as loss payee
- certificate of title
- copy of the bill of sale

The abbreviated policy statement shown in exhibit 14.4 provides clear guidance to all lenders regarding some of a bank's requirements for a home equity line account.

It is helpful to supplement a policy statement with a procedures manual that provides further guidance regarding the proper preparation and handling of all necessary documents. For example, detailed procedures may be developed to explain how to get the bank's lien on a car title and how to verify insurance coverage before the loan is made. The two items—policies and procedures—are often presented in a single manual that can provide answers to virtually any question lenders may have.

EXHIBIT 14.3 Sample Marine Loan Policy

Eligible collateral: All boats that are titled in the states of Maryland or Virginia or are documented with the U.S. Coast Guard. Outboard motors and trailers may be financed if they are purchased with the boat.

Ineligible collateral: Wooden vessels, boats to be used for charter, and vessels used for business purposes.

Age	Maximum Advance	Maximum Term
New boats	100 percent invoice	180 months
Used boats		
1-5 years old	80 percent of high book value	180 months (for advance over $15,000)
		12 months per $1,000 (for advance under $15,000)
6-10 years old and older boats	75 percent of high book value or marine survey	180 months (for advance over $15,000)
		12 months per $1,000 (for advance under $15,000)

Rates:

New boats: Fixed—11 percent for loans up to 60 months only
Variable—Prime + 2 percent

Used boats: Fixed—12 percent for loans up to 60 months only
Variable—Prime + 2.5 percent

Refinancing: 1 percent over the rates just quoted

Marine Survey: A marine survey is required to establish the value of all boats more than five years old or when the advance is $10,000 or more.

Federal Documentation: Required on all loans with a cash advance of $35,000 or more, or when the boat will be operated outside of the state. All other boats must be titled with the state.

EXHIBIT 14.4 Sample Home Equity Loan Policy

Eligible collateral: Owner-occupied homes located in Maryland, Virginia, and the District of Columbia
Lien position: The bank must have either a first or second mortgage position
Maximum advance: 75 percent of the appraised value of the home, minus the first mortgage balance
Rate: Wall Street Journal prime rate plus 2 percent
Other requirements:

- property must be appraised by a certified appraiser and approved by the bank
- property must be the applicant's primary residence
- property must not be used for commercial purposes
- properties located in a flood zone must be covered by proper flood insurance
- the three-day Truth in Lending recission period may not be waived under any circumstances
- bank must be named as loss payee on the homeowner's insurance policy

Loan policies should provide clear guidelines, but they should not be completely inflexible. Provisions must be made for identifying and handling situations that justify an exception to the standard loan policy. For example, although an applicant may fail to meet the bank's credit requirements, an exception may be warranted when the loan is to be fully secured by a savings account with the bank. In this case, the bank may want to make an exception contingent upon the customer having an acceptable credit history and meeting the bank's debt-to-income ratio.

Requests for exceptions often arise when the applicant is a "good" customer of the bank. In these cases, it is important that the bank define "good" by using quantitative measures, such as balances in depository accounts, number of services used, length of account relationship, or profitability of the customer's accounts.

Compliance and Loan Review

Loan policy should establish responsibility for the compliance and loan review functions. A compliance officer—the individual charged with establishing controls necessary to ensure compliance with regulations and the bank's policies—must be identified. The tasks performed by the loan review department should also be itemized.

Collection and Charge-Off

The lending policy should also define the bank's practices regarding the handling of delinquent accounts and charge-offs. Specific attention should be given to defining the point at which delinquent accounts will be charged off as a loss to the bank. More detailed collection department policies and procedures should be distributed to those responsible for actually collecting delinquent accounts. A sample policy statement is shown as exhibit 14.5.

EXHIBIT 14.5 Sample Loan Charge-Off Policy

Closed-end loans: Loans will be charged off no later than 120 days past due unless one of the following conditions exists:

- the collateral securing the loan will be sold within the next 30 days, resulting in a full recovery of the balance due
- firm arrangements have been made with the customer to bring the account current or pay off the balance within the next 30 days

Open-end accounts: Open-end accounts will be charged off no later than 180 days past due unless the line is secured, and one of the conditions just noted applies.

Summary

A bank's loan policy plays a key role in guiding the lending and support personnel in making decisions. A loan policy should improve uniform decision-making and operational efficiency by clearly communicating goals and objectives. Lending policy should be viewed as a dynamic, rather than a static, process. To optimize results in the consumer credit market, policy may be adjusted in response to changing market conditions and bank objectives.

It is important that the bank's loan policy be clear and comprehensive enough to cover the major aspects of each loan type. However, policies should not be too restrictive, allowing loan officers flexibility when appropriate.

Review Questions

1. Why should a bank institute a formal loan policy? Does a formal policy interfere with a consumer lender's ability to exercise judgment in the lending process? ~Page 281
2. In what way does a formal lending policy help curb regulatory violations? How does it help improve the bank's efficiency? ~Page 284
3. List six categories that should be covered in the bank's lending policy statement. ~ Page 284
4. What are some of the items typically spelled out under the terms and conditions for various types of loan products? ~ Page 287
5. Why is it important to spell out clearly how the bank's credit authority policy works? ~ Page 285-286

Optional Research

1. How is your bank's credit authority policy structured? Briefly summarize the various lending authorities specified. What requirements exist for being granted a given level of credit authority?
2. Does your bank's loan policy specify desirable and undesirable types of loans?
3. Compare your bank's terms and conditions for several types of loans—cars, second mortgages, credit cards—and identify any differences. Can you explain why the differences exist?

15   Managing the Consumer Credit Function

After reading this chapter, you will be able to

- ❏ list the elements of the management and planning process
- ❏ discuss the steps in the planning process and describe their implications for managing the consumer credit operation
- ❏ identify the types of objectives that should be established for consumer credit and give examples of typical objectives
- ❏ discuss the importance of developing and maintaining controls and give examples of how such controls are used to achieve optimal performance

The Management and Planning Process

Managing the consumer credit business involves planning, organizing, directing, and controlling the bank's activities in the market. The management and planning process for consumer credit has a cyclical nature and relies on the close interrelationship of the parts of the process. Exhibit 15.1 presents the elements of the process and illustrates the flow of activities.

Planning

The consumer credit management process begins with planning. The plan identifies the direction in which the bank wishes to go and the strategies it will use to reach its objectives. The planning process involves three basic steps: situation analysis, establishment of objectives, and formulation of the marketing mix.

EXHIBIT 15.1   The Management and
                Planning Process

Question #1

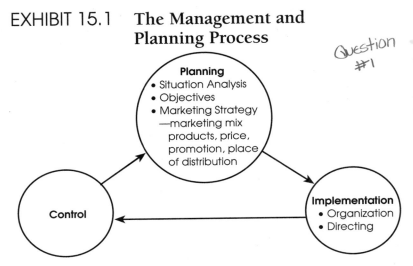

Planning
- Situation Analysis
- Objectives
- Marketing Strategy
  —marketing mix
  products, price,
  promotion, place
  of distribution

Control

Implementation
- Organization
- Directing

Conducting a Situation Analysis

A situation analysis answers the question, "Where are we now?" Finding the answer involves an analysis of the external and internal environments to identify both opportunities and problems.

A study of the competitive environment reveals who the bank's major competitors are, what products they are offering, their pricing practices, and their general strategies. Note that the bank's competitors may be different for each product. This analysis enables the bank to compare its products and strategies with those of the competition, and also identifies the bank's strengths and weaknesses in the market.

A study of the economic environment reveals the status of and trends in the economy of the bank's market area. This helps the bank focus on opportunities—such as market areas that are growing rapidly and may be underserved—or problems— such as rising unemployment or inflation possibly resulting in reduced demand for credit and an increase in delinquencies and losses. The study of the economic environment should also identify which segments of the market are growing most rapidly and which are stagnant or declining. The bank may then wish to focus on the segments it has identified and offer product lines that possess the greatest future growth potential.

A study of the social environment reveals changing attitudes, life-styles, and values that may affect the market. The trend toward smaller family units, more single-parent heads of households, and more two-income families may have some effect on the need for credit and on credit underwriting practices. Therefore, trends like these should be monitored and responded to by the bank. For example, rising divorce rates and increases in the number of women pursuing careers led some banks to change their underwriting policies in the 1960s, years before these changes were mandated by the Equal Credit Opportunity Act.

Another element the bank should study is the regulatory environment. The bank should anticipate regulatory changes that will help its efforts in the market and also prevent unwanted legislation. The bank must also act defensively to fight legislation that would damage its position in the market. For example, suppose a state legislator introduces a bill that would prohibit lenders from repossessing cars other than between the hours of 9 a.m. and 5 p.m. Such legislation would greatly increase the cost of repossession and the ability of consumers to hide the bank's collateral. Consequently, banks in the state might decide to join together to prevent the bill from becoming law.

The bank must also study its internal environment to identify its strengths and weaknesses. Relevant issues include staffing, training, support systems, products, asset quality, and profitability. As part of this process, the role consumer credit is to play in relation to the bank's other services should be delineated.

After analyzing its internal environment, the bank might find that its costs are lower than many of its competitors, giving it an advantage in the market. On the other hand, it may find that its home equity line product is priced higher and has higher monthly payment requirements than competing products. These findings may lead to changes in the bank's pricing practices.

Establishing Objectives

Once the situation analysis is completed, the bank should address the question, "Where do we want to go?" Objectives may be established for a number of key aspects of the consumer credit portfolio, including

- loan diversity
- loan outstandings
- loan volume
- delinquency and loss levels
- recoveries
- fee income
- operating expenses
- profits

The level of detail in the statement of objectives varies from bank to bank, but it is generally desirable to establish specific objectives for each product in the consumer credit portfolio. This helps managers perform their management tasks more effectively. For example, if delinquencies and losses are higher than the objectives specify for indirect automobile loans, corrective action can be focused on that part of the portfolio without detracting from other products. The bank could change its underwriting policies only on indirect loans, or only in regard to a particular dealer, to resolve the problem.

Formulating a Marketing Strategy

Having established where the bank wants to go, managers may focus on the strategies to be used or, "How are we going to get there?"

To achieve marketing objectives, managers manipulate the elements of the marketing mix—products, price, promotion, and the place of distribution. This is the creative part of the management process because it entails developing strategies to create a unique market position designed to meet the objectives. It is also a dynamic, rather than static, process since it must respond to changes in the external environment.

For example, as the 1986 Tax Reform Act moved toward final approval, many banks developed aggressive new strategies to market home equity line products. Banks that did not yet offer the product had to quickly develop one; others quickly intensified their promotional programs to bring their existing product to the attention of more potential customers. Moreover, the more aggressive banks adjusted all of the elements of the marketing mix to achieve their objectives. For instance, many adjusted their prices—offering low introductory rates and no-fee plans—and changed their place of distribution to include applications by telephone and mail.

In specifying its marketing mix, a bank blends products, pricing, promotion, and place of distribution to achieve the best marketing plan. Let's look at some recent trends in the elements of the marketing mix.

❑ **Products** The consumer credit product line has expanded with the biggest change coming in the development of open-end revolving credit products. Product features have also changed, with wider use of simple interest, simple language documents, and more flexibility for consumers and lenders in structuring loans.

❑ **Pricing** Consumer credit products are now offered on both a fixed- and variable rate basis by many banks. Loan fees have also become an important source of income on many types of loans. Finally, creative pricing, low introductory rates, and loan sales, have been used to achieve bank objectives.

❑ **Promotion**   Consumer loan products are still promoted through all available media, but the themes have changed, in many cases, to more effectively target selected segments of the consumer market. The use of direct mail and telemarketing has been increased, and banks have successfully used aggressive prescreened and preapproved promotional programs.

❑ **Place of distribution**   Increased emphasis has been given to providing credit to consumers when, where, and for whatever purposes they deem appropriate. Open-end products do this, but lenders have also enhanced their ability to provide nearly the same level of service on many closed-end loans. Finally, banks have moved beyond their branch and dealer distribution systems by delivering loan products by mail directly to the consumer's home.

Implementation

The implementation phase of the planning process entails the activities of organizing and directing.

Organizing

Organizing involves structuring the lending process to be effective and efficient. An effective organization is one that accomplishes the objectives established at the beginning of the planning process, reaches the market in a manner that generates the desired level of business, and provides quality service to the bank's customers at the lowest possible cost.

The bank needs to tailor its organization to the unique characteristics of the market it serves and the products it offers. For example, in organizing the management of its direct loan portfolio, a bank might emphasize its branch network and the personal selling skills of customer contact employees. The same bank might manage its credit card operation through a centralized department that uses direct mail with a reach far beyond the bank's branches.

The **effectiveness** of the bank's management organization is measured by the

- growth of loan outstandings

- generation of loan applications and volume
- level of delinquencies and losses
- additional business brought in by cross-selling and loan structuring efforts
- compliance with regulations and bank policy

A successful management organization is able to meet the bank's goals and objectives in each of these areas. An **efficient** organization, on the other hand, is one that provides a high level of service at the least possible cost. Efficiency is measured by the

- manner in which applications are taken
- time and expense to make a credit decision
- service turnaround time—from application, to decision, to loan closing
- accuracy and timeliness of loan servicing, including payment processing and error resolution
- cost of collecting past-due and charge-off accounts

Ultimately, measuring organizational effectiveness and efficiency involves both quantitative and qualitative factors that have an impact on the overall success of the consumer credit function.

Directing

Directing is the second part of the implementation stage. Management must ensure that the organization remains focused on the objectives and is moving in the right direction at the required pace. Direction begins with establishing policies and procedures that guide decision making and actions, ensuring consistency and soundness in the operation. Clear and well-conceived policies result in the development of loan portfolios that enable the bank to achieve its asset quality objectives, while encouraging the development of profitable business.

Providing direction is a daily activity. It includes training and developing the skills of lenders, collectors, loan interviewers, accountants, customer service representatives, and other personnel to perform their jobs in efficient and effective ways. The task of directing also includes continually looking for ways to improve the operation.

Control

Management must monitor the performance of the consumer credit department to ensure that all of the elements are functioning as they should and that the bank is moving toward its objectives. The consumer credit operation has several vital control points. These include

- the loan review group, which monitors loan documents for accuracy, completeness, and compliance with the regulations and bank policy
- the compliance officer, who reviews the bank's policies, procedures, forms, and other elements of the bank's programs to ensure regulatory compliance
- the collection department, which provides data regarding loan quality and any adverse patterns that may be developing
- management reports, which identify how lenders, branches, and the bank as a whole are performing in relation to objectives

Deviations from objectives call for an analysis of the problem and corrective action. The following examples show how a bank's consumer credit objectives can be derailed, and the actions needed to get them back on track:

- If the consumer credit department is not meeting its objectives for loan outstandings and volume, it may need to reduce its rates, increase promotional efforts, or pursue other segments of the market that offer greater growth potential.
- If the indirect loan department is not meeting its service objective to provide three-hour turnaround on all applications, it may need to increase staff or improve the flow of credit investigations.
- If delinquencies and losses on unsecured lines of credit accounts are higher than targeted, the bank may need to change its underwriting policy or improve the quality of the collection effort.
- If a particular loan employee is making an unacceptable level of documentation errors, he may need additional training or be relieved of this responsibility.

If these deviations from objectives are resolved quickly, the consumer credit operation should remain efficient and effective and the bank should attain its profit objectives.

Summary

The management and planning process is a dynamic one in which the bank constantly adjusts to the market while remaining focused on its key objectives. The process affects every aspect of the consumer credit department; indeed, it ties all of the various tasks, functions, and strategies into a meaningful whole.

Sound management and planning systems are critical considerations in assuring the bank's success in an increasingly challenging and complex consumer credit market. As the market continues to evolve, it is clear that the successful bank will need to effectively manage change and find a niche in the market that will enable it to meet its short- and long-term objectives.

Review Questions

1. What question does situation analysis address? Page 294
2. List some areas in which management should set specific objectives for the consumer credit portfolio? — Page 295
3. Briefly define the four elements of the marketing mix. Pages 296+297
4. Name some control tasks that are built into a typical consumer credit operation? — Page 299
5. List the steps in the management and planning process. In which area do managers spend most of their time? — Page 293 & 298

Optional Research

1. Find out what your bank's objectives are for the current year in the area of loan growth and loan volume. Are specific objectives set in these areas?
2. What are some of the ways your bank controls its consumer credit operation? What happens to lenders who have excessively high loan losses?

Notes

1. Michaelman, Irving S., *Consumer Finance: A Case History in American Business,* 2d Ed., Frederick Fell, Inc. (New York, 1966), p. 88.
2. Ibid., p. 88.
3. Ibid., p. 89.
4. Plummer, Wilbur C., "Consumer Credit in Colonial Philadelphia," *The Pennsylvania Magazine of History and Biography,* (October 1942), p. 396.
5. Michaelman, op. cit., p. 74.
6. Michaelman, op. cit., p. 80.
7. Ibid., p. 108.
8. Porter, Sylvia., *New Money Book for the 1980s,* Doubleday & Company, Inc. (Garden City, 1979), pp. 78-79.
9. Fousek, Peter G., "Prerequisites for the Growth of Consumer Installment Credit," *Journal of Finance,* Volume 13 (May 1958), pp. 166-67.
10. Tobin, James., "Consumer Debt and Spending: Some Evidence from Analysis of a Survey," *Consumer Installment Credit,* Volume I, Part II, p. 543.
11. Dunkelberg, William C., and F. P. Stafford., "Debt in the Consumer Portfolio: Evidence from a Panel Study," *American Economic Review,* Volume 61 (September 1971), p. 611.

Glossary

account balance   The difference between the total credits and the total debits to an account.

account holders   The owners of an account who have the authority to deposit and withdraw funds.

accounts receivable   The amount of money owed to a business by its customers for goods and services already provided.

accrue   To accumulate between payments. In consumer credit transactions, interest charges accumulate from the date one payment is due until the due date of the next payment.

acquisition costs   The amount of money spent to make a loan, including marketing, interviewing applicants, investigating the credit risk, gathering and processing documents, and making the credit decision.

actuarial interest   Interest costs that allow a lender to take the amount of a missed or insufficient payment and add it to the unpaid principal of the loan. All subsequent interest charges are calculated against this new sum and not the original principal.

add-on interest   A method for calculating interest costs by taking a percentage of the desired loan amount and adding it to the principal to calculate the total amount the borrower will repay.

adverse action   The refusal to grant credit either in the amount or according to the terms requested by the applicant.

adverse action notice   A document that explains to an applicant the reason credit has been denied.

amortization schedule   A table that shows the amount of principal and interest due for each loan payment and the remaining unpaid balance after each payment is made.

annual percentage rate (APR)   The total interest costs of a loan expressed as an annualized percent and computed by multiplying the periodic rate of interest (the rate charged each billing period) by the number of periods in a year. Truth in Lending regulations set specific formulas for computing the APR.

applicant   A person or business that requests or receives funds from a lending institution.

appraisal   A report prepared by an expert estimating the current market value of a property.

appreciating value collateral　Assets pledged as collateral that increase in value over the life of the loan.

Article 9　The sections of the Uniform Commercial Code that govern the documentation of loans secured by personal property.

B

balance sheet　A detailed listing of the financial condition of an individual or a business at a given point in time, including total assets, total liabilities, and net worth.

Bankruptcy Code　The federal laws that govern legal proceedings of those who are no longer able to pay their debts. Under Chapter 7 of the code, the debtor is relieved of financial obligations, and assets are liquidated to pay creditors. Chapter 13 of the code allows the debtor to "reorganize" the debt and make partial or full repayment over a 5-year period without fear of legal action from creditors.

basis point　A change in interest rates or yields expressed as 1/100 of one percent.

bill consolidation　The borrowing of funds to pay off multiple and often overdue debts. The borrower then owes only one creditor with loan payments usually extended over a longer period of time.

billing cycle　The period between regularly scheduled dates or days when customers' bills are mailed.

blockbusting　The practice of directing prospective home buyers to a specific neighborhood in an effort to scare property owners into selling at below market prices.

bond　A certificate of debt issued by a corporate or municipal organization, usually with a maturity of 5 years or more, that promises to pay interest at regular intervals and to repay the principal at a future date.

book　To enter an account or loan into a bank's records.

brokerage firm　A financial company that handles the purchase and sale of stocks, bonds, and other securities for its customers.

buy rate　The rate of interest a bank will charge on loans it buys from dealers of consumer goods such as autos and mobile homes.

call provision　A clause in a loan contract that allows the lender to demand payment in full at any time.

captive finance company   A finance company, owned by a large corporation, that finances consumer purchases of the parent company's products.

cash flow   The amount of money available to a company or individual for spending after operating expenses are deducted from gross income.

cash management account (CMA)   A customer account that combines traditional brokerage services (the ability to buy and sell stocks and invest in money market funds) with traditional banking services (check-writing privileges, a credit card, and a line of credit). The CMA was first introduced in 1977 by Merrill Lynch.

cash value life insurance   The value of an insurance policy based on the dollar amount of premiums paid.

certificate of deposit   A document issued when funds are deposited into an interest-bearing account at a financial institution for a specified time ranging from 7 days to 7 years.

charge-off   The process of writing off debts that a bank no longer expects to be able to collect.

chattel mortgage   A loan made for personal property, such as equipment or automobiles, rather than for real estate, such as buildings or land. In these loans, the personal property is pledged to the lender to guarantee that the debt will be repaid.

check overdraft line   A line of credit on a checking account. Checks that exceed the balance of the account are paid out of the line of credit and not returned because of insufficient funds.

Civil Rights Act of 1968   A law prohibiting discrimination on the basis of race, color, religion, sex, or national origin.

close   The process by which all pertinent loan documents are signed and funds are disbursed to the borrower.

closed-end loan   A credit arrangement in which the borrower and lender agree on the total amount being loaned and the number, size, and due dates of each payment.

closing costs   The costs a borrower must pay when a mortgage loan is finalized, including an origination fee, title insurance, attorney's fees, a property survey, and prepaid expenses, such as taxes and insurance.

coapplicant   A person who joins with one or more others in requesting or receiving funds from a lending institution.

collateral   Assets pledged by a borrower to a lender to guarantee a loan. These assets become the property of the lender if the borrower fails to repay the borrowed funds.

comaker A person who signs for a loan made to another person. The comaker does not receive the funds but is jointly and equally liable for repaying the debt if the borrower fails to do so.

commercial bank A financial company with chief functions of accepting deposits and making loans.

commission Compensation computed as a percentage of new business or sales for which an employee is responsible.

community property Property that is owned jointly and equally by a husband and wife as a result of marriage.

Community Reinvestment Act (CRA) A law that encourages financial institutions to meet the credit needs of their local communities, especially the needs of low- and moderate-income neighborhoods. Regulatory agencies are authorized to evaluate CRA performance when considering an application from an institution. The law, Title VIII of the Housing and Community Development Act, became effective November 1978. Major amendments to CRA were released August 9, 1989, and additional regulatory requirements were consequently developed.

compliance program The policies and procedures followed by a financial institution to assure it is obeying all federal and state laws and regulations.

Comptroller of the Currency A federal office responsible for chartering, examining, and regulating national banks.

conspicuous consumption Lavish or wasteful spending thought to enhance social prestige.

consumer credit market The segment of the population that borrows money for personal purposes.

consumer credit outstandings The total dollar amount of unpaid balances on all consumer credit products, including loans, lines of credit, and credit cards.

Consumer Credit Protection Act A 1969 federal statute covering consumer credit activities. Popularly known as the Truth in Lending Act, this act requires disclosure of certain pertinent facts about loan rates and charges and applies to all lenders that extend credit to consumers.

Consumer Credit Restraint Program A federal program announced in March 1980 as part of a general government effort to curb inflation. The action imposed restraints on certain types of consumer credit and increased banks' reserve requirements.

consumer credit transaction The transfer of funds by a financial institution to an individual for personal use. The funds are made available for a specified period and the borrower agrees to pay a sum of money to the lender for their use.

Consumer Leasing Act   A 1976 law requiring that those who lease property for personal, family, or household use receive clear and accurate information about the item being leased and the terms of the lease agreement.

consummation   The point in time when the contractual relationship between borrower and lender begins.

cost of funds   The price a bank must pay to have funds available for loan, including factors such as the amount of interest it must pay on deposits and on funds it borrows from investors. This figure is an important consideration in setting loan interest rates.

counteroffer   A proposal to grant credit on terms different from those requested by the applicant.

coupon book   A set of forms that the borrower sends, one at a time, with each loan payment. Each coupon includes the borrower's name, loan number, and amount of payment due.

credit card   A plastic card (or its equivalent) used by the cardholder to obtain money, goods, or services, possibly under a line of credit established by the card issuer. The cardholder is billed for any outstanding balance.

credit clinic   A company in the business of advising consumers how they can improve their credit rating and resolve bad debts with their lenders.

credit decision   The process of determining whether to grant credit, to offer credit on terms other than those requested, or to deny credit.

credit disability insurance   Insurance offered to loan and credit card customers that will pay the balance of their debt if they become unable to earn an income.

credit life insurance   Insurance, offered to loan and credit card customers, that will pay the balance of their debt if they die before completing their payments.

credit limit   The maximum allowable unpaid balance on open-end credit such as credit cards or lines of credit.

credit record   A history of a prospective borrower's ability and willingness to pay debts on time.

credit report   A confidential report prepared for lenders that provides factual data about a prospective borrower's financial condition and standing with creditors.

credit reporting agency   A company hired by a lender to prepare a report on a prospective borrower's credit history and creditworthiness.

credit scoring   A statistical formula used to evaluate and rate credit applicants.

credit standards   Guidelines used by a lending institution to determine if an applicant is eligible to receive credit.

credit union   A financial institution formed by depositors with a common affiliation (for example, the same employer) in order to promote savings and offer short-term personal loans. A credit union is a cooperative organization in which depositors are called members and their deposits are treated as shares of ownership.

cross-selling   The practice of promoting financial services in addition to the one being used by an existing customer.

Cs of credit   Criteria, all beginning with the letter c, used by lenders to evaluate an applicant's creditworthiness. The number of criteria varies but generally includes character, capacity, capital, collateral, and conditions.

curtailments   Payments required by a bank from a dealer who has received a floor plan loan because the merchandise financed has depreciated to a value below the amount owed on it.

D

daily periodic rate   The interest rate that a creditor imposes on a daily basis on the outstanding balance in open-end credit such as a credit card or revolving charge account.

dealer floor planning   A loan for financing a retailer's inventory. The bank disburses funds to the dealer after specific goods sitting on the showroom floor are pledged as collateral. When this merchandise is sold, the lender is repaid.

dealer plan of operation   A business arrangement in which a financial institution buys loans from a dealer who sells consumer goods, such as automobiles and boats. The consumer buys and obtains financing from the dealer but directly repays the loan to the financial institution.

dealer recourse   The right of a bank to collect funds from a dealer who sold it a loan that has gone bad.

dealer reserve account   An account set up by a bank to hold the funds that accumulate because a dealer is granting loans at one rate of interest and selling them to the bank at a lower rate.

debt service   The total amount of interest and principal due on borrowed money.

debt-to-income ratio   A measure of creditworthiness computed by dividing the dollar amount of debts by total income.

default   The failure to comply with any of the terms of a loan agreement.

delinquency   The failure to make a loan principal or interest payment on time.

demand loan   A loan that does not have a specific due date but is repaid when the creditor asks for payment or when the borrower decides to make payment.

deposit base   The total dollar amount of customer deposits held by a financial institution.

depreciating value collateral   Assets pledged as collateral that decrease in value over the life of the loan.

depreciation   The process of decreasing in value or usefulness.

deregulation   The process of removing or liberalizing legal restrictions to promote competition. In recent years, the financial services industry has experienced price deregulation (removal of interest rate ceilings), product deregulation (regulatory approval to offer more diversified products and services), and geographic deregulation (expansion across state lines).

direct loan   A two-party lending arrangement in which the borrower obtains financing by dealing directly with a financial institution.

direct verification   An investigation of an applicant's credit history conducted by direct contact with creditors and employers.

disburse   To pay out money.

discount rate   A method of calculating interest costs by deducting the interest charges from the total amount of money being loaned.

Discover Card   An all-purpose credit card with related services created in 1985 by Sears, Roebuck and Company and marketed to merchants and consumers nationwide by their banking subsidiary Greenwood Trust Company.

disintermediation   The flow of funds out of interest-bearing accounts in financial institutions into other types of investments that yield a higher return.

disposable personal income   The amount of an individual's income available for spending and investment after payment of taxes.

dollars outstanding   The total dollar amount of all unpaid debts.

double financing   The fraudulent practice in which dealers or other borrowers apply for and receive loans for the same customer from two different banks.

dowry   The property that a woman brings to her marriage.

durable goods   Items, such as appliances, automobiles, and furniture, purchased by individuals for their use over a period of time, generally three years or longer.

economic cycle   A pattern of fluctuation in economic activity characterized by the four stages of expansion, contraction, recession, and recovery.

effective yield   The real, as opposed to the quoted, rate of interest. For example, a rate quoted as 8 percent may actually mean an annualized rate of 12 percent.

endorser   One who either signs or rubber stamps the back of a financial instrument that bears his or her name, such as a check or money order, in order to transfer the right to those funds to someone else.

Equal Credit Opportunity Act   A law that prohibits discrimination against credit applicants on the basis of their race, color, religion, national origin, sex, age, marital status, or receipt of income from public assistance programs. This law was passed as Title VII of the Consumer Credit Protection Act when it was amended in 1975.

Equal Housing Lender poster   A poster lenders must publicly display declaring that their lending practices comply with both the Fair Housing Act and the Equal Credit Opportunity Act.

equity   The difference between the amount of unpaid loan principal on a property and its current market value.

escrow account   An account established during a real estate transaction into which a borrower deposits funds either to cover future payments, such as taxes and insurance, or to put on hold until certain conditions of the contract have been met.

evergreen loan   A loan in which no provisions have been made to pay of the principal.

exposure   The amount of loss (the net principal amount still owing) that a lender would have to absorb if a borrower defaulted.

Fair Credit Billing Act   A law that requires creditors to notify customers of their rights and the procedure for making complaints about billing errors. The act, a 1974 amendment to the Truth in Lending Act, also sets requirements for resolving these errors within a specified time.

Fair Credit Reporting Act A 1971 law that gives an individual the right to examine his or her file at a credit-reporting agency and establishes procedures for resolution of any errors in that file.

Fair Debt Collection Practices Act A law prohibiting abusive and deceptive practices by debt collectors. It is Title VIII of the Consumer Credit Protection Act, which went into effect in 1978.

Fair Housing Act A section of the Civil Rights Act of 1968 that prohibits discrimination on the basis of race, color, religion, national origin, or sex when making mortgage, construction, or home improvement loans.

family life-cycle The progressive stages of a family's spending and investment behavior as identified by marketers. The stages include single person, young married couple, young married couple with children, older married couple with older children, older married couple with no children at home, and widow or widower.

Federal Aviation Act A 1958 law that contains documentation requirements for loans secured by aircraft.

federal box A model format, in the shape of a rectangular box, that is used to inform borrowers of the annual percentage rate, total finance charges, amount being financed, and total amount of payments in a loan transaction.

Federal Deposit Insurance Corporation (FDIC) An independent government agency organized in 1933 to insure depositors' accounts at all national and most state-chartered banks. The FDIC also has the authority to supervise state banks that are not Federal Reserve members and rule on merger and branching applications.

Federal Reserve The central banking authority established in 1913 to monitor and regulate the commercial banking system, set U.S. monetary policy, provide a national check collection and payments system, and serve as financial agent for the federal government. The system consists of 12 Federal Reserve banks, each in a different region of the country, and a board of governors in Washington, D.C.

fee-splitting The illegal practice of paying someone to refer potential loan customers.

fictitious loans The fraudulent practice by automobile dealers and other borrowers of submitting loan applications from nonexistent people or real people who do not have a sales contract with the dealer.

finance charge   The total interest costs a consumer pays to obtain credit.

finance charge income   Income received from interest charges on unpaid credit balances.

finance company   A company that specializes in making small- and medium-sized loans to consumers, especially those who might have trouble obtaining credit otherwise.

first mortgage loan   The real estate loan that takes precedence over all other mortgage loans on a property. If the borrower fails to pay, the first mortgage lender has first claim against the property (subject to state law).

fixed-rate loan   A loan with an interest rate that remains the same over the life of the loan.

Flood Disaster Protection Act   A law authorizing lenders to make federal flood insurance a requirement on loans secured by real estate located in a flood zone.

floorplanning   A loan for financing a retailer's inventory. The bank disburses funds to the dealer after he or she has pledged specific goods sitting on the showroom floor as collateral. When this merchandise is sold, the lender is repaid. *Also called* inventory financing or wholesale line of credit program.

fluctuating value collateral   Assets pledged as collateral that rise and fall in value over the life of a loan.

foreclosure   A legal procedure allowing a creditor to sell real estate property given as collateral on a mortgage loan if the borrower defaults.

full recourse   A dealer recourse option requiring the dealer who sold a loan to reimburse the bank the full amount if the borrower defaults.

Functional Cost Analysis   An annual sampling survey conducted and published by the Federal Reserve Board, which compares various asset, income, and cost ratios for banking functions, such as trust, installment lending, commercial lending, and safe deposit.

gross monthly income   The total dollar amount of income before taxes, insurance, and other deductions.

guaranteed loan   A loan, made by a financial institution to an eligible business or individual, that is guaranteed against default by a federal agency.

Guaranteed Student Loan Program   A program sponsored by the U.S. Department of Education, which guarantees a loan

made by a financial institution to a student. While the
student is in school, the department also makes interest
payments on the loan.

guarantor   One who takes responsibility for the debts and
obligations of another. The guarantor becomes liable only
after all attempts to convince the first person to pay or
perform fail.

hologram   A three-dimensional image, created by a technology
using lasers and precise optical equipment, that appears on
credit cards and makes them difficult to counterfeit.

home equity line of credit   A line of credit based on the
borrower's equity in a home, for example, the market value
of the home minus the amount of mortgage principal
remaining to be paid. The borrower can access all or any
part of this credit by writing a check or using a credit card.

Home Mortgage Disclosure Act   A 1975 law requiring lenders to
make public the geographic location of their mortgage
loans.

Housing and Community Development Act   A 1977 law
implementing federal housing policy and programs and
containing the provisions of the Community Reinvestment
Act.

indirect loan   A loan involving three parties including the
borrower who obtains financing from a merchant who then
sells the loan to a financial institution.

indirect verification   An investigation of an applicant's credit
history conducted by contacting a third party such as a
credit bureau.

index rate   A leading economic indicator, such as the prime rate
or the 90-day Treasury bill rate, that is used as a
benchmark for setting variable loan interest rates. As the
index rate rises and falls, the loan rate follows.

inflationary spiral   An economic condition where higher prices
for goods and services mean higher costs for buyers, which
results in demands for higher wages and, eventually, still
higher prices from producers and suppliers paying those
wages.

insolvent   The inability to pay debts when due.

installment loan   A loan that is repaid in two or more periodic, fixed payments.

interchange fee   A handling charge collected by either the merchant's bank or the card-issuing bank for processing credit card transactions that have occurred outside their local market area.

interest-earning assets   Bank funds that are invested in loans, Treasury bills, municipal and corporate bonds, and other investments that earn interest income.

interest rate   The price one must pay to borrow money. The rate is generally computed on a percentage-per-year basis.

interest rate sensitivity   The degree to which behavior is influenced by fluctuations in current interest rates. For example, interest-sensitive consumers borrow money when loan rates are low and invest more funds in certificates of deposit (CDs) when CD rates are high.

interest subvention program   A program through which a manufacturer of goods pays a portion of the bank's loan interest charges so that the company can offer below market rates to its customers.

kickback   An illegal payment by the borrower to the lender in return for granting credit.

leasing   A contractual arrangement through which the owner of property or goods, such as automobiles and equipment, rents them to someone else.

lessee   One who rents and uses property or goods owned by someone else.

lessor   The owner of property or goods that are rented to someone else.

lien   A legal claim giving a lender the right to take possession of collateral if a borrower fails to repay the loan.

limited recourse   A dealer recourse option requiring the dealer who sold a loan to provide partial reimbursement to the bank if the borrower defaults.

line of credit   The amount of money a financial institution is willing to lend over a specified period without requiring additional loan applications. The customer can borrow, repay, and borrow again any or all of the credit extended and may be required to keep a certain level of funds in the bank or offer personal property as security.

liquid assets   Assets that can be easily and quickly converted into cash without a loss in value.

liquidation costs   The amount of money spent to remove a paid up loan from the bank's records and return the note to the borrower.

liquidity   The ease with which assets an be converted into cash without a loss in value.

loan balance   The total amount still owed on a loan after deducting the total amount of payments made.

loan contract   The written agreement between borrower and lender that spells out the amount and terms of the loan.

loan decision   The outcome of determining whether to grant a loan, to offer credit on terms other than those requested, or to deny credit.

loan documentation   The process of gathering and completing all the papers necessary to secure the lender's interest and comply with the legal requirements of making a loan.

loan loss rate   A measure of a lender's previous experience with bad loans computed by dividing the dollar amount of total losses by the dollar amount of total loans made.

loan outstandings   The total dollar amount of unpaid balances on all types of loans.

loan policy   A written statement of the goals, guidelines, standards, and procedures a lender follows in determining who will receive credit and under what specified terms and conditions.

loan portfolio   The total of all loans held by a financial institution and managed as a collective whole.

loan shark   A person or firm that lends money to a poor credit risk at an excessively high or illegal rate of interest.

loan structuring   The process of constructing a loan interest rate that results in enough income to cover the costs of lending and earn a reasonable profit.

loan volume   The total dollar amount of loans made in a given period.

loss exposure   The amount of money a lender could lose if loans go bad.

maintenance costs · The amount of money spent to maintain a loan until its maturity date. This includes overhead expenses (such as rent and utilities), salaries for loan processors and customer service representatives, coupon books and other office supplies, and computer expenditures.

margin account   Credit provided by a brokerage firm to its customers to enable them to pay for stocks and other securities they may want to purchase. These funds can only be a portion of the total sale and interest must be paid to the broker for the use of the borrowed funds.

marginal loan   A loan that is considered a borderline credit risk.

mass market   To offer and promote a product or service to the general public.

MasterCard International   An independent, not-for-profit association that contracts with financial institutions to offer an internationally accepted credit card, credit insurance, traveler's checks, and other related credit card services to their customers.

maturity date   The date a loan is due.

maturity structuring   The process of determining a loan maturity date that results in enough interest income to cover the cost of lending and to earn a reasonable profit. Common maturities are 36, 48, and 60 months.

merchant discount   The amount a merchant pays to a bank for processing its credit card transactions, generally figured as a percentage of the dollar amount of each sale.

money market rates   The interest rates paid on short-term private and government obligations, such as Treasury bills, commercial paper, and tax-exempt securities.

Morris Plan bank   A type of financial institution that was first established in 1910 by Arthur J. Morris to make small- and medium-sized unsecured loans to consumers who could convince two others to cosign the loan with them. Since most banks in that day only made loans to businesses, Morris Plan banks were one of the earliest institutions that provided consumer credit.

negative amortization   An increase in the unpaid balance of a loan, which occurs when unpaid interest is added to the loan principal.

net investment   The total expenditure to acquire or use an asset minus the value of the asset.

net worth   The value of an individual or a business after deducting the total of liabilities from the total of assets.

nonrecourse   A dealer recourse option where the dealer who sells a loan has no liability to the bank that bought the loan if the borrower defaults.

note   A written promise to repay a specified amount of money by a specific date.

O

open-end loan   A credit arrangement allowing the borrower to make purchases and take cash advances up to a previously agreed limit. Repayment is made at fixed intervals and will vary in size depending on the amount of credit extended. Lines of credit and credit cards are two examples.

over-limit charge   A fee paid by a credit card holder who charges more than the authorized credit limit.

P

pay down   To reduce a debt by making payments.

pay out   To pay off a loan before its due date.

payroll deduction   A plan that allows an employee to authorize that specified sums of money be deducted from his or her pay to be credited to financial obligations, such as health insurance, loan payments, or savings programs.

perfect a lien   A procedure for protecting a lender's claim to loan collateral in the event of default. When collateral is handed over to the lender, as in the case of stocks and bonds, the claim is secure. When the lender does not have possession of the collateral, the lender must file a financing statement, which describes the collateral and the terms of the loan agreement, with the appropriate legal authorities. By taking this step, a security interest is "perfected."

periodic rate   The interest rate that a creditor charges on a daily, weekly, or monthly basis on the outstanding balance in open-end credit such as a credit card or revolving charge account.

periodic statement   A summary, usually mailed monthly, of the activity in an open-end credit account, including the previous balance, new transactions, finance charges, new balance, and minimum payment due.

personal banker   A bank employee who provides personalized customer service to highly valued customers. Personal bankers are banking professionals informed about the financial needs of customers and have the authority to handle all nonroutine transactions.

personal loan company   A company that specializes in short-term, small- and medium-sized loans to consumers.

point-of-sale (POS) verification terminal   An electronic device, found at retail locations but connected by telephone to a bank's computer system, that checks a customer's account to verify that adequate funds are available to pay for goods or services. Some POS terminals are also capable of transferring the funds from the customer's to the merchant's account in the same transaction.

portfolio liquidity   The ease with which a financial institution's collective holdings can be converted into cash without a loss in value.

prescreening   The practice of examining credit bureau files for individuals who meet credit requirements and targeting efforts to market at these consumers.

primary borrower   The person who receives the direct benefit of borrowed funds in a loan signed by one or more comakers.

prime rate   A benchmark from which a bank computes an appropriate rate of interest for a loan contract. Generally, the benchmark is based on numerous factors, including the bank's supply of funds, what it costs the bank to keep those funds, its administrative costs, and competition from other suppliers of credit.

principal   The amount of a loan or deposit excluding fees and interest.

principal balance   The amount of unpaid balance of a loan excluding fees and interest.

product line   A group of products that are closely related because they have similar functions, for example, passbook savings, statement savings, and money market savings accounts.

product packaging   The practice of marketing a group of financial services as a single customer product. For example, a product package may include free checking and a line of credit accessed by the bank's credit card.

profit margin   A ratio computed by subtracting expenses (or total dollars of expenses) from the sales price (or total dollars of sales) and dividing the result by the sales price (or total number of sales).

purchase-money loan   A mortgage granted by the seller to the buyer of the seller's property.

pyramiding debt   Taking on a significant amount of debt in a short period of time, or steadily increasing the amount owed on loans.

qualify   To meet a lender's criteria for granting credit.

range of balances   The lowest to the highest dollar amount on open-end credit balances that will be charged a specific rate of interest. When the range changes to a new low and high dollar amount, the rate changes. For example, on a balance from $1 to $2,500, a monthly interest rate of 2 percent will be charged, but this rate drops to 1.5 percent on a balance of $2,501.

rate cap   The maximum allowable interest rate a financial institution may charge on a loan.

rate floor   The lowest interest rate a financial institution will agree to charge on a loan.

rate subsidy program   A program in which a manufacturer of goods pays a portion of the bank's loan interest charges so that the company can offer below market rates to its customers.

reage an account   An arrangement for allowing a delinquent borrower to skip one or more payments and then extending the life of the loan by the same number of payments.

real estate broker   A licensed professional authorized to represent clients involved in real estate transactions and to facilitate the sale or leasing of a property.

Real Estate Settlement Procedures Act   A 1975 law that requires lenders to provider borrowers with accurate and timely information on the costs of the real estate settlement process and protects borrowers against abusive uses of their escrow funds.

rebate   To return interest to the borrower because the loan has been repaid early.

recession proof   The ability to maintain a level of consumption despite a general slowdown or decline in economic activity.

recovery department   The offices within a lending institution responsible for getting whatever repayment is possible on a defaulted loan.

red flag   Information given on a credit application that appears suspicious and alerts the lender to further check the veracity of the information.

redlining The practice of restricting or refusing to make loans in certain neighborhoods because they are considered a bad investment.

refinance The process of obtaining a new loan, usually at a lower interest rate, in order to pay off an existing loan and reduce monthly payments.

regional banking The establishment of a banking presence in nearby states by merger, acquisition, or new charter.

Regulation B The Federal Reserve rule that prohibits credit discrimination, sets guidelines for gathering and evaluating credit information, and requires written notification when credit is denied. Regulation B implements the Equal Credit Opportunity Act.

Regulation C The Federal Reserve rule requiring financial institutions to make public the geographic locations of their mortgage loans. Regulation C implements the Home Mortgage Disclosure Act.

Regulation O The Federal Reserve rule that prohibits a bank from making loans to its executive officers and officers at banks with which it does business.

Regulation U The Federal Reserve rule that governs the amount of money a bank may lend for buying stocks.

Regulation X A rule of the Department of Housing and Urban Development that requires full and accurate disclosure of credit terms in real estate transactions. Regulation X implements the Real Estate Settlement Procedures Act.

Regulation Z The Federal Reserve rule that requires disclosure of credit terms, including finance charges, service charges, and payment schedules, and sets procedures for resolving billing errors. Regulation Z implements the Truth in Lending Act.

relationship banking A program designed to develop long-term client relationships with bank customers by offering them a package of products that serves their total financial needs.

repayment period The time interval between when a debt begins and when it is due.

repossession The act of claiming property or goods given as security on a loan when the borrower has defaulted.

repurchase recourse A dealer recourse option requiring the dealer who sold a loan to repurchase it if it becomes delinquent within the first 90 days.

residential loan A loan in which real estate, such as an owner-occupied home, is pledged as security.

residual value The value of an asset at the conclusion of a lease agreement.

retail banking   Products and services offered by a bank to individual consumers as opposed to those offered to businesses or other organizations.

retail installment loan   A loan made to an individual for personal use and repaid in periodic, fixed payments.

retail paper   Dealer installment loan contracts that are sold to banks.

retention rate   The rate of interest a bank will charge on loans it buys from a dealer.

revolving line of credit   A prearranged loan that can be activated by writing a check or using a credit card. The payment due is always less than the total balance due and any unpaid balance is subject to finance charges.

right of offset   A provision in loan contracts that allows the lender to use funds deposited in the borrower's accounts for payment of delinquent loans.

right of rescission   The right of a borrower or buyer to cancel a contract within 3 business days without penalty and with refund of all deposits. This privilege is a provision of the Truth in Lending Act.

rule of 78s   A method used to determine how much interest to refund to the borrower when a loan is repaid early.

sales draft   A sales slip used in credit card transactions to document that the card holder owes money to the card issuer.

salvage department   The offices within a lending institution responsible for getting whatever repayment is possible on a defaulted loan.

savings institution   A financial institution that accepts savings deposits and invests them by offering long-term mortgage loans. This is a general term that refers to savings and loan associations, savings banks, and credit unions.

second mortgage   A loan on a property that was made after the first mortgage loan. If a borrower fails to pay off loans, the second mortgage holder must wait until the claims of the first mortgage lender have been satisfied (subject to state law).

secondary market   A national market where a financial institution's loans, primarily mortgages, can be bought and sold to other investors. The secondary market enables the institution to convert long-term loans back into cash.

secured loan A loan requiring the borrower to pledge specific assets that become the property of the lender if the loan is not repaid.

securities Documents that show evidence of ownership or indebtedness. Stocks and bonds are two kinds of securities.

securities broker One who acts as an agent for others in the buying and selling of stocks and bonds.

security agreement A document signed by a borrower establishing a lender's right to take possession of loan collateral in the event of default.

sell up To convince a borrower to accept a loan for more money than requested.

service To perform those activities related to collecting loan payments, including handling and securing loan documents, sending billing statements or coupon books, receiving payments, responding to customers' inquiries, and following up on delinquencies.

Ship Mortgage Act of 1920 A law that sets documentation requirements for loans secured by seagoing vessels.

short-term equity advance A loan granted for a short period on the basis of the equity in the borrower's home.

skip tracing The process of locating borrowers who have stopped making their loan payments and cannot be located at their last known address or employer.

simple interest A method of calculating a loan interest rate by taking a percentage of the loan balance each month, not including previous interest charges, and expressing this figure as an annualized rate.

single-payment loan A loan that requires full payment on a specific date.

stable value collateral Assets pledged as collateral that remain constant in value over the life of a loan.

statement of waiver A document signed by a borrower relinquishing rights to rescission (privileges to cancel a loan contract within three working days).

steering The practice of directing a prospective home buyer away from a specific neighborhood.

stock A certificate showing evidence of ownership in a corporation.

straw purchaser An individual who allows someone with a poor credit rating to use his or her name and credit report to obtain a loan.

surety A person who agrees to be responsible for the debts and obligations of another.

tangible assets   Property and goods that are in a physical form and can be touched or seen, such as an automobile or a piece of land.

term   The period between the commencement and termination of a debt or contract.

thrift   A financial institution that accepts savings deposits and invests these funds in long-term mortgages. The three types of thrifts are savings and loan associations, savings banks, and credit unions.

tie-in selling   The practice of offering a buyer products or services in addition to the one requested.

transfer of title   To change ownership from one party to another.

triggering terms   Words or phrases that, when used in bank advertising, "trigger" or set off certain Truth in Lending disclosure requirements.

Truth in Lending Act   The law that requires clear and accurate disclosure of credit terms in a lending transaction, including interest, fees, and all other costs. Truth in Lending is the popular name of the Consumer Credit Protection Act of 1969.

Truth in Lending Simplification and Reform Act   A 1982 law designed to streamline the original Truth in Lending legislation by easing and simplifying disclosure requirements so that disclosure statements can be more easily understood by consumers.

unauthorized transaction   The illegal use of a credit card or bank account by someone other than the card or account holder.

underwriting guidelines   Criteria used by a lending institution to determine if an applicant is eligible to receive credit.

Uniform Commercial Code (UCC)   A set of laws drafted to give consistency to the legal aspects of business and financial transactions, including bank deposits, the sale of goods, stock transfers, and secured loans. Every state except Louisiana has adopted the UCC.

uniform disclosure   A standardized format for informing consumers about the terms of a credit agreement.

Uniform Small Loan Law   A law adopted on the state level that spells out uniform guidelines on maximum allowable interest rates, loan size, and the licensing of small loan companies. A model of this law was drafted and promoted by the Russell Sage Foundation to encourage consistency and credibility in state consumer credit legislation.

unsecured line of credit   The amount a financial institution is willing to lend over a specified period of time without requiring additional loan applications. The borrower can withdraw all or part of the amount, repay and withdraw again on the basis of his or her credit history and ability to repay, and not because he or she has pledged specific assets to the lender.

unsecured loan   A loan made on the basis of a borrower's credit history and ability to repay and not on the requirement of pledging assets to the lender.

unsolicited credit card   A credit card issued to a consumer who has not requested it. The practice of issuing unsolicited credit cards is now prohibited by law.

usurer   Someone who charges a higher rate of interest than that allowed by law.

usurious interest   A rate of interest on a loan that is higher than that allowed by state law.

usury law   A law that sets the maximum interest rate that can be charged on different types of loans.

usury limit   The maximum interest rate allowed by law.

valuation guide book   A reference book used by lenders to determine the market value of collateral that may depreciate over time (for example, used cars, mobile homes, and boats).

variable rate loan   A loan with an interest rate that can change over the life of the loan. The loan rate is tied to an important money market indicator, such as the prime rate on the 90-day Treasury bill rate, and rises or falls with that rate.

Visa International   An independent, not-for-profit association that contracts with financial institutions to offer an internationally accepted payment systems including credit cards, traveler's checks, and other related credit card services to their customers. The credit card used domestically is called a VISA card.

wage attachment   A court order for seizing a person's wages as security for his or her debts.

wage garnishment   A court order requiring an employer to withhold a portion of an employee's wages to pay his or her creditors.

warranty   A guarantee of quality made by the seller of a product or service.

Index

C

Capacity, in credit evaluations, 173–75
Capital, in credit evaluations, 176–78
Captive finance companies, 31–32
Central information systems (CIS), 255
Character, in credit evaluations, 167–72
Charge-offs
    and collection cycle, 274–75
    and loan policy, 290
    and recovery operations, 276
Chicago Tribune, 7–8
CIS. *See* Central information systems
Civil Rights Act of 1968, 59
Closed-end loans
    background, 67–68
    comaker loans, 70
    defined, 65
    home improvement loans, 70–71
    outstandings share, 20
    secured, 71–75
    Truth in Lending disclosures, 49–52
    types, 68–69
    unsecured, 69–70
    volume for commercial banks, 22
Collateral
    appreciating value of, 74
    in credit evaluations, 178–79
    in credit investigations, 157
    depreciating value of, 71–72
    fluctuating value of, 72–73
    and loan policy, 287–89
    perfecting, 250–52
    possessory vs. non-possessory, 248
    stable value of, 73–74
    verification, 148–49
Collection
    cost efficiency, 260–61
    cycle, 266–72

Fair Debt Collection Practices Act, 261–62
    and loan policy, 290
    objectives, 257–61
    organization of, 265
    remedies, 268–71, 272
    techniques in 1800s, 7
Comaker loans, 70
Commercial banks
    advantages, 30
    challenges, 30
    market share, 29–30
Community Reinvestment Act (CRA)
    and application process, 129
    background, 57–58
    and federal laws and regulations, 41
    and guaranteed loans, 75
Competition, consumer credit, 197–98
Compliance officer, 290
Compliance programs
    loan policy and review, 290
    objectives, 62
    overview, 62–63
    and Regulation B, 62–63
Comptroller of the Currency, 41, 274
Conspicuous consumption, 13
Consumer
    legal defined, 3
Consumer credit. *See* Credit
Consumer Credit Counseling, 270
Consumer Credit Protection Act of 1968, 3, 12, 42
Consumer Credit Restraint Program, 12–14
Consummation, defined, 49
Cost of funds, and loan pricing, 201–2
Counteroffer, 47
CRA. *See* Community Reinvestment Act
Credit
    benefits, 17–19
    compliance programs, 62–63

Home Mortgage Disclosure Act
(HMDA), 60
Housing and Community
Development Act, 57

I

Income
    and credit evaluation requirements,
        45–46
    credit investigation verification,
        153–54
Index, 210
Indirect loans
    advantages, 88–90, 94
    application process, 87–88, 132
    background, 83–84
    bank perspective, 88–92
    characteristics, 84–85
    consumer perspective, 94–95
    dealer perspective, 92–93
    disadvantages, 90–92, 94–95
    lending process, 85–88
    and loan structuring, 233–35
    maturity stretching, 227–28
    payment schedules, 93
    recourse options, 89
Industrial Revolution
    and the history of credit, 7–8
Inflation
    effects on consumer credit, 28
Insurance policy agreement, 244
Interchange fees, 121–22
Interest subvention programs, 28–29
    and indirect loans, 90
International credit cards, 107–8

J

Job rankings
    in credit evaluation, 172
Joint applicants, credit evaluation, 45
Judgmental system of credit
    evaluation, 167–81
    capacity variable, 173–75

capital variable, 176–78
character variable, 167–72
collateral variable, 178–79
conditions variable, 179–80

K

Kickbacks
    and Real Estate Settlement
        Procedures Act, 59

L

Leasing
    background, 100–2
    defined, 100
Legal environment
    and loan policy, 196–97
    and loan pricing, 196–98
    overview, 41–62
Lending authority, 285–86
Liens, 248–50
Life-cycle stages
    and credit behavior, 25–26
    and decision making, 165–66
Lincoln, Abraham, 7
Liquid assets, 176
Liquidity, 117–18
Loan closing
    completion of documentation,
        240–41
    ensuring customer understanding,
        242–43
    objectives, 239–44
    and regulatory compliance, 241–42
Loan committees, 286
Loan costs
    average vs. marginal cost analysis,
        202–3
    categories, 200
    Federal Reserve Functional Cost
        Analysis, 200–2
Loan documentation
    advantages, 246–47
    for automobile loans, direct, 244

Notes

Notes

Notes

Notes

Notes

Thank you for using this American Bankers Association/American Institute of Banking textbook. Your responses on the following evaluation will help shape the structure and content of future editions. <u>Return your completed form to your instructor or fold in three and mail to</u>: American Institute of Banking, Attn: Manager, Product Development, 1120 Connecticut Avenue, N.W., Washington, D.C. 20036.

Name of Chapter _____

Name of Bank _____

TEXTBOOK/COURSE ATTRIBUTES

Importance Factor					Satisfaction Level			
Very Important			Not Important		Completely Satisfied			Not Satisfied
1	2	3	4	Textbook covered all important topics	1	2	3	4
1	2	3	4	Content was easy to read and understand	1	2	3	4
1	2	3	4	The graphics and examples were helpful	1	2	3	4
1	2	3	4	I can use what I've learned in this course in my work	1	2	3	4

	Excellent			Poor
What was your overall opinion of the textbook?	1	2	3	4

Did your instructor use any additional materials to teach this course?
( ) Yes   ( ) No

If Yes, please check all that apply
( ) Transparencies/Overheads   ( ) Handouts
( ) Other textbook (please specify)_____

Number of AIB courses you have taken in past three years:
( ) 0   ( ) 1-2   ( ) 3-5
( ) More than 5

AIB course taken through: (Please check all that apply)
( ) AIB Chapter/Study Group
( ) AIB Correspondence Study Program
( ) Other (please specify)_____

Currently working toward an AIB Diploma/Certificate?
( ) Yes   ( ) No

If yes, please specify:
( ) Bank Operations   ( ) Consumer Credit
( ) Commercial Lending   ( ) General Banking
( ) Mortgage Lending   ( ) Accelerated Banking
( ) Customer Service   ( ) Securities Services
( ) Supervisory

Asset size of your bank:
( ) 0-$75m   ( ) $76-$250m   ( ) $251-$500m
( ) $501-$1b   ( ) over $1b

Number of employees in your bank:
( ) 1-10   ( ) 11-20   ( ) 21-40
( ) 41-90   ( ) 91-200   ( ) 201-350
( ) 351-2,000   ( ) over 2,000

Job Title:_____

Major Job Responsibility:
( ) Lending   ( ) Marketing   ( ) Operations
( ) Compliance   ( ) Auditing   ( ) Human Resources
( ) Trust   ( ) Customer Svc.   ( ) Branch Admin.
( ) Securities Processing   ( ) Security/Risk Management

( ) Other (Please specify)_____

Years in Banking:
( ) 0-2   ( ) 3-5   ( ) 6-10
( ) Over 10

Highest Education Level:
( ) High School   ( ) Some College   ( ) BA/BS Degree
( ) Advanced Degree

Age:
( ) under 25   ( ) 25-35   ( ) 36-45
( ) over 45

Name_____
Bank_____
Address _____
City _____ State _____ Zip _____
Telephone (____) _____

( ) Please send me more information on AIB's Diploma/Certificate Program.

( ) Please send me more information on AIB's Correspondence Study Program.

Comments (please identify any specific suggestions you have that may improve the overall effectiveness of this publication):

_____

_____

_____

_____

_____

_____

_____

_____

_____

BUSINESS REPLY MAIL
FIRST CLASS MAIL PERMIT NO. 10579   WASHINGTON, DC

POSTAGE WILL BE PAID BY ADDRESSEE

American Bankers Association
Attn: Manager, Product Development, AIB
1120 Connecticut Avenue, N.W.
Washington, DC 20077-5760